Effective Selling
Through Psychology

NEW EDITION

Effective Selling Through Psychology

DIMENSIONAL SALES AND SALES
MANAGEMENT STRATEGIES

V.R. BUZZOTTA, PH.D.

R.E. LEFTON, PH.D.

MANUEL SHERBERG

Published by

PSYCHOLOGICAL ASSOCIATES, INC.
8201 Maryland Avenue
St. Louis, MO 63105
(314) 862-9300

International Standard Book Number: 0-9630421-0-6

Library of Congress Catalog Card Number: 82-16308

Printed in the United States of America

Library of Congress Cataloging in Publication Data

Buzzotta, V. Ralph, 1931–
  Effective selling through psychology.

  Bibliography: p.
  Includes index.
  1. Selling—Psychological aspects. 2. Sales management.
I. Lefton, Robert Eugene, 1931– II. Sherberg, Manuel.
III. Title.
HF5438.8.P75B89 1982   658.8′1   82-16308
ISBN 0-9630421-0-6
        92 PCP 18 17 16

Contents

Introduction

Three things should be said about this book at the outset:

1. The book has been written for both salespeople and sales managers (and, of course, for anyone interested in selling in the broadest sense of the word). Both sets of readers will benefit by reading *all* of it. The information on "selling skills," which is found mainly in the middle chapters (5-15), is indispensable to sales managers as well as salespeople; the information on "sales management skills," mainly in chapters 16-19, will prove useful to any salesperson seeking to work more effectively with his or her superior.

In particular, sales managers will profit by reading the "selling skills" chapters carefully. If, say, probing skills are essential for salespeople, they're equally essential for sales managers; a manager who skips the chapter on probing will get very little out of the later chapters. The same is true of all the other "selling skills" chapters; they deserve close reading by *all* readers.

The reason for this, which will become clearer during the course of the book, is that salespeople and sales managers are both charged with the same fundamental task: *to get better results from their work with other people.* To accomplish that task, they must be able to *interact effectively with others.* And this requires one fundamental set of skills — whether exercised by salespeople or sales managers. This is not to say that selling and managing are identical; far from it. But selling and managing demand the ability to exercise the same interactional skills. In fact, it might be more accurate to say that chapters 5-15 deal not with selling skills but with interactional skills. The examples in those chapters are taken from the field of selling, but the skills themselves can and should be used in *any* situation

1

where two people are supposed to work together effectively. For that reason, we strongly recommend that all readers read all the chapters through 15 and that sales managers keep on reading till the very end; we also think that salespeople will find the four final chapters well worth their time.

2. A few paragraphs back, we used the phrase "his or her." It would obviously be cumbersome to continue using such dual-gender phrases ("he or she," "him or her," "herself or himself") throughout the book. But it would be much worse to make the pronouns all male or all female; after all, very large numbers of both men and women are in selling and sales management. Since the English language provides very few neuter pronouns, we've resolved this problem by changing gender in alternating chapters. Thus, Chapter 1 is written in masculine gender, Chapter 2 in feminine, and so on. We think that once you get accustomed to this usage, you'll find it seems both natural and sensible.

3. Some, but not all, of the chapters conclude with summaries. Where a wealth of material in a chapter seems to require a summary, we've included one. Where a chapter is written in what is essentially outline form (the chapters on the Q4 strategies are a good example), a summary would only prove redundant, and so we've omitted it. Throughout, our sole purpose has been to make the book *convenient* to read and use.

VRB
REL
MS

1

Selling, People Skills, and You

Selling is another word for *persuading*. It's something *all* of us do. Some people, of course, are paid to concern themselves with selling. Salespeople and sales managers are obvious examples. But just about *anybody* who works for a living must occasionally sell—persuade.

Take Helen Wright. She manages the accounting department in a trucking company. Ordinarily, you wouldn't think of her as doing saleswork. But today she's going to have a talk with the company's data-processing manager; she wants to persuade him that cash-flow reports should be processed semi-weekly instead of weekly. He's not likely to be enthusiastic; he thinks his department is already "overloaded." Helen has some *selling* to do. Or take Lou Parrish. He's shipping foreman for a major shoe manufacturer. As a rule, you wouldn't think of him as doing saleswork. But today he's going to have a talk with one of his packers; he wants to persuade him that he can pack more shoe boxes into cartons each day by changing the way he places cartons on the floor. The packer's likely to argue; he's a hothead who doesn't like getting advice. Lou has some *selling* to do. There are countless similar examples. In fact, it's hard to think of people who *don't* have to do some selling—persuading—as part of earning a living.

We can go even further: nearly every day, all of us do some selling *off* the job. We try to persuade family, friends, or neighbors, to accept an idea, an attitude, a proposal. We may not think of ourselves as selling, but that in fact is what all of us do. While this book is directed mainly at people who sell for a living or who manage those who sell for a living, it should be useful to anyone who wants to become *more persuasive.*

WHAT THE BOOK'S ABOUT

This book explains how to get better sales results through people skills. We'll define *people skills* in a minute. First, a word about *sales results.* Different companies define *sales results* differently. Some define sale results in terms of dollars ("I just concluded a $10,000 sale"), others in terms of units ("He sold 500 sets"). Sales results can be measured in many ways: by volume, by cost of sales (how much is the company spending for the sales it's getting?), by closure rate (what percentage of sales calls results in sales contracts?), by repeat business (how many customers keep on buying after their first purchase?), by competitive comparisons (what's our share of the market compared to Company B's?), and by product mix (are we selling the most profitable blend of products or services?)—to mention only a few. This book does two things:

1. It explains how salespéople can use people skills to *improve* sales results—*no matter how defined.*
2. It explains how sales managers can use people skills to get *improved* sales results—no matter how defined—from their salespeople.

(We'll use the words *salesperson* and *salespeople* throughout because they're widely accepted terms for people whose major responsibility is to *sell.* Your company may use other terms: account executive, sales representative, calling officer, and so on.)

PEOPLE SKILLS

People skills is an "umbrella" term. It covers four sets of skills which are indispensable for maximizing sales results: (1) sizing-up skills, (2) strategy-planning skills, (3) communication skills, and (4) motivation skills.

- **Sizing-up skills.** Sales aren't just "made"; they're made to *somebody in particular*. When you call on a customer, you always call on somebody *unique*: Customer A is sarcastic; he's got a house-size chip on his shoulder. Customer B is tense; he seems eager to get the whole thing over with. Customer C is genial; he's apparently got all day to talk. And so on. Sales are always made to *special* people with special characteristics. Sales managers are in exactly the same situation; each of their salespeople has special characteristics: Salesperson X is convinced he knows all there is to know about selling; Salesperson Y is so unsure of himself that he avoids calling on tough customers; Salesperson Z knows his own strengths but also knows he's got a lot to learn. And so on. Obviously, then, whether you're a salesperson on a sales call or a sales manager in a coaching session, you want to keep some key questions in mind: What's *this* person—the one I'm facing right now—like? What special characteristics must I deal with? What obstacles can I anticipate? Which traits should I pay particular attention to? *Sizing-up skills* help answer these questions. After all, there are *many* ways to deal with people; sizing-up skills help you "figure out" the person you're dealing with, so you can pick the *best* way.

- **Strategy-planning skills.** Once you have figured out the other person, the question becomes: What *is* the best way to deal with him? How can I overcome the obstacles he's likely to place in my path? How can I most effectively respond to his needs, concerns, doubts? How can I persuade him *without* wasting time and energy? To answer these questions, you need *strategy-planning* skills. The difference between sizing-up skills and strategy-planning skills is the difference between diagnosis and prescription. Sizing-up skills *diagnose*; they help you "make sense" out of what the other person's saying and doing. Strategy-planning skills *prescribe*; they help you *deal* with what he's saying and doing. Strategy-planning skills help you lay out the right plan-of-action—the one that will *work best*—for working with Customer J or Salesperson M. They enable you to deal *flexibly* with people. Your strategy for Customer J will differ— maybe a little and maybe a lot—from your strategy for Customer K or Customer L. Your strategy for Salesperson M will be tailored to him—so you'll have to re-fashion it for Salesperson N or Salesperson O. Strategy-planning skills help you *personalize* your dealings with people. That makes persuasion a great deal easier.

- **Communicating skills.** Once you've planned the right strategy—worked out the best way to deal with Customer R or Salesperson S—you'll have to *get through* to him. Before people can be persuaded (not intimidated or coerced or pressured, but actually *persuaded—convinced*), they must *understand* what they're being asked to do. Before they'll buy, customers want the answers to certain questions: "*Why* should I spend money on *this* product? What will it *do* for me? Why should I prefer it over competitive products?" And before they'll exert themselves to change and improve, salespeople want the answers to certain questions, too: "What *exactly* am I being asked to do? Why should I bother doing it? What's in it for me?" Answering these questions so the answers are really understood takes *communication* skills.

- **Motivation skills.** Generating understanding isn't all there is to persuasion, however. Understanding must be followed by *action.* A customer who says, "I see perfectly what I'm being asked to buy . . . and why . . . but I want to think about it for six months," may understand, but he's not *committed.* A salesperson who tells the boss, "I know what you mean . . . and I know what you expect of me . . . but I just don't think it's worth the effort," may understand, but he's not committed either. Understanding means: "I get it . . . I catch on." Commitment means: "I intend to do something about it . . . to *follow through.*" Generating commitment takes *motivation* skills.

ARE PEOPLE SKILLS ENOUGH?

Let's make something plain: *by themselves*, people skills won't produce better sales results. They're no substitute for product knowledge or for time-and-territory management. But, if you have the other things it takes to produce results—the technical and administrative skills and the drive to succeed—people skills can make it much easier. They can make the difference between success and mediocrity. We'll present evidence for this statement in Chapter 4. Right now, we'll simply reiterate: important as they are, people skills can't do the job alone.

WHAT'S IN IT FOR YOU?

Why bother reading this book? We've already said that whether you're a salesperson or a sales manager, it'll help you get better *sales* results. But it'll help you get *other* results, too:

- **Tangible results.** Whatever tangible rewards you're working for –
  more money, a promotion to sales manager, a bigger district to
  manage, the Salesperson-of-the-Year or the Sales-Manager-of-
  the-Year award – you'll improve your chances of getting them if
  you use people skills. People skills will pay off not only for your
  company, but for *you.*

- **Intangible results.** By using people skills, you can also get more
  satisfaction out of your job. The ability to persuade a wider range
  of people should help you feel more secure, develop smoother
  working relationships, win new respect, and enhance your feeling
  of competence and accomplishment.

HOW IT STARTED

How do we *know* people skills can do what we've said? We know it
because we've *seen* them work; we've seen them produce better results for thousands of salespeople and sales managers in hundreds of
companies.

Here's the story: in the 1960s, Dimensional Training Systems, a
division of Psychological Associates, the training organization with
which the authors are affiliated, introduced Dimensional Sales Training (DST), a program to help salespeople master people skills and improve sales results. DST (and its counterpart, Dimensional Sales Management – DSM) found prompt acceptance in many companies, not
only in the United States, but in other countries of North and South
America and Western Europe. Every one of the hundreds of DST and
DSM seminars since then has taught the ideas and skills described in
this book. When the people who have gone through these seminars
have returned to their jobs and used their people skills, we've had a
"natural laboratory" in which to study the effectiveness of the skills.
The *real world* – where these salespeople and sales managers *work* –
has been the crucible in which the skills have had to prove themselves.

And they have. A whole series of follow-up studies by client companies has shown that people skills *do* by and large boost sales results
and *do* by and large pay off as we've described. Some of these studies are described in Chapter 19. So we can say with assurance that
people skills are likely to help *you* get better results – for your company and yourself.

THE SCIENTIFIC BACKGROUND

Where did the ideas in this book come from? And why did Dimensional Training Systems believe the ideas would work?

The ideas came from psychologists, communication specialists, marketing and management specialists, and researchers in related fields, who spent years testing them out. These researchers are too numerous to mention here, although the key contributors are named in the bibliography. By the 1960s they'd developed a large body of evidence to *prove* that people skills *work* (much more evidence has been added since). Thus, follow-up studies in companies using DST and DSM only confirmed what we (and most behavioral scientists) already knew.

The evidence for our ideas, then, comes from two sources: the scientific community and our own experience. In the end, of course, you yourself must be the final judge of the validity of these ideas. We predict that they'll match your experience and your common sense, but only *you* can say whether they really do.

PEOPLE SKILLS CAN BE LEARNED

One crucial fact is implied in everything we've said: people skills *can* be learned. They're not innate or inherited; nobody brings them into the world at birth. They're *acquired* by men and women willing to expend the necessary time and energy.

This means there's nothing mysterious about people skills. They're not vague, indefinable qualities like "charm" or "magnetism" or "charisma." They're *techniques* which have been learned—and mastered—by thousands of people. *Nobody* can say, "I don't have what it takes to size up people" or "I'm not the sort of person who can motivate others." "What it takes" is *not* a special sort of person; what it takes is learning the necessary *skills*, practicing them, getting feedback, and then using the skills until they become "second nature." This book zeros in on what the skills are. The practice and the use are up to you.

Let's get started.

2

Getting Down to Cases

As we've said, before deciding on the best way to deal with some-body, it's a good idea to *size up* her behavior. Diagnosis first, then prescription. The same is true of *yourself.* Before starting on a course of self-development, it's a good idea to size up your own behavior. See where you're *at*, then decide where to *go*. This chapter will help you do it.

SOME PRELIMINARIES

1. This chapter contains three questionnaires:

- Questionnaire I is for sizing up *customer* behavior. If you're a salesperson, use it to size up your *toughest* customer or prospect — the one you have most trouble making sales to. If you're a sales manager, use it to size up one of your salespeople's toughest customers — one you've actually observed out in the field. (If you're a sales manager who manages a territory instead of salespeople, or who does a considerable amount of selling, size up your *own* toughest customer.)

- Questionnaire II is for sizing up *sales* behavior. If you're a salesperson, use it to size up the way *you* typically act during a sales call. If you're a sales manager, use it to size up the typical sales behavior of one of your salespeople. (It might be worthwhile to pick someone who's "hard to handle" or who's not performing up to potential.) If you're a sales manager who manages a territory or does a lot of selling, size up your *own* sales behavior.

• Questionnaire III is for sizing up *sales management* behavior. If you're a sales manager, use it to size up your *own* behavior — the way you *typically* interact with your salespeople. If you're a salesperson, use it to size up your boss's behavior — the way she typically interacts with *you.*

2. The idea behind these questionnaires — and this whole book — is that you're *already* selling or managing effectively. If you weren't, you probably wouldn't be in your present job or bother to read this book; as a rule, people who are already effective are most interested in becoming more so. The questionnaires will give you an overview of your current sales or managerial behavior, or both. Once you know which skills you're using now, you can begin building on them.

3. The questionnaires won't yield *precise* "measures" — only rough ones. These rough measures may not be completely valid. That's because the questionnaires partly measure your view of your *own* behavior, and it's hard to be objective about your own behavior. Thus, the "profiles," especially those on your *own* behavior, may be somewhat crude. Of course, the more *candid* your answers, the more refined the profiles. So muster all the objectivity you can.

4. When you finish this book, you may want to answer the questionnaires again. If you do, you'll probably draw a truer profile because you'll have acquired insights that will help you see your behavior in a truer light.

5. This doesn't mean your first response to the questionnaires will be worthless. Far from it. By thinking carefully about each item *in the light of your everyday experience*, and by being candid, you'll draw profiles that are approximately "true." For now, an approximation will do fine.

HOW TO DO IT

Pages 13 – 17 contain three questionnaires. The first two are about what happens in a sales call, so they're organized around the five basic steps to the sale: (1) opening, (2) exploring customer needs, (3) presenting the product or service, (4) managing objections, and (5) closing. The third is about what happens in a coaching session between a sales manager and a salesperson (a "curbstone conference," for example), so it's organized around the five basic steps to effective coaching: (1) starting, (2) getting the salesperson's views, (3) presenting your own views, (4) resolving disagreements, and (5) working out the action plan.

On each questionnaire, for each step listed above, you'll find four statements describing typical ways of interacting during that step. For example, on Questionnaire I, "My Toughest Customer," on the horizontal line next to "Opening," you'll find four statements, each describing one way your toughest customer might interact with you during the opening of a sales call. The next horizontal line has four statements describing how she might interact when you're exploring needs. And so on.

Here's what to do on each questionnaire:

1. Take one questionnaire at a time. Read each group of four statements *across*. Compare them with the actual behavior of the person being profiled. The statements are extreme, so none of them may *exactly* describe the actual behavior, but one or more of them should come close.

2. After reading each group of four statements, apportion 100 points among them so as to reflect the degree to which each statement describes the *actual* behavior of the person being profiled. Write the number of points allotted to each statement on the blank line inside each box. The point allotment for any one statement should be *proportionate* to how closely that statement fits the actual behavior. For instance, if the first statement on the first row across of Questionnaire I "perfectly" fits your toughest customer's behavior during the opening of a sales call, and if the three remaining statements don't fit at all, allocate the points this way: 100, 0, 0, 0. In most cases, you'll probably see something of the actual behavior in several or maybe all of the four statements. So your point allotments could be 10-30-20-40 or 25-25-0-50 or 60-10-10-20, *or whatever best describes the actual behavior*. Be sure to use *all* 100 points for each horizontal row of four statements.

3. Don't allot most of your points to what you consider the "ideal" answer. Make a candid allocation of points, even if the resulting profile isn't "complimentary." You want to end up with three *realistic* — not idealized — profiles. You're going to *use* these profiles; the more accurate they are, the more useful they'll be. Be candid.

4. There are no "right" or "wrong" responses. There are only *more descriptive* and *less descriptive* statements.

SUMMING IT UP

If you add the points in each vertical column on each profile, you'll probably see that you've assigned more points to one kind of behavior than to others. These point assignments should give you some important clues:

- Suppose, for example, that for "My Toughest Customer" you've assigned a preponderance of points to Customer Behavior A. This might mean you have trouble handling *most* customers who are stubborn, closed-minded, and argumentative — all characteristics of Customer Behavior A. If so (and a little reflection on the behavior of your *other* tough customers should tell you if it is) it means you need people skills that'll help you deal more effectively with that kind of behavior.

- Now, suppose you've also assigned a preponderance of points to Sales Behavior A (on the "How I Sell" questionnaire). If this assignment of points is fairly accurate, it means a sizable part of your sales behavior is brash, high-pressure, unbudging — all characteristics of Sales Behavior A. This might help explain *why* you have trouble selling your toughest customer — the one who's stubborn, closed-minded, and argumentative. After all, if you're brash and she's argumentative, if you're high-pressure and she's stubborn, if you're unbudging and she's closed-minded, you'd *expect* trouble. (This is only an example, of course. The point is that *whatever* your profile, and *whatever* your toughest customer's profile, the *interaction* between your behavior and hers probably sheds some light on *why* you have a hard time selling this particular customer.)

- If you're a sales manager, you'll probably find it useful to compare your managerial profile with the profile of your "hard-to-handle" salesperson. The *interaction* between your typical behavior and hers could shed light on *why* you're having problems.

To repeat: the profiles you've developed may be quite rough. That's why you want to be careful — at this point — about the conclusions you draw from them. But, rough or not, they should give you some idea of why sizing-up skills are important. As you go through this book and sharpen your ability to size up behavior, you'll see clearer patterns in your own behavior and that of others. These patterns will help you "make sense" out of your everyday experience.

Questionnaire I
MY TOUGHEST CUSTOMER

Steps to the Sale	Customer Behavior A	Customer Behavior B	Customer Behavior C	Customer Behavior D
1. Opening	Resists, interrupts, belittles, challenges, tries to grab control.	Quiet, aloof, suspicious, hard-to-read.	Very agreeable, talky, rambling, relaxed, eager to please.	Cordial, attentive, candid, ready to talk business.
2. When salesperson tries to explore customer's needs	Resists salesperson's efforts; gives belligerent, sarcastic, or overbearing answers.	Unwilling to disclose information; gives short, unrevealing answers or shrugs off questions.	Gives windy but incomplete answers; skirts touchy issues; tries hard to be pleasant and up-beat.	Willingly gives full, candid answers without wasting time.
3. When salesperson presents product/service	Interrupts, argues, objects, or tries to rattle salesperson; shows no desire to learn.	Silent, noncommittal, impassive; shows no curiosity.	Agrees with almost everything; strong enthusiasm doesn't always reflect real understanding.	Listens carefully and analytically; asks searching questions; shows real desire to learn.
4. When customer raises objections	Hops from objection to objection; argues vigorously; ignores facts and logic.	Offers no objections or weak ones; mostly just clams up and doesn't respond at all.	Offers no objections or a few apologetic ones; agrees readily with any answer or tries to change subject.	Offers candid objections and reasons; listens to answers; discusses them reasonably.
5. Closing	Tries to dictate terms or "make a deal", or refuses to buy in spite of good reasons to do so.	Postpones decisions with vague, noncommittal statements or gives in and unenthusiastically signs order.	Let's self be pressured into buying, makes token purchase to avoid saying "no," or promises to buy sometime in future.	Realistically assesses value and benefits after getting the facts, then makes reasonable, businesslike decision.

Remember: each row across should total 100 points.

Questionnaire II
HOW I SELL

Steps to the Sale	Sales Behavior A	Sales Behavior B	Sales Behavior C	Sales Behavior D
1. Opening	I do most of the talking, exert tight control, make strong claims, and try to dazzle with my drive and knowledge.	I'm reluctant to assert myself or set a direction; I prefer to let customer take the initiative.	I show I'm eager to please. I'm sociable, good-natured, and careful not to push or come on strong.	I explain why I'm there and what I expect to do for customer, and try to get a reaction.
2. Exploring needs	I usually know what the customer needs without much discussion, so I lay it on the line and expect her to take my word for it.	I hesitate to dig into the customer's needs; she knows what they are, so there's no good reason to explore them.	The customer's major need is for warm, genial treatment, so I give her that; all the rest is secondary.	I dig hard to uncover customer's needs, asking relevant questions and letting her do most of the talking.
3. Presenting product/service	I make a hard-driving presentation, with lots of claims, because that's what impresses people; I want to sound like an expert.	I describe the product and let the customer decide; its my job to describe and hers to make decisions.	I'm casual, sometimes barely referring to the product; instead, I concentrate on making a pal out of the customer.	I explain the product and what it'll do for the customer, so she sees how it'll solve problems and make her better off. I encourage questions.

4. Managing objections	I put down objections by burying the customer under an avalanche of facts or out-arguing her.	I ignore objections or go along with the customer; if I explore the objections, I may annoy her or create problems.	I gloss over objections, or compromise; if that doesn't work, I agree with the customer; I don't want to hurt our relationship by arguing.	I make sure I understand the objection, then discuss it till it's answered to the customer's satisfaction.
5. Closing	I push hard, using pressure if I must. Closing is a test of strength, so I do what I must to overpower the customer.	The close is up to the customer, not me; she'll buy when she's ready, so it's foolish to try for an order beforehand.	I go along with the customer; as long as we part on friendly terms, I know I'll get my share of the orders eventually.	I sum up what the customer will gain by buying, clear up any confusion or doubt, and ask for the order.

Remember: each row across should total 100 points.

Questionnaire III

HOW I COACH MY SALESPEOPLE

Steps to Effective Coaching	Managerial Behavior A	Managerial Behavior B	Managerial Behavior C	Managerial Behavior D
1. Starting the session	I lay it on the line, letting the salesperson know what's wrong, and that I'll explain how to correct it.	I'm reluctant to coach for fear I'll stir up problems; I play it safe by just skimming the surface.	I look at the bright side; I start by telling her how well she's doing; my aim is to boost morale.	Coaching is a learning experience, so I tell her we're going to explore pluses and minuses, and why that will benefit her.
2. Getting the salesperson's views	I don't fool around with getting the salesperson's views; I know what's wrong and what to do about it, so I spell it out.	I don't push to get her views; that'll only complicate things. If she wants to say something, she'll bring it up on her own.	I'm always ready to hear her out; a relaxed chat — on any topic — is a good way to ease tension and boost morale.	I try to learn what she thinks about the subject; I ask questions and allow time for response; that broadens my perspective.
3. Presenting my views	I explain, in no uncertain terms, that I want improvement, and I tell her how to achieve it; I don't waste time on discussion.	I've usually got a good idea of what the company "line" is, so I tell her and let it go at that.	I focus on pluses, so I don't discourage her; as long as I keep her morale high, she's sure to do her best.	I try to be objective, candid, helpful; I encourage questions, and try to show how she'll benefit from improving her performance.

4. Resolving disagreements	I put a quick end to disagreements by explaining that things must be done my way; that's what being boss is all about.	I don't discuss disagreements, because there's no reason to; she'll do as she wants, no matter what I say.	I play down disagreements and try to focus on other things; arguing is demoralizing, so I head off arguments.	I encourage full, frank discussion of disagreements, so as to come up with the best solution for everybody.
5. Working out an action plan	I voice my conclusions, make sure she knows they must be carried out, and end the session.	I don't worry about an action plan, because whatever's decided today may be undone tomorrow. It's best to leave things a bit vague.	I favor a plan we'll both feel comfortable with, which usually means a compromise.	I work toward a plan that'll bring her closer to her sales goals — one she'll feel committed to.

Remember: each row across should total 100 points.

HOW YOU STACK UP

You may be interested in knowing how your profile compares with those developed by other readers. We don't know what the profiles of all our readers look like, but we can tell you something about the profiles of a large and representative group of readers: the salespeople who have taken part in our Dimensional Sales Training seminars.

When preparing to attend a DST seminar, salespeople develop a self-profile, using a questionnaire something like the one you've just used. At the end of the seminar, they develop another self-profile, using the same questionnaire but ignoring their previous point allotments. The idea is to see if the second profile has changed as a result of insight acquired in the seminar. Over the years, Dimensional Training Systems has kept records on these profiles, both pre- and post-seminar, for thousands of salespeople, so by now we've got some very reliable norms. Here's what they show:

- Before attending DST, salespeople allocate most of their points to Sales Behavior D (which, as you've no doubt realized, is the most *idealized*, the behavior that exemplifies a widely accepted view of how salespeople *should* act). By comparison, they allocate the next largest number of points to Sales Behavior C, then A, then finally, B.

- At the end of DST, salespeople allocate a *significantly* different number of points to each behavior. Why? Because in the seminar they acquire insights which *change* the way they see themselves. As a result of feedback—candid reports from others on how they come across—they become more *aware* of their *actual* sales behavior. (We can't reveal the actual point allocations. If we did, we'd spoil an important part of DST for those readers who will attend a seminar after reading this book. We'll only say that the differences between the pre-seminar and the post-seminar point allocations are evidence of a dramatic—and valid—change in the way salespeople see their behavior. The same change occurs in sales managers who attend Dimensional Sales Management seminars.)

Thus, if you retake the questionnaire after reading this book, there's a good chance your second profile will differ from the first. That's not surprising. Just as salespeople acquire insights in DST which cause them to see their behavior differently, you'll acquire insights in reading this book which will cause you to see *your* behavior (and others') differently. That's why we said your first profiles might be "rough"—and why we've cautioned against drawing hard-and-fast conclusions from them.

If you read this book and then attend a DST or DSM seminar, you can expect your profile to change yet *again*. Thus, this book should help you see your present behavior more clearly, and a DST or DSM seminar would almost surely help you see it even more clearly. This increasing self-awareness is an important part of developing people skills.

3

Four Patterns of Behavior

Chapter 2 briefly described four ways of selling, of buying, and of managing. Why *four?* Because research shows that interactional behavior usually falls into one or more of *four patterns.* There are four basic ways to deal with customers or with salespeople. Once you know what they are, you'll have an easier time sizing up behavior — and prescribing behavior that gets results. This chapter describes the four patterns of interaction by means of what we call the Dimensional models.

THE DIMENSIONAL MODELS

A model is a way of *organizing* observations. We constantly observe people — customers, managers, salespeople, ourselves — behaving in various ways. And we classify these people on the basis of their behavior: "She's a show-off" . . . "He's a hard guy to deal with" . . . "I'm easy to get along with." Like it or not, this is just the way our minds work; categorizing is part of being human.

The Dimensional models do two things: (1) they organize our observations into more *useful* categories than we might come up with on our own; (2) they categorize *behavior* — not *people.* Let's explain.

- The models are useful for two reasons. First, because they deal with *interactional* behavior, they help us understand why some interactions "work out okay" and others "go bad" or "don't work out." Second, once we know *why* certain interactions don't work out, we can prescribe behavior that *will* work out. The Dimensional models are a tool for *improving results.*

- The models categorize behavior—not people. That's because people are enormously complex; sticking a label on a customer or anyone else is almost sure to be misleading because it reduces an intricate human being to a mere phrase. Moreover, people are changeable, but labels tend to be permanent; once we categorize a customer as a "pipsqueak," we may be surprised—and unprepared—when he stops squeaking and starts shouting. By categorizing behavior, not people, the Dimensional models avoid both traps.

The models are dependable. They're based on very solid research. The original research was done by psychologists in the late 1940s and 50s (it's described in Appendix C); since then, it's been amplified and reinforced by many behavioral scientists. The Dimensional models apply this research to the world of work. We think you'll be impressed by how well they "fit" your own observations. The models meet the test of experience.

The Basic Dimensional Model

Here's the basic model:

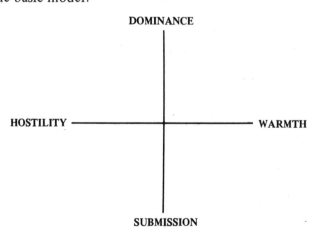

We'll separate the two intersecting dimensions and define their identifying terms: *dominance, submission, hostility, warmth.*

Dominance: Dominance is control or influence. It's asserting yourself, putting yourself or your ideas forward, trying to affect other people's thinking or behavior. It's taking charge and staying in charge, guiding and leading, convincing and moving others to action.

Submission: Submission is going along with others without first asserting your own ideas. It's ready compliance, giving in with little or no effort to exert influence.

One way to distinguish between *dominance* and *submission* is this: dominant behavior tries to *make* things happen while submissive behavior *lets* things happen. Dominant behavior is active; submissive behavior is passive.

Hostility: Hostility is self-centeredness and lack of regard for others. Hostile behavior is insensitive and unresponsive to people's needs, feelings, and ideas. It disparages their motives and their abilities.

Warmth: Warmth is regard for others coupled with trust, or at least openmindedness. Warm behavior is sensitive and responsive to people's feelings, needs, ideas. It's optimistic about their motives and abilities.

A good way to distinguish between *hostility* and *warmth* is this: hostile behavior is based on a *negative* or *pessimistic* view. It holds that you shouldn't expect much of other people, and shouldn't offer much of yourself in return. Warm behavior is more *positive* or *optimistic.* It holds that you should approach people, at least initially, in an open, receptive way. Hostile behavior considers most other people undependable at best, threatening or hurtful at worst. Warm behavior takes a much more favorable view.

Neither of the behaviors on either dimension shows up *alone.* Each *combines with* one of the behaviors on the other dimension. In combining, they're *modified,* so the actual *expression* of the behaviors always differs somewhat from our definitions. This will become clearer as we go along.

Combining the Dimensions

Combining the two dimensions gives us *four* basic patterns of behavior. These patterns are what the Dimensional models are all about.

Actually, there are as many different behaviors as there are people. But, because many of them are *similar* (*never* identical), we can group them into four basic patterns: (1) dominant-hostile, (2) submissive-hostile, (3) submissive-warm, (4) dominant-warm. Each pattern has countless variations.

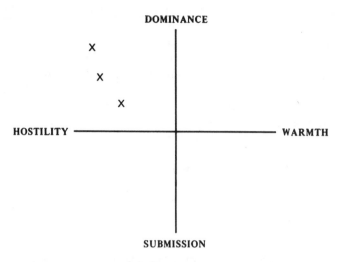

In any of the patterns, behavior becomes more *intense* as it moves away from the intersection. As behavior gets farther from the midpoint of the model, it becomes more pronounced, more clearly distinguishable.

Applying the Models

The rest of this chapter describes the four basic patterns of sales behavior, of customer behavior, and of sales management behavior. In all likelihood, *nobody's* behavior is exactly like any of our descriptions. That's because (a) the descriptions are "caricatures"; they lack subtlety and shading; and (b) each of us manifests *each* of the behaviors at various times. Still and all, most of us favor some one pattern over the others. For example, in the model of sales behavior, you'll probably recognize more of your own behavior in one description than in the other three.

From now on, because the behaviors fall into four quadrants, we'll call them, for short, Q1, Q2, Q3, and Q4:

Q1 = dominant-hostile
Q2 = submissive-hostile
Q3 = submissive-warm
Q4 = dominant-warm

You'll recognize these as the same behaviors—under new names—that we described in the questionnaires in Chapter 2.

CUSTOMER BEHAVIOR

Let's look at the first of our three models, the Dimensional Model of Customer Behavior. It's organized around the five steps to the sale used in the last chapter: (1) opening, (2) exploring customer needs, (3) presenting the product or service, (4) managing objections, and (5) closing. We'll describe each pattern of typical customer behavior in each step, and the attitudes underlying the behavior. Remember, our descriptions are caricatures, more extreme than most behavior you'll encounter on the job. We suggest you read the model first (Figure 1), and then the explanations which follow.

Q1 (Dominant-Hostile) Customer Behavior

As Figure 1 shows, Q1 is *adversary* behavior. The customer takes an *oppositional* stance:

> Let's face it: most salespeople are out to make a sale—whether it's in my best interest or not. That's why I'm determined to get—and keep—the upper hand. As long as *I'm* in control, as long as I can keep the salesperson off-balance, there's not much danger I'll get stuck with something I don't want or need. Most sales are win–lose situations; I do what I must to make sure I don't lose.

Thus, Q1 customer behavior tries to seize the initiative early in the sales call and maintain it throughout:

> If you can fluster the salesperson . . . keep him on the defensive . . . make him follow your game-plan . . . you can call the shots and make a decision on *your* terms—not his.

You're dealing with Q1 when the customer:

- Brags a lot, tries to impress you by dropping "big" names
- Tries to monopolize the discussion
- Interrupts, listens impatiently
- Is unreasonably stubborn and argumentative
- Offers dogmatic I-know-better-than-you-do opinions
- Reacts negatively before hearing the whole story
- Makes sarcastic or cutting comments
- Belittles you, your product, or your company
- Seems to be looking for an argument
- Claims to have all the answers
- Has a strong need to win arguments

Figure 1.   The Dimensional Model of Customer Behavior.

DOMINANCE

Q1 Customer Behavior

Basic premise: Keep the salesperson off-balance or you'll end up buying something you don't want or need.

Opening. Abrasive, defiant: "I dare you to sell me."

Exploring needs. Cocky, uncooperative: "I already know what I need, so why waste time talking about it?"

Presenting. Argues, interrupts: "I'll show you you're not as smart as you think."

Objections. Stubborn, belligerent, hops from objection to objection: "I'm not going to let you win."

Closing. Flatly refuses to buy or tries to dictate terms: "Don't forget who's in charge around here."

Q4 Customer Behavior

Basic premise: I expect a salesperson to explore and identify my needs, and show me how to satisfy them.

Opening. Receptive, attentive: "I'm hoping to get something out of this."

Exploring needs. Candid, cooperative: "I'll answer any questions designed to further my interests."

Presenting. Attentive, inquiring: "I expect a clear, organized explanation of what I stand to gain by buying."

Objections. Straightforward, businesslike: "I won't buy until my doubts have been cleared up."

Closing. Decision based on evidence: "I'll buy if I'm persuaded it's in my interest, but not otherwise."

HOSTILITY ———————————————————— WARMTH

Q2 Customer Behavior

Basic premise: The less you say to a salesperson, the less chance you'll get stuck with a bad buy.

Opening. Apathetic, hard-to-read: "I don't want to encourage you."

Exploring needs. Curt, tense: "I'm not going to reveal anything you can use against me."

Presenting. Silent, indifferent: "Go ahead and say what you want – I can't stop you."

Objections. Vague, vacillating: "I'll use any excuse to avoid making a firm decision."

Closing. Gives in without conviction, makes vague commitment, or postpones decision: "I just don't feel sure."

Q3 Customer Behavior

Basic premise: I always enjoy talking to salespeople, even if I don't intend to buy anything.

Opening. Friendly, genial: "Let's relax and chat a while."

Exploring needs. Talky, highly positive: "Why spoil things by dwelling on sticky issues?"

Presenting. Agreeable, encouraging: "I don't want to ruin your presentation by being negative."

Objections. Doesn't object or does so very weakly: "I don't see any value in giving salespeople a bad time."

Closing. Makes enthusiastic purchase or alibis for not buying: "I want to preserve our good relationship."

SUBMISSION

Q2 (Submissive-Hostile) Customer Behavior

Q2 is *protective* behavior. The customer takes a *defensive* stance:

> If I'm not careful, a salesperson may pressure or maneuver me into buying something I don't want or need. To prevent this, I'm very careful not to say anything that can be used against me. The more a salesperson *knows* about me, the more ammunition he can fire at me. So, as far as I can, I keep my mouth shut and my ideas to myself.

Thus, Q2 customer behavior is a safeguard against exploitation:

> As soon as I open up to a salesperson, I run the risk of being outsmarted or outtalked. Salespeople are experts at using words to their own advantage. Why play the game their way?

You're dealing with Q2 when the customer:

- Shrinks back and says little
- Picks words very cautiously, refuses to commit himself
- Is reluctant to take even calculated risks
- Seems tense, ill-at-ease, or reticent
- Backs away from new ideas; is more inclined to go along with established ideas
- Procrastinates or responds pessimistically to most suggestions
- Shies away from discussing personal matters
- Won't deviate from routine

Q3 (Submissive-Warm) Customer Behavior

Q3 is *acceptance-seeking* behavior. The customer works at being *liked*:

> I don't like cold, calculating business relationships. I want to get along with people—including salespeople—so I try hard to please. I'm friendly with everyone who calls on me, even though I frequently have no intention of buying anything, in which case the salesperson gets nothing out of it except some sociability. But, if I can, I try to spread my orders around, so that, over time, everyone gets a share.

Because Q3 customer behavior is designed to make the salesperson "feel good," it's long-winded, rambling, and cheerful:

> If you want people to enjoy being with you, you can't dwell on unhappy subjects. I talk about cheerful things. That's what makes friends.

You're dealing with Q3 when the customer:

- Is mainly intent on being pleasant
- Agrees quickly and heartily, even if he hasn't heard the whole story
- Responds optimistically to most suggestions
- Is a lot more talkative than the situation calls for
- Roams illogically from topic to topic
- Seems to have "all the time in the world" to talk
- Has a good word for nearly everybody and everything
- Avoids touchy subjects
- Dodges disagreements by suggesting quick compromises
- Is easily swayed

Q4 (Dominant-Warm) Customer Behavior

Q4 is *pragmatic* behavior. The customer tries to derive a *payoff* from the sales call:

> I'm busy, and I don't have time to waste. If I'm going to take time to talk to a salesperson, I expect to get something for it—to be better off as a result. If the salesperson can show how his product will make me better off, fine. I'll listen, cooperate, and probably buy. If he can't, I'll call off the discussion and go on to more important things. That's only practical.

Thus, Q4 customer behavior is businesslike and candid:

> When I'm talking to a salesperson, I expect to talk business. As long as he sticks to the subject and relates it to me and my concerns, I'll be as attentive, helpful, and straightforward as I can.

You're dealing with Q4 when the customer:

- Is self-assured but not cocky
- Is candid and open without being a know-it-all
- Readily defends his own ideas and listens to yours
- Acts decisively after hearing all the evidence
- Refuses to be overwhelmed by "experts"; wants to consider the facts for himself
- Asks tough but pertinent questions; tries to get the whole story
- Willingly takes intelligent risks if the return seems worth it
- Responds favorably or at least curiously to new ideas
- Discusses differences open-mindedly
- Openly answers questions and shares information
- Doesn't mind being proven wrong

Figure 2.   The Dimensional Model of Sales Behavior.

DOMINANCE

Q1 Sales Behavior

Basic premise: The surest way to make a sale is to overpower the customer.

Opening. Hard-driving, exaggerated: "The first thing to do is dazzle or intimidate the customer."

Exploring needs. Superficial: "I know what's best for the customer without asking lots of questions."

Presenting. Fires barrage of facts, exaggerations, claims, with little give-and-take: "Keep up the pressure till you wear down the customer."

Managing objections. Bulldozes, belittles, out-argues: "Bury the objection before it buries you."

Closing. Intense, overbearing: "Keep the pressure on till the customer gives in."

Q4 Sales Behavior

Basic premise: To make a sale, prove your product will make the customer better off.

Opening. Informative, results-oriented: "I tell the customer why I'm there, and what I expect to do for him, and find out if he's ready to work with me."

Exploring needs. Questions and analyzes: "Unless I know the customer's needs, I can't make a presentation that meets his concerns."

Presenting. Fits products to customer's needs: "I show how my product will fill his need and make him better off."

Managing objections. Patient, searching, confronts hard facts: "I try to understand and remove the customer's doubts."

Closing. Systematic, instructive, results-oriented: "I sum up, clear up final doubts, stress what's in it for the customer, and ask for the order."

HOSTILITY ——————————————————————— WARMTH

Q2 Sales Behavior

Basic premise: You can't create sales; you can only take orders.

Opening. Mechanical, colorless: "Why knock myself out? The customer will buy when ready—in spite of anything I say."

Exploring needs. Superficial, indifferent: "If the customer needs something, he'll say so without my asking."

Presenting. Spiritless, apathetic: "I present the facts and let the customer draw his own conclusions."

Managing objections. Ignores or goes along: "I can't do much to change a customer's mind, so why try?"

Closing. Weak or non-existent: "Whether or not to buy is up to the customer. If he's ready to place an order, he'll tell me."

Q3 Sales Behavior

Basic premise: If you make yourself liked, you'll eventually make the sale.

Opening. Very sociable, relaxed, may not mention business at all: "I let the customer know I'm there as a friend."

Exploring needs. Superficial, unsystematic: "As long as I keep the conversation going, I'll learn the customer's needs sooner or later."

Presenting. Longwinded, unfocussed: "I'm more concerned with fostering a relationship than discussing the product."

Managing objections. Agrees, glosses over, or changes topic: "Why dwell on things that could spoil our relationship?"

Closing. Weak, compliant: "I go along with the customer. As long as we're friends, I'll get my share of the business."

SUBMISSION

SALES BEHAVIOR

We're ready now to shift from *customer* behavior to *sales* behavior. The sales model (Figure 2) follows the same format as the customer model. Once again, our descriptions are extreme; there are actually innumerable individual variations of each behavior.

Q1 (Dominant-Hostile) Sales Behavior

Q1 tries to *power* its way to results. It marshals all available resources — energy, knowledge, verbal agility, aggressiveness, pressure — to overwhelm the customer. It tries to bulldoze opposition, or, if that doesn't work, grind it down. The idea is to get the order by being stronger, tougher, more durable than the customer:

> There's a tendency on just about everyone's part to resist buying. To overcome it, you must show the customer you won't take no for an answer. Selling is a contest of wills, and the stronger will usually prevails. Most customers are like immovable objects; they can't be budged unless they come in contact with an irresistible force. It's my job to be the irresistible force.

Q1 selling is hard-driving and tenacious:

> If I can't bowl the customer over, I try to wear him down, outlast him. Sooner or later, someone has to give in. As long as it's not me, I know I'll get the order. And getting the order is what counts.

You're seeing Q1 when a salesperson:

- Overwhelms the customer with facts, figures, "expert" opinions
- Argues even before he gets the whole story
- Twists the facts to suit his own purpose
- Turns on and keeps on the pressure
- Keeps tight control of the subjects he "permits" the customer to discuss
- Dominates or monopolizes the discussion
- Hears what he wants, disregards the rest
- Tries to convey the impression that he "knows it all"
- Puts down, belittles, taunts, or embarrasses the customer

Q2 (Submissive-Hostile) Sales Behavior

Q2 is a *fatalistic* approach to selling:

> I don't kid myself about my powers of persuasion. In fact, I don't believe in the power of persuasion. Most people buy things when they're good and ready—not before—and a salesperson can't do much to get them ready; it's all up to the customer. What a salesperson can do is make plenty of calls—be

on hand when customers decide to buy. As long as I'm out knocking on doors and making myself available, the law of averages will work for me, and I'll pick up some orders.

Q2 selling is lackluster, almost indifferent. Much of the time, the salesperson seems to go through the motions, repeating memorized lines without zest or conviction:

> Why knock myself out? Nothing I say or do will make much difference; the initiative lies with the customer—not me. When he's ready to buy, he'll do it regardless of what I say or don't say. About the only useful thing I can do in a presentation is explain how the product works and answer technical questions. Beyond that, it's all up to the customer.

You're seeing Q2 when a salesperson:

- Makes a listless presentation, as if he's not convinced of what he's saying
- Doesn't respond to the customer, or responds mechanically
- Makes vague statements that can't be pinned down
- Backs off if the customer objects; quickly takes "no" for an answer
- Seems tense, awkward, ill-at-ease
- Doesn't give evidence of hearing everything that's said
- Won't make firm commitments
- Seems dour and humorless
- Doesn't dig for information or follow up promising clues

Q3 (Submissive–Warm) Sales Behavior

Q3 believes that making sales is mostly a matter of *gaining acceptance*:

> People prefer to do business with people they like. That's only human. And it's truer than ever today, when competitive products are so much alike. Lots of times, what makes the difference between getting the order and not getting it isn't the product—it's the relationship between the customer and the salesperson. So, the important thing in every sales call is to cultivate the customer—make a friend. The way to do it is to be sociable, easygoing, and eager to please.

Q3 selling is talkative, agreeable, and lopsided—attentive to "cheerful" subjects while ignoring or downplaying "troublesome" ones:

> Why introduce tension into a congenial relationship? I try to avoid, or at least minimize, disagreeable subjects. I guess I'm like a musician who prefers harmony to discord. Everyone hits a sour note occasionally, but, as far as I'm concerned, the fewer the better.

You're seeing Q3 when a salesperson:

- Meanders from subject to subject
- Sees only the bright side
- Readily agrees with almost anything the customer says
- Has trouble sticking to business; likes to digress
- Injects lots of upbeat phrases, like "That's terrific" and "Glad to hear it," as the customer talks
- Discusses the product in general terms, but is weak on details
- Backs away from any sign of disagreement; suggests easy compromise
- Uses far more words than necessary
- Seems to hear only cheerful information, tunes out the rest

Q4 (Dominant-Warm) Sales Behavior

Q4 is *results-oriented*:

> Why should any customer listen to me unless he gets something in return? Customers are like investors; they'll give you their time and attention *if* they think they'll get something back for it. My job is to make sure each customer's investment pays off. The way to do it is to show him that buying my product will make him *better off* by filling one or more of his *needs*. If I can do that ... if I can deliver a plus to the customer ... I'm fairly sure to get the order.

Q4 is *analytic*:

> How do I know what will make the customer better off? I *don't*—unless I dig for information. Selling isn't just a matter of describing a product—it's a matter of asking questions and analyzing the answers, so I can make the description *fit* the customer. Unless I can find out what he needs, I can't show how my product will *fill* his need—and I can't prove that buying it will make him better off. Selling isn't overpowering customers; it's *understanding* them.

You're seeing Q4 when a salesperson:

- Gets the customer seriously involved in the presentation
- Listens carefully and shows he's trying to understand
- Asks plenty of pertinent questions, especially about the customer's needs and objections
- Tries to discover the real needs instead of imposing his own ideas
- Explains how buying the product will help satisfy the needs
- Comes across as a problem-solver, not a pitchman
- "Rolls with the punches" by quickly adapting to changes in the customer's behavior

SALES MANAGEMENT BEHAVIOR

There's one more model to look at—on managerial behavior. It follows the same format as the questionnaire on managerial behavior in the last chapter. It's based on the five steps to effective coaching: (1) starting the session, (2) getting the salesperson's views, (3) presenting the manager's views, (4) resolving disagreements, and (5) working out an action plan (These steps will be fully explained later.) As you go through the model, see if you can recognize your own (or your manager's) behavior.

Q1 (Dominant-Hostile) Sales Management

Q1 is *coercive* behavior; it relies on the sales manager's *power* over the salesperson:

> Let's be realistic. Most salespeople have to be pushed to work hard. They have to be told what to do. That's *my* job. If I don't prod my people and exert close control, they're bound to sluff off or make mistakes. The surest way to have a successful sales organization is to use clout—*make* people perform the way they should.

Thus, Q1 management moves in one direction: from manager to salesperson, with very little traffic the other way:

> Look, that's the way it has to be. I'm paid to *know best*—that's why *I'm* the manager. It's my job to call the shots. Discussions and debates only waste time. The important thing is to tell people what to do and then make sure they get out there and do it.

You can recognize Q1 when a manager:

- Refuses to consult his salespeople before making decisions involving them
- Handles many tasks on his own that could easily be delegated
- Exerts tight control, even down to small details
- Tells his salespeople what to do and how, without bothering to get their reactions
- Uses threats—overt or implied—to get his people to do what he wants
- Makes his people feel "pushed around" or "treated like kids"
- Resists new ideas by belittling the salesperson who originated them ("You're not being paid to run this operation"); sometimes, however, "appropriates" new ideas and passes them off as his own.

Figure 3. The Dimensional Model of Managerial Behavior.

DOMINANCE

Q1 Managerial Behavior

Basic premise: If you want results from salespeople, run a tight ship and let them know who's boss.

Starting. Blunt, accusatory: "I let them know I'm dissatisfied and intend to straighten things out."

Getting views. Superficial or non-existent: "I'm not interested in alibis. I know what's wrong, and I intend to spell it out."

Presenting views. Hammers away at faults: "I tell them what they're doing wrong and how to change it. That's my job."

Resolving disagreements. Squelches and suppresses: "I don't tolerate backtalk."

Action-planning. Autocratic, demanding: "The point is, I want to see things done my way."

Q4 Managerial Behavior

Basic premise: Show your people what they'll gain by meeting their sales goals; give them an incentive to get the job done.

Starting. Candid, results-oriented: "I explain we're going to talk about pluses and minuses, so the salesperson can improve performance and meet his goals."

Getting views. - Inquiring, analytic: "If I can get the salesperson to analyze his own performance, he's more likely to accept the analysis."

Presenting views. Candid, thorough, instructive: "I try to solve problems by encouraging questions and discussion."

Resolving disagreements. Explores, discusses: "I don't care whose ideas prevail as long as they're the best ideas."

Action-planning. Clear, workable: "I strive for an understanding of the plan and commitment to it."

HOSTILITY ──────────────────────────── WARMTH

Q2 Managerial Behavior

Basic premise: Salespeople are what they are; if you've got some good ones, you're lucky; if you haven't, you can't do much about it.

Starting. Vague, apathetic: "Coaching doesn't accomplish much, but it's something a manager's expected to do."

Getting views. Superficial, uninterested: "The more questions I ask, the more likely I'll open up problems best left closed."

Presenting views. Routine, indifferent: "I know what the company expects me to say, so I say it."

Resolving disagreements. Avoids and ignores: "Why stir up trouble? I won't change anyone's mind anyway."

Action-planning. Vague, vacillating: "Most actions plans are empty talk; people go on doing what they've always done."

Q3 Managerial Behavior

Basic premise: If I keep morale up, I can keep performance up; a positive attitude is what counts in selling.

Starting. Cheerful, vague: "I explain that I just want to chat about how things are going."

Getting views. Talkative, unfocused: "The salesperson can say whatever he wants, but I try to skirt touchy subjects."

Presenting views. Longwinded, upbeat: "I look at the bright side. Focusing on negatives is demoralizing."

Resolving disagreements. Minimizes, glosses over, changes subject: "Arguments weaken the positive attitude I want to create. And discussing differences can lead to an argument."

Action-planning. Easygoing, compromising: "Why make strong demands? They only cause tension."

SUBMISSION

Q2 (Submissive-Hostile) Sales Management

Q2 is *pessimistic*; it takes a bleak view of people and their potential for change:

> I think we mostly kid ourselves about motivation. There's very little any sales manager can do to motivate or change or improve salespeople. Good sales-people—those who want to do the job and know how—will do it. The others won't. And nothing I do will make much difference. As I see it, there are two things a sales manager can do: monitor the handling of the company's policies and procedures, so everything runs smoothly, and look out for himself. Beyond that, you pretty much have to accept whatever comes your way.

Thus, Q2 focuses on *routines*. It's *passive*:

> Managers go through a lot of rituals that leave things pretty much the way they were. Sure, I do what's expected: coaching, performance appraisal, all the rest. But I don't fool myself that any of it will improve sales results. So why knock myself out to do something that can't be done?

You can recognize Q2 whenever the manager:

- Rarely conveys his own views, acting instead as a mouthpiece for top management
- Exerts little direction unless passing along routine instructions or trying, too late, to keep things from getting out of hand
- Puts off all but the most routine decisions
- Says little; keeps most communication superficial
- Resists new ideas by citing tradition ("The way we've been doing it works, so let's not change it") or by indefinitely postponing a decision ("Let's think about it for a while")
- Takes things as they come, without seriously trying to motivate improved performance

Q3 (Submissive-Warm) Sales Management

Q3 is *lenient*, even *indulgent*. That means it's also *selective*: it emphasizes positives, and plays down or overlooks negatives:

> The way to get better sales results is to make sure your salespeople feel good—about themselves, their jobs, their company. Selling is a matter of attitude; the salesperson with high morale is more enthusiastic and relaxed, and customers like that. Cheerfulness, optimism, zest—these things make sales. It's my job to see that my salespeople are cheerful, optimistic, zesty. The surest way to do it is to focus on positives. Nothing can be gained by knocking or criticizing or finding fault.

Thus, Q3 management is fairly *loose* and *unstructured*:

> The whole idea of systems and organization has been overdone. All the systems in the world won't do much good if your salespeople have the wrong attitude. Sales managers would be better off if they concentrated on good relationships with their people and worried less about procedures. You can't boost morale with a procedures manual.

You can recognize Q3 when a manager:

- Sets goals that won't "trouble" anybody because they're easy to achieve
- Exerts little or sometimes no control
- Is very concerned that salespeople "like" his decisions
- Eagerly discusses cheerful or encouraging news, and ignores or downplays bad or ominous news ("It'll work out fine—just wait and see")
- Enjoys long, relaxed talks which focus largely on non-business
- Motivates by personal appeals ("Do it as a favor to me") or by "cheerleading" ("I know you've got what it takes, so go to it")

Q4 (Dominant-Warm) Sales Management

Q4 is *realistic* and *pragmatic*:

> Most salespeople will work hard if they have a good reason, and they'll work effectively if they know how. My job is to see that they *do* have a good reason and that they *do* know how. I try to know what my people *want* from their jobs, I show them how they can *get* it by attaining their sales goals, and I help them develop the skills for doing it. I see myself as a motivator and a trainer; I don't think the two roles can be separated.

Thus, Q4 management is highly *individualized*:

> People want different things from their work. An incentive for one may not be an incentive for another. And people need to develop different skills. One may lack product knowledge, another may not know how to ask questions, and a third may have trouble handling objections. So, before I can motivate and train, I've got to know each of my salespeople as a *unique* person.

You can recognize Q4 when a manager:

- Involves his salespeople in decisions that concern them or to which they can contribute something (experience, insight, information, etc.)
- Delegates whenever delegation makes sense for the company, the salesperson, and himself

- Motivates his salespeople by helping them see "what's in it for them" if they hit their goals
- Involves his salespeople in businesslike discussions; asks searching questions and listens carefully
- Tries to discuss all topics candidly, omitting nothing pertinent and including nothing distorted

VARIATIONS IN BEHAVIOR

Obviously, nobody behaves the same way all the time. For one thing, many people behave differently in different roles; somebody who mostly "Q1s it" as a *customer* may mostly "Q3 it" as a *subordinate.* For another thing, even in a single role, our behavior often changes with circumstances:

- As long as things "go well," most of us stick fairly close to the behavior we feel most comfortable with. This "standard" behavior — which people who know us come to *expect* of us — is called *primary* behavior. Because it seems "natural" to us in a particular role, we use it again and again in that role.

- When things don't "go well," and we feel frustrated or tense, we frequently *shift* to a different — and unplanned — behavior. (Think of the "nice guy" who under a lot of stress suddenly "blows up" and starts shouting.) These reflexive behaviors, which "just happen," are called *secondary* behaviors. They're usually short-lived.

- At other times, we shift to another behavior *intentionally* — in response to pressure or to attain a goal. (Think of the soft-spoken salesperson who, pressured by the boss to "toughen up," adopts a loud, brash manner. Or the low-key salesperson who, eager to win a sales contest, adopts hard-hammering tactics.) These deliberate shifts are called *masks.* Most masks (not all) are worn only a short time. When we "remove" a mask, we usually revert to our primary behavior.

It's often very difficult to tell whether a behavior is primary, secondary, or mask. And, *for all practical purposes,* it doesn't matter. What does matter is that you deal with the behavior you see and hear *in front of you.* If you call on a customer who Q1s it, deal with the Q1 behavior. If that same customer suddenly starts Q3ing it, deal with the Q3 behavior. (The rest of this book explains *how.*) Don't worry about which is primary or secondary or mask. It makes no *practical* difference. All that counts is that you deal with the behavior you observe *as you observe it.* We'll talk a lot about this later.

SOME DISTINCTIONS

If you think back to the basic model, you may be puzzled by the fact that each dimension can take two basic forms. There's Q1 dominance and Q4 dominance, Q2 submission and Q3 submission, Q1 hostility and Q2 hostility, and Q3 warmth and Q4 warmth. You can recognize each member of these pairs this way:

- Q1 dominance is *me*-centered. The idea is to exert control to gain your own ends. Q4 dominance is more *us*-centered. The idea is to exert control to gain—or come close to—*both* people's ends. Q1 dominance is aggressive; Q4 dominance is assertive. Q1 dominance aims at a *win–lose* result; Q4 dominance aims at a *win–win* result.

- Q2 submission is *self*-protective. The idea is to give in to keep yourself out of trouble. Q3 submission is *relationship*-protective. The idea is to give in so as not to endanger a good relationship.

- Q1 hostility is usually very apparent; it can be seen and heard, because it's directed *outward*. Q2 hostility is *less* apparent; it takes the form of silence and withdrawal. Q1 hostility is blustery and overt; Q2 hostility is remote and covert.

- Q3 warmth is eager to *please* and willing to *go along*; the idea is to make yourself *liked*. Q4 warmth is *respectful, concerned*, and *responsive*; the idea is to do what's in everyone's *best interest*—even though it may not make you very popular.

SUMMARY

1. The Dimensional Models do two things: (a) organize our observations of interactional behavior so that we can make use of them; (b) categorize behavior—not people.

2. The dimensions used in the models are dominance-submission and hostility-warmth.

3. Dominance is control or influence; submission is compliance without prior assertion. Dominance is active; submission is passive.

4. Hostility is self-centeredness and lack of regard for others; warmth is regard for others coupled with trust or openmindedness. Hostility is negative or pessimistic about others; warmth is positive or optimistic.

5. The four patterns in the Dimensional Model of Customer Behavior are: Q1—adversary behavior; Q2—protective behavior; Q3—acceptance-seeking; Q4—pragmatic behavior.

6. The premise of Q1 customer behavior is: "If you don't keep salespeople off-balance, you're liable to end up buying something you shouldn't."

7. The premise of Q2 customer behavior is: "If you don't open up to salespeople, you'll have a better chance of not getting stuck with a bad purchase."

8. The premise of Q3 customer behavior is: "It's always nice to spend time with salespeople, even if a sale doesn't result."

9. The premise of Q4 customer behavior is: "A salesperson should do three things: explore my needs, identify them, and show me how to fill them."

10. The four patterns in the Dimensional Model of Sales Behavior are: Q1 – which tries to power its way to results; Q2 – a fatalistic approach; Q3 – which focuses on gaining acceptance; Q4 – business-like, need-filling behavior.

11. The premise of Q1 sales behavior is: "There's one sure way to make a sale: overpower the customer."

12. The premise of Q2 sales behavior is: "Forget about creating sales, since you can't do much to create them anyway; just be around to take the order when the customer's ready to give it."

13. The premise of Q3 sales behavior is: "Concentrate on making yourself liked, and the sale will take care of itself."

14. The premise of Q4 sales behavior is: "To make a sale, show the customer that your product will make him better off."

15. The four patterns in the Dimensional Model of Sales Management Behavior are: Q1 – coercive; Q2 – pessimistic and passive; Q3 – lenient; Q4 – individualized.

16. The premise of Q1 management is: "To get results out of salespeople, exert tight control; make sure they know who's boss."

17. The premise of Q2 management is: "You can't do much to change the salespeople who work for you; the good ones are good, and the others aren't, and there's not much you can do about either."

18. The premise of Q3 management is: "Keep morale up and you'll keep sales up; salespeople perform effectively when they've got a good attitude toward their jobs."

19. The premise of Q4 management is: "Salespeople perform effectively when they've got an incentive to do so and know how; it's the manager's job to provide the incentive – the reason to do good work – and the know-how."

20. Primary behavior is the interactional behavior we most typically manifest. Secondary behavior is unintentionally manifested when we're sufficiently frustrated. Mask behavior is deliberately manifested to cope with frustration or pressure. For all practical purposes, the distinctions don't really count. What counts is that you deal with the behavior that confronts you.

4

What's the Difference?

If you think you've detected a Q4 bias in the previous chapters, your're right. We *do* favor Q4 behavior—in selling and in sales management. Why? Because research, experience, and common sense all point to the same conclusion: Q4 gets *better results*, over the long haul and on the average, than other behaviors. We'll back up this claim in this chapter. And we'll try to persuade you (*sell* you on the idea) that, whether you're a salesperson or a sales manager, Q4 skills are worth learning—and using.

We'll start by asking you to look at your own experience. Whether you sell or manage, you've probably been around long enough to see all kinds of customer behavior, all kinds of sales behavior, and all kinds of sales *results*. The question now becomes: Is there a *connection* between the behaviors and the results? Here's how to get the answer:

1. First, review Figures 4 and 5. They recap the four basic sales and customer behaviors, and will help you fix them in mind.

2. Then go to Figure 6 and fill in each box. If you think one of the interactions on the chart typically produces *above average* results, put a plus sign (+) in the box. If you think an interaction typically produces *average* results, put an "A" in the box. And if you think an interaction typically produces *below average* results, put a minus sign (–) in the box. Base all judgments on your own experience—on what you've actually seen or heard in the field.

3. What *kind* of results should you consider? We suggest:
   - Volume (dollars or units)
   - Cost of sales
   - Closure rate
   - Repeat business
   - Maintenance rate in face of competition
   - Product mix
   - Target accounts sold
   - Customer loyalty
   - Referrals

Once you've reached your conclusions, we'll give you ours. Remember, focus on *typical* results, even though they may not happen in every single case.

Figure 4. The Basic Sales Behaviors.

Steps to Sale	Q1	Q2	Q3	Q4
Opening	Pushy	Mechanical	Social	Purposeful
Exploring needs	Assumes them; doesn't check assumptions	Reluctant to explore	Tries to make friends	Questions and analyzes
Presenting	Hard-hitting monologue	Routine recitation	Rambling chat	Instructive dialogue
Handling objections	Bulldozes	Backs away	Glosses over	Analyzes, then answers
Closing	High-pressures	Hesitates	Gives away store	Proves benefit

Figure 5. The Basic Customer Behaviors.

Steps to Sale	Q1	Q2	Q3	Q4
Opening	Stubborn	Hard-to-read	Sociable	Results-oriented
Exploring needs	Feisty, uncooperative	Unresponsive	Rambling, unfocussed	Candid, cooperative
Presenting	Quarrelsome, interruptive	Quiet, indifferent	Agreeable, talkative	Attentive, inquiring
Objections	Numerous, unreasonable	Vague, uneasy	Alibis, changes subject	Candid, reasonable
Closing	Argues and horse-trades	Vacillates, postpones	Agrees or makes big promises	Buys if committed

Figure 6

TYPICAL SALES–CUSTOMER INTERACTIONS

CUSTOMER BEHAVIOR

	Q1	Q2	Q3	Q4
Q1				
Q2				
Q3				
Q4				

SALES BEHAVIOR

Now that you've gauged sales-customer results in the light of your own experience, we'll share our experience with you. The results we've posted on Figure 7 are generalizations, as yours are. They don't forecast the result of any *specific* interaction. They're simply results *over the long haul* and *on the average.* They're based on our experience with thousands of salespeople in Dimensional Sales Training courses and on research, some of which we'll cite later in this chapter.

A glance at Figure 7 explains why we advocate Q4 sales behavior. But it doesn't explain why the various interactions so often turn out the way they do. Why, for instance, is Q1 sales behavior likely to get better results with Q3 customer behavior than with Q2? Figure 8 gives the reasons.

Figure 8 makes three vital points:

1. Q4 sales behavior, as a rule, produces above average results *no matter what* the customer's behavior. This isn't true of the other sales behaviors. Q1, for example, frequently runs into trouble with customers who Q2 it. Q2 is very often stymied by customers who Q1 or Q4 it. And Q3 usually has a hard time with customers who Q1 it. Only Q4 has a high "payoff rate" with *all kinds* of customer behavior.

2. It's impossible to explain the results of any sales interaction by looking *only* at the salesperson's behavior or *only* at the customer's behavior. A sales interaction "makes sense" only when *both* behaviors are examined. What's critical is the *interaction*—the "mix"—between the two. (We're not saying, of course, that sales results can be fully understood simply by looking at the behavior involved. Many other factors must be examined: product quality, reputation, service, price, the competitive situation, the salesperson's technical knowledge, and so on. Our concern is with behavior, but obviously, these other factors are also significant—and sometimes decisive.)

3. Q4 is most likely to pay off, across the board, because it answers a whole series of critical questions which trouble many, probably most, customers: "What's in it for me? How will this purchase make me better off? What do I stand to gain from it? Why should I bother listening to this salesperson? Why should I trust her? Why should I cooperate with her during the presentation? Why should I share information and ideas with her? Why should I accept her guidance and advice?" Other sales behaviors either *don't* answer these questions, or they answer them the *wrong way* (as we'll see later, for example, other behaviors sometimes persuade the customer that she *shouldn't* trust the salesperson).

Figure 7

TYPICAL SALES–CUSTOMER INTERACTIONS

		CUSTOMER BEHAVIOR		
SALES BEHAVIOR	Q1	Q2	Q3	Q4
Q1	A	−	+	A
Q2	−	A	A	−
Q3	−	A	+	A
Q4	+	+	+	+

Figure 8

TYPICAL SALES–CUSTOMER INTERACTIONS

		CUSTOMER BEHAVIOR			
SALES BEHAVIOR		*Q1*	*Q2*	*Q3*	*Q4*
	Q1	(A) Scrappy, hard-hitting exchange produces mutual respect, much heat, but little understanding.	(–) Customer made uneasy by fast talk and lavish claims; figures it's safer not to buy.	(+) Customer cannot withstand pressure and torrent of claims; "goes along" to please salesperson.	(A) Customer respects salesperson's strength, but may not fully trust her or see good reason to buy.
	Q2	(–) Customer overpowers salesperson, who quickly caves in and calls it quits.	(A) Salesperson's low-key, undemanding manner reassures customer, who may place an order.	(A) Salesperson's aloofness baffles customer, who may decide to "give her a break" anyway and buy.	(–) Salesperson's recital generates neither understanding nor commitment.
	Q3	(–) Salesperson agreeably goes along with customer's objections, so customer sweeps the field.	(A) Customer finds salesperson's warmth and refusal to pressure reassuring; may place an order.	(+) Both people hit it off from the start; sale seems to "come naturally."	(A) Customer will buy if able to discern "what's in it for me" amid excessive verbage.
	Q4	(+) Salesperson guides customer while letting her maintain self-esteem; customer feels she can submit to guidance without "losing face."	(+) Salesperson quickly demonstrates trustworthiness; customer confident of salesperson's reliability, willingly listens and cooperates.	(+) Salesperson is suitably sociable but doesn't lose sight of main objective; customer feels accepted and able to trust salesperson.	(+) Salesperson is businesslike and instructive; customer understands proposal and "what's in it for me."

Later chapters will explain how Q4 does all this; for the moment, the important point is that, of all sales behaviors, only Q4 consistently provides *good reasons* to cooperate with the salesperson and to buy her product or service.

SOME ADDITIONAL EVIDENCE

Our conclusions about Q4 are confirmed by research. Some years ago, Dimensional Training Systems developed the DSA—Dimensional Salesperson Analysis—questionnaire. People using it are asked to think of both the "best" salesperson and the "worst" salesperson they've known, and then to identify the behaviors of each by assigning points to behaviors listed on the questionnaire. Each behavior on the list is Q1, Q2, Q3, or Q4. The end result is a numerical behavioral profile. By asking hundreds of participants in Dimensional Sales Management courses to fill out the questionnaire, and then combining and averaging the profile "scores," Dimensional Training Systems has developed composite portraits of the "best" and the "worst" salesperson. These profiles are shown in Figure 9.

Two points about Figure 9 are important:

1. In general, people see the "best" salesperson they know as someone who manifests *much more* Q4 behavior than any other kind. And they see the "worst" as someone who manifests *much less.* Q4 behavior does make a favorable impression.

Figure 9

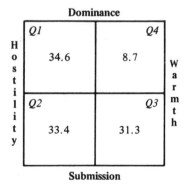

(Because of scoring system, figures do not total 100.)

2. The fact that someone's considered the "best" salesperson doesn't mean she couldn't become even better. And the fact that someone's the "worst" doesn't mean she's fated to stay the worst. Salespeople aren't locked into their present behaviors. As we'll see, sales (and managerial) behavior *can* be changed; interactional skills *can* be learned. If that weren't so, there'd be no point in reading any more of this book.

SALES MANAGEMENT RESULTS

If you're a sales manager, you may want to gauge the results of various *managerial* behaviors. You can do so on Figure 10. Our own conclusions can be found on Figure 11. (If you're a salesperson, you may also enjoy filling out the chart, basing your judgments on what you've observed in your own company.) Here's how to use Figure 10:

1. Ask yourself two questions: (a) If I were mainly to Q1, Q2, Q3, or Q4 it with my salespeople, how would that affect sales results, costs, morale, turnover, teamwork, innovation, and development over the long haul? (b) Whenever I've seen other sales managers Q1, Q2, Q3, or Q4 it with their salespeople, what effect (as far as I can tell) has that had on sales results, etc.?

2. Where you think the result would be above average, write "high"; where average, write "average"; and where below average, write "low."

Our conclusions, based on experience with many managers in Dimensional Sales Management courses and on independent studies, are on Figure 11. Once again, we're generalizing, not trying to forecast the outcome of any specific interaction.

CONCLUSION

In general, Q4 — whether in sales or sales management — pays off best for four reasons:

1. Q4 is realistic. Q4 selling recognizes that customers want to *maximize the benefit* they'll derive from a purchase, so it shows them how they can do it. Q4 sales management recognizes that salespeople want to *maximize the benefit* they'll derive from their jobs, so it shows them how to do it.

Figure 10

	MANAGERIAL BEHAVIOR			
Results	*Q1*	*Q2*	*Q3*	*Q4*
Sales results				
Costs				
Morale				
Turnover				
Teamwork				
Innovation				
Development of salespeople				

Figure 11

	MANAGERIAL BEHAVIOR			
Results	*Q1*	*Q2*	*Q3*	*Q4*
Sales results	High to average over time	Low	Low	High
Costs	High to average	High to average	High	Average to low
Morale	Low	Low	High	High
Turnover	High	Low	Low	Average
Teamwork	Low	Low	Low	High
Innovation	Low	Low	Low	High
Development of salespeople	Low	Low	Low	High

(For explanation of results, see Chapter 16.)

2. Q4 *demonstrates* trustworthiness. Salespeople and sales managers who behave in *other* ways may also be trustworthy, but their behavior doesn't always convey the fact. Q4 *makes it plain* that "You can rely on me — because I have your interests at heart as well as my own." For this reason, people are usually more ready to "open up" in the presence of Q4 behavior, to cooperate, to believe what's said. There's nothing adversarial about Q4 interactions; they're more like "working partnerships."

3. Q4 is skilled. It doesn't "just happen." Behaving in a Q4 way takes certain skills. People who practice Q4 consistently do so because they've mastered the skills. They know *how* to "Q4 it."

4. Q4 is flexible. Since one person's enlightened self-interest isn't necessarily the same as another's, Q4 always tries to understand — and appeal to — *individual* interests. It tries to get past stereotypes and cliches and come to grips with the real living-and-breathing person. This requires a high degree of flexibility.

Starting in the next chapter, we'll explain *how* the appeal to enlightened self-interest and the demonstration of trustworthiness, combined with skills and flexibility, can pay off for you.

5

Q4 Selling

We've referred several times to "the five steps to the sale." In this chapter, we'll take a closer look at them, because they're the framework—the "skeleton"—of Q4 selling.

The five steps to the sale are actually a special version of the *five steps to successful interaction*—no matter what the purpose of the interaction. That's why, in Chapter 2, we organized our *sales* questionnaire around one version of the five steps and our *management* questionnaire around a parallel version:

Steps to the sale	Steps to effective coaching
1. Opening	1. Starting
2. Exploring customer needs	2. Getting the salesperson's views
3. Presenting the product or service	3. Presenting the manager's views
4. Managing objections	4. Resolving disagreements
5. Closing	5. Working out an action plan

Both sets of steps, in spite of their different labels, involve doing basically the same things. So, while this chapter zeros in on selling, it's also about a *basic format* for making *all kinds* of interaction pay off. The format can be adapted to *any* meeting between any two people. Later, in Chapter 18, we'll show how sales managers can use it when coaching salespeople—or in most other kinds of manager-salesperson interaction.

Q4 SELLING

We've titled this chapter "Q4 Selling." Why *Q4?* Don't Q1 and Q2 and Q3 use the same five steps? Not necessarily. Q1, Q2, and Q3 either *skip* certain steps (Q1, for instance, often ignores Step 2 – exploring customer needs) or treat them *superficially* (in Step 4, for instance – managing objections – Q2 doesn't so much "manage" objections as dodge them). What distinguishes Q4 is that it follows the five steps as a matter of course; it treats *all* of them seriously. The five steps are the framework on which Q4 is built.

To see what Q4 selling is like, we'll go through each of the five steps briefly in this chapter. Then, in later chapters, we'll examine the *skills* needed to make the steps work. After that, we'll return to the steps themselves and go through them more thoroughly – explaining how to adapt them to different kinds of *customer* behavior – Q1, Q2, Q3, and Q4.

THE STEPS TO THE SALE

Step 1: *Opening*

Objectives. A Q4 opening does five things:

   a. It sets the tone of the call.
   b. It explains why you're there.
   c. It arouses customer interest.
   d. It gets the customer involved.
   e. It makes sure the customer is ready to go ahead.

All this takes special skills:

   a. You can't set the "right" tone unless you know what's "right" for *this* customer. Should you spend a minute on small talk? Or get right down to business? Should you be formal or relaxed, outgoing or reserved? In Q4 selling, tone is always pitched to the customer the salesperson's dealing with here and now. Setting an individual tone – either on a first call or a repeat call – takes *sizing-up* skills.

   b. Explaining why you're there – stating the purpose of the call – isn't as easy as it sounds. First, you *yourself* must know why you're there ("I was just in the neighborhood and thought I'd drop in" is hardly a statement of *purpose*). Then you must state the purpose clearly and briefly, so the customer doesn't get the idea you're beating around the bush, unwilling to admit your purpose. This takes *presentation* skill—the ability to say things in plain, confidence-building language.

c. Arousing the customer's interest may be even tougher. In all probability, he's someone with lots on his mind who's wondering: "Why should I bother listening to this?" Chances are he *won't* listen without a good reason. That's why you must explain—very early on—"what's in it" for him, what he can expect to get out of the sales call. *Your* purpose must be linked to his interests. That takes sizing-up skills and skill at phrasing *benefit statements*—statements that give the customer an *incentive* to listen and cooperate.

d. That brings us to the next objective—getting the customer involved. Q4 wants more than the customer's interest; it wants his *involvement.* It wants him to listen, analyze, discuss, answer questions, be open and candid. Getting this involvement—and getting it early—takes *probing* skill—skill at framing good questions, overcoming reticence, setting the customer at ease, drawing him out.

e. Finally, before concluding the opening, you have to make sure the customer is ready to go ahead. Does he really understand why you're there? Does he really *care?* Will he cooperate? If not, you're going to spin your wheels in Step 2, because in Step 2 you want to explore the customer's needs—and you can't do that if he won't *work with you.* To make sure he *will*—or to get him to that point—takes probing skills and *receptivity-raising* skill, the skill to convert unwilling or apathetic adversaries into willing and interested *partners.*

Any opening that doesn't do these five things—set the tone, explain the purpose, arouse interest, get involvement, and check willingness to go ahead—isn't Q4.

Step 2: *Exploring the customer's needs*

Objectives.   Q4 exploration of needs does two things:

a. It uncovers the customer's *tangible* needs—the ones that might be satisfied by your product or service.
b. It uncovers the customer's *intangible* needs—the ones that can be satisfied by the way you *handle* the sales call and present your product or service.

Once again, achieving these objectives takes special skills.

a. Every customer has two sets of needs. We call them *tangible* and *intangible.* They could just as well be called *external* and *inter-*

nal, or *objective* and *subjective*, or *material* and *psychological* needs. Whatever they're called, Q4 tries to satisfy *both* sets. It satisfies tangible needs with *what's* being sold; it satisfies intangible needs by *how* it's sold.

b. Before you can satisfy a tangible need, of course, you must know what it is. A need cannot be satisfied if it's secret—known only to the customer. To make it known to yourself, you need probing skills.

c. Many times, however, the customer *himself* doesn't know his tangible needs. He may be confused about them or completely unaware of them. So exploring tangible needs involves more than getting the customer to disclose what he already knows; it involves helping him learn things he wasn't aware of before. It involves uncovering buried or hidden needs. This, too, requires *probing* skills.

d. Uncovering *intangible* needs takes not only probing skills but *sizing-up* skills. To determine the right "psychology of the sale," you must listen carefully to the customer, observe his behavior, and figure out what it all means. Only then can you make the sale significant to him by linking your product and adapting your presentation to his intangible needs.

Q1, Q2, and Q3 selling may or may not uncover tangible needs during a call; they very rarely uncover intangible needs. Q4 does both, as a matter of course.

Step 3: *Presenting the product or service*

Objective. A Q4 presentation does two things:

a. It proves that the customer will be *better off* if he buys what you're selling, because his needs—tangible and intangible—will be *filled.*
b. It does this in a way that gratifies his intangible needs *here and now*—during the sales call.

Both objectives require special skills:

a. To prove your product or service will make the customer better off, you need *benefit-proving* skills (to connect his needs to what your're selling), *receptivity-raising* skills (to keep him attentive), and *explanatory* skills (to get your message across).
b. To respond to the customer's intangible needs here and now, you need *Q4 strategy* skills—the ability to tailor your approach so it

fits *this* customer on *this* call. These skills help you do what we recommended in the last chapter: *customize* your behavior to mesh with the customer's, and *change* your behavior if the customer's changes.

In presenting the product or service, every Q4 sales call does both these things.

Step 4: *Managing objections*

Objective. In dealing with objections, Q4 does four things:

    a. It acknowledges the objection—candidly admits that the customer's *not* convinced.
    b. Digs until it really understands what the objection's all about.
    c. Answers the objection.
    d. Gets the customer to confirm the answer.

To achieve these objectives takes several special skills:

    a. You must isolate the real objection (which may be hidden beneath a phony one) and then make sure you understand it. Knowing that the customer's "bothered" isn't good enough; you must know *what's* bothering him. This takes *probing* skills—the ability to ask searching questions and elicit frank, informative answers.

    b. Once you know *why* the customer is resisting, you must overcome the resistance. This can be done only by *answering* the objection or *solving the problem* that prompted it. The customer must be convinced the objection is unimportant or groundless. This takes *explanatory* skills.

    c. You can't be sure the customer is convinced, however, until *he* says so. An objection hasn't been fully disposed of until the *customer* confirms your answer—admits that he understands and "buys" it. Getting this confirmation takes *probing* skills.

    Q1, Q2, and Q3—all in different ways—seldom manage objections to the full satisfaction of the customer. As a result, the objections often come back to haunt the salesperson and spoil the sale. Q4 manages objections *completely.*

Step 5: *Closing*

Objectives. A Q4 close does four things:

    a. It *restates* the reason to buy—the ways in which the product or service will make the customer better off.

b. It asks for a commitment—a statement that the customer's ready and willing to buy—or it creates conditions in which he volunteers a commitment.

c. It *defines* the commitment—pins down what the customer is agreeing to.

d. It paves the way to future business.

All of this requires special skills.

a. Restating the reasons to buy calls for *explanatory* skills. The final statement must be clear and compelling.

b. Getting the customer to affirm his commitment calls for *probing* skills. If he doesn't volunteer his commitment (and there's a good chance he won't), you'll have to elicit it.

c. Defining the commitment calls for *explanatory* skills. You'll have to spell it out in language the customer understands and can agree to.

d. Paving the way to future business calls for *all* the skills mentioned so far. Unless each of the five steps has been skillfully handled, you may end up paving the way for competition.

A LOOK AHEAD

In the following chapters, we'll take a hard look at all the people skills mentioned in this one. Then we'll return to the five steps and tie them and the skills together. Right now, the key point is that whenever we talk about Q4 selling, we're talking about selling that follows the five steps—without omissions—in the order we've described.

6

Why People Buy

The logical way to begin a discussion of selling skills* is to explain *why people buy*. Once that's done, we can more easily explain the skills for *getting* people to buy. So in this chapter we'll explain what motivates customers to say, "Okay, I'll sign the order." In answering the question, "Why do people buy?", we'll lay the groundwork for the chapters that follow.

MOTIVATION AND Q4

Q4 sales behavior is motivating behavior. As we said in the last chapter:

> A Q4 presentation does two things: It proves that the customer will be better off if she buys what you're selling, because her needs—tangible and intangible—will be filled. It does this in a way that gratifies her intangible needs here and now—during the presentation.

---

*The skills we'll discuss from now on have one ultimate purpose: to *persuade*. We'll focus on persuading people to buy, but the skills can be used for other kinds of persuasion as well. If you're a sales manager, for example, you can use them to persuade your salespeople to try new sales techniques or to change their work habits. So, while the next few chapters talk about *selling*, the key points can be generalized to *any kind* of persuasion.

This, in a nutshell, is what motivation is all about, and why people buy. The whole idea can be very simply expressed in a diagram:

Figure 12. What Happens in a Q4 Presentation.

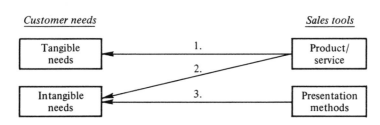

Figure 12 makes three points:

1. Every qualified prospect has two kinds of needs — tangible and intangible.

2. You have the tools for filling these needs: your product or service and your method of presentation.

3. You can fill the tangible needs by your product or service. You can fill the intangible needs by your product or service *and* your presentation method. When you've filled *both* the tangible and intangible needs — which is what Q4 selling is all about — the customer should be *motivated to buy.*

Thus, Figure 12 says graphically what we said verbally in the last chapter:

> Every customer has two sets of needs. We call them *tangible* and *intangible*. They could just as well be called *external* and *internal*, or *objective* and *subjective*. Whatever they're called, Q4 tries to satisfy *both* sets. It satisfies tangible needs with *what's* being sold; it satisfies intangible needs by what's being sold and *how* it's sold.

Another way to say this is: there are *three pathways* to a sale (designated by the three arrows in Figure 12). The first and second pathways are the use you make of your *product* or *service*; if you can connect *it — what* your're selling — to the customer's tangible needs (Pathway 1) and to her intangible needs (Pathway 2), you'll be on your way to a sale. The third pathway is the way in which you handle the *presentation*; if you can connect *it —* the way you *interact* with the customer—with her intangible needs (Pathway 3), you'll be even further along on your way to the sale. Q4 selling is a matter of moving along *all three* pathways at *one* time—which, as we hope to show, isn't as difficult as it sounds. After all, in any sales presentation, you want to talk about your product or service (the "what" of the sale), and you want to arouse the customer's understanding and commitment while doing it (the "how" of the sale). The way to do it is to link both the "what" and the "how" to the customer's tangible and intangible needs. To make this point clearer, let's look closer at what these needs are.

Tangible Needs

Tangible needs can be satisfied directly by your product or service. A plumbing contractor who has to replenish his supply of welding torches has a tangible need; if you sell welding equipment, you can fill it. A recent college graduate who wants to begin an investment program has a tangible need; if you sell securities, you can fill it. A bowling center which needs new scoring machines has a tangible need; if you sell bowling equipment, you can fill it. And a couple who have just moved into a new home and need fire insurance have a tangible need; if you sell casualty coverage, you can fill it. Tangible needs are always needs for something *objective*, something that exists "out there"—not in the customer's mind but in the world outside. (Many salespeople are familiar with the terms "tangible selling" and "intangible selling" to distinguish the selling of *things* from the selling of *services.* Thus, tangible selling is the selling of anything *physical*: shoes, sheet steel, office furniture, food products, oil-field equipment, dental supplies, and so on, while intangible selling is the selling of anything *non*-physical: insurance, investment counseling, advertising services, computer programming, personnel testing, and so on. The distinction is far from perfect—is someone who sells advertising on matchbooks selling a tangible or an intangible?—but, for all practical purposes, it's fairly useful. However, when *we* talk about "tangible" needs in this book, we're talking about needs that can be satisfied by products *or* services; a need for professional engineering advice—a "service"—is as much a tangible need as a need for steel girders—a "thing." *Any* need that can be satisfied by something "out there"—something *external* to the customer, something with its own *objective* existence apart from the customer—is a *tangible* need. Thus, both salespeople who sell "tangibles" and those who sell "intangibles" are in the business of filling tangible needs.)

Intangible Needs

Intangible needs are always needs for something *subjective*, something that exists in "the customer's head"—a feeling, an emotion, a frame of mind. They can be satisfied by your product or service *and* by your method of presentation—the way you interact with the customer. A couple of examples will make this clear:

1. Joe Hawthorne, purchasing agent for Acme Manufacturing, is looking for durable transmission belts to replace some that haven't worn very well. That's a *tangible* need; transmission belts exist "out there." Joe, who's usually tense around salespeople, is especially nervous about making this purchase, because he feels he was "taken" the last time be bought transmission belts, and doesn't want to repeat the experience. He wants to feel secure with whatever he buys. That's an *intangible* need; the feeling of security, the confidence that one's made a "good buy," exists in "the customer's head." A need for transmission belts is a need for something *objective*; a need for a feeling of security is a need for something *subjective*.

When Carol Melville, a salesperson for Consolidated Belting Company, calls on Joe and shows him that Consolidated's new Super-ply belt outlasts all competitive belts in laboratory tests, she uses her product to fill Joe's tangible need for a durable transmission belt (Pathway 1) and his intangible need for security (Pathway 2). But she does something more, she makes her points in a deliberate, helpful way, without overstating her case or applying pressure. This helps Joe relax and feel unthreatened. Thus, Carol fills Joe's intangible need for security by her method of presentation (Pathway 3) as well as by her product.

2. Martha Emerson's working at her first job since getting a business school degree, and wants to start an investment program that'll produce some quick returns—"put my money to work making money," as she puts it. That's a *tangible* need; an investment program is something objective, something "out there." Having majored in finance at college, Martha considers herself a bit of an expert on investments. She'd like to "make a killing" on her first investment and earn admiration for her know-how. That's an *intangible* need; the need to be admired is internal, not external. Furthermore, when she talks to an investment broker, she wants to be looked up to as someone who "knows the score." That's another example of the same *intangible* need; the feeling that "I'm admired and looked up to" can only exist in her head. It's subjective, not objective.

When Dave Channing, an investment broker, calls on Martha, he explains a new stock issue that's likely to produce sizable returns faster than more conservative investments; if Dave is right, this should fill her *tangible* need for quick dividends (Pathway 1), and her *intangible* need for feeling that she's "made a killing" (Pathway 2); Dave does something else; he asks for Martha's ideas and opinions, listens carefully, and gives her full credit for "knowing what's what." Thus, she realizes that Dave admires her competence; she feels "looked up to." So Joe's *method of presentation* (Pathway 3) as well as the service he provides fills Martha's intangible need for respect.

THE PYRAMID OF NEEDS

It's impossible to enumerate *tangible* needs; they're literally countless. Individuals or companies or institutions or governments (all of which have tangible needs) may need items as small as a microchip

Figure 13. The Pyramid of Needs.

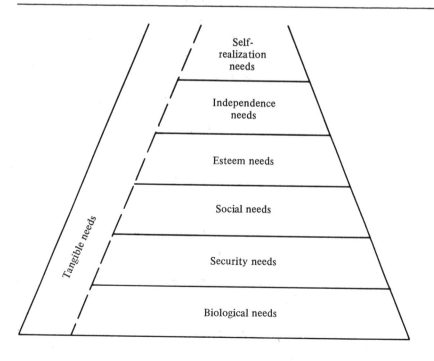

Figure 14. A Closer Look at Intangible Needs.

Intangible Needs	Definition	What Happens When Need Is Not Filled
1. Biological needs	Physical requirements for healthy functioning	Pain, discomfort, impairment, illness, death
2. Security needs	Needs for stability, predictability, safety	Tension, anxiety, worry, fear, panic, danger
3. Social needs	Needs for companionship, love, belonging, affection, acceptance	Loneliness, boredom, feelings of being unloved or unlovable, low self-image, estrangement
4. Esteem needs	Needs for recognition, reputation, status, prestige, approval, self-respect	Loss of confidence, low self-image, self-doubt, guilt, shame, resentment
5. Independence needs	Needs for privacy, responsibility, autonomy, self-assertion, control of our own lives and work	Feelings of frustration, entrapment, exploitation, despair, resentment
6. Self-realization needs	Needs to develop, learn, mature, make use of personal resources, increase competence and mastery, become what we're capable of	Feelings of futility, alienation, bitterness, wasted chances, being at a dead-end, hopelessness

or as large as a tandem-trailor truck, as commonplace as a paper clip or as rare as a space satellite, as simple as an ice cream cone or as complex as a textbook on non-Euclidean geometries. There's just no way to generalize about tangible needs, except to say that they're needs for something objective—something "outside our heads"—and they can therefore be satisfied by the appropriate product or service.

Intangible needs are different. They can be enumerated, and they're easier to generalize about. One scheme for enumerating and generalizing about them is the well-known Pyramid of Needs, developed by psychologist Abraham Maslow in the 1950s. It's proven so useful that it's still widely used today. Although some psychologists would modify the pyramid in various ways, it still serves to identify the intangible needs people are likely to encounter in ordinary face-to-face interactions. Our own slightly modified version of Maslow's pyramid is depicted in Figure 13. The intangible needs are represented by the horizontal layers; we've added tangible needs on the diagonal to show that the two kinds of needs go together.

WHY PEOPLE BUY

Let's go back to our original question: why do people buy? To answer it, let's recall the basic premise of Q4 selling, as spelled out in Chapter 3 by a fictitious salesperson:

> Why should anyone listen to me unless she gets something in return? Customers are like investors; they'll willingly give you their time and attention *if* they think they'll get something back for it. My job is to make sure their investment pays off. And the only way to do that is to show them that buying my product will make them *better off.* If I can do that . . . if I can deliver a plus to the customer . . . I'm fairly sure to get the order.

That helps us tie together all we've said so far, and explain why people buy. People buy because they think or feel it will make them (or the company or institution they represent) *better off.* In other words, they buy when they have what *they* consider a good reason to buy. The reason may be *rational*; they may actually be able to spell it out, clearly and logically. Or it may be *emotional* — a gut-feeling or a hunch. Whether the reason's rational or emotional, whether the customer thinks it or feels it, the end result is the same: the customer decides, "This purchase will produce a *plus* for me or my organization or both of us together." This "plus" will be all the bigger — and more compelling — the more the salesperson succeeds in filling *both* the customer's tangible and intangible needs. To put it a bit differently, unfilled needs — tangible and intangible — are a *minus*; they mean something is lacking. People buy to convert this minus into a plus — to fill the lack. And the surest way to fill the lack — deliver the plus — is to follow *all three* pathways to the sale.

This helps us explain what motivation is all about:

1. People buy when they have what they consider a *good reason* — rational or emotional — to buy. A good reason — anything that'll make them (or their organization) *better off*, anything that'll product a "plus" — is an *incentive.* People who have that incentive are *motivated.*

2. Whenever you give a customer a reason to buy — by filling her tangible and intangible needs — you *motivate* her. Motivation is nothing more than supplying the *incentive* that makes customers think or feel, "There's a *plus* in this for me (and my organization)."

This is why salespeople are constantly advised to "sell benefits." Selling benefits means showing the customer "what's in it for me (and my organization) if I buy." It means demonstrating — to the customer's satisfaction — that "If I buy, I (or we) will be better off." Selling benefits *is* motivating.

THREE MOTIVATIONAL PATHWAYS

We can now see that the three pathways to the sale (Figure 12) are actually three *motivational* pathways. What Figure 12 says, in effect, is that during any sales presentation, there are three ways to motivate the customer — give her a good reason (or reasons) to buy:

1. You can motivate her by showing how your product or service will fill her tangible needs (Pathway 1).
2. You can motivate her by showing how it will fill her intangible needs (Pathway 2).
3. You can motivate her by presenting the product or service in a way that fills her intangible needs (Pathway 3).

One thing that distinguishes Q4 selling from other kinds is that only Q4 follows *all three* pathways. Most other selling follows Pathway 1 — and *only* Pathway 1. If the customer needs, say, widgets, the salesperson tries to explain why *her* company's widgets will fill the bill better than any competitor's. She tries, in other words, to fill the *tangible* need. But she gives very little thought to the customer's *in*tangible needs. Pathway 2 and Pathway 3 are mostly ignored, while the salesperson travels down Pathway 1. In Q4, the salesperson travels down all three pathways in the *same* call.

Uncovering Tangible Needs

Obviously, you can't fill any needs — tangible or intangible — if you don't know what they are. How can you find out? In the case of *tangible* needs, the customer may volunteer them; if not, you'll have to ask; if that doesn't produce an answer, you'll have to dig.

1. The customer, with little or no urging, may simply *tell* you what the tangible need is: "We're looking for extrusion dies that'll give us sharper definition than we're getting now." If this happens, fine. You may want to ask a few questions to determine if this is the only tangible need, but at least you have something definite to work with.

2. Many times, however, the customer won't volunteer the need. Instead, she'll conceal it behind Q1 behavior ("I'm gonna make this

salesperson *work* for every bit of information she gets"), or Q2 ("I'm gonna be very careful about telling her anything until I'm sure I can trust her"), or Q3 ("I'll get around to talking about my needs after we've had a chance to chat"). In cases like these, you'll have to ask about the need. A simple, direct question ("What are you looking for in extrusion dies?") may be all it takes.

3. Sometimes, however, a simple, direct question won't work because the customer either won't know the answer or won't be sure of it. In this case, you'll have to *dig*—probe—ask a *series* of questions to clarify her thinking. We'll talk a lot about probing in a later chapter.

In any case, the important thing is that tangible needs can be *openly discussed*. Whatever the tangible need may be, it can be *talked* about.

Uncovering Intangible Needs

*In*tangible needs can seldom be talked about, because they aren't apparent; they're *buried* under behavior. *Behavior*—what the customer *says* and *does*—is a clue to intangible needs; it's circumstantial evidence—indirect evidence—but it's the only evidence you're likely to get. By analyzing it, you can usually infer the customer's intangible needs.

But why go to this trouble? Don't *all* of us have all six of the intangible needs on the pyramid? Sure we do. But in each of us, one or two needs are usually stronger, more intense, than the others. And it's our *strongest* needs that we most want satisfied. That's because they're the ones that "bother" us. Strongly-felt needs make us uncomfortable, tense, uneasy. They nag at us, press us, refuse to be ignored. So it's the customer's *strongest* intangible needs—her most intensely-felt needs—that you want to fill. The uncomfortable feeling the customer experiences from her unfilled intangible needs is a *minus*; the satisfied feeling that *you* provide by filling those needs (Pathways 2 and 3) is a *plus*.

During a presentation, then, you want to remove, or at least lessen, the customer's discomfort or anxiety or uneasiness. You want her to be *satisfied*—literally. But you can't satisfy a need unless you know what it *is*. That's why you must look for clues in her *behavior*—in what she says, how she says it, what she does, and how she does it. In most cases, the customer's behavior will give away her most pressing intangible needs. (Whenever we use the word *behavior* in this book, we mean both *words* and *actions*. What a customer says is as much behavior as what she does. In fact, in a typical sales presentation, most of the customer's behavior is verbal, not physical. So *listening* is a big part—a very big part—of observing and analyzing the customer's needs.)

Generally, customer behavior—as described on the Dimensional Model—correlates with the intangible needs on the pyramid. There's a fairly predictable "fit" between Q1, Q2, Q3, and Q4 behavior and certain intangible needs. The correlations are shown on Figure 15 (the two broken lines leading from Q3 indicate that esteem and security needs correlate fairly closely with Q3 behavior, but not as closely as social needs, which, in the case of Q3, are predominant):

Figure 15. Needs and Behavior.

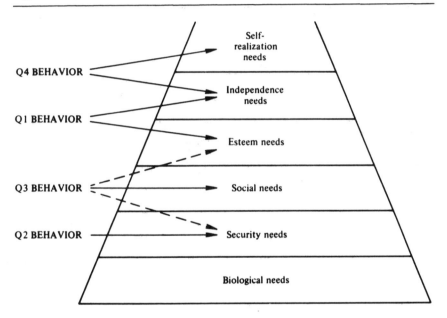

This diagram is useful—up to a point. It doesn't tell you which specific behaviors to look for. So we've listed them on Figure 16. It's not infallible, but it should prove helpful. While none of the behaviors is a sure clue to a particular intangible need, a cluster of the behaviors, all happening in the same interaction, *is* strong evidence of a particular intangible need. As a rule, strong evidence is all you need.

Figure 16. Behavioral Clues to Intangible Needs.

Needs	*CUSTOMER BEHAVIOR*
Security (Q2)	1. Shrinks back. 2. Says little. 3. Speaks very cautiously. 4. Won't take risks. 5. Doesn't commit self. 6. Procrastinates. 7. Ill-at-ease. 8. Leans heavily on past experience. 9. Dislikes innovation. 10. Pessimistic, strongly negative. 11. Keeps discussion impersonal. 12. Won't deviate from routine.
Social (Q3)	1. Outgoing, eager to please. 2. Quick to agree. 3. Optimistic, strongly positive. 4. Talkative. 5. Roams from topic to topic. 6. Unhurried. 7. Has good word for everybody. 8. Quick to compromise. 9. Has trouble making up mind. 10. Easily swayed. 11. Dodges touchy subjects.
Esteem (Q1) and Independence (Q1)	1. Brags a lot. 2. Tries to monopolize conversation. 3. Interrupts, listens impatiently. 4. Stubborn, argumentative. 5. Dogmatic. 6. Strongly negative. 7. Drops "big" names. 8. Takes credit belonging to others. 9. Likes status-symbols. 10. Hates to lose. 11. Sarcastic. 12. Belittles. 13. Chip on shoulder. 14. Has all the answers. 15. More concerned about short-term than long-term.
Independence (Q4)	1. Self-assured, not cocky. 2. Cooperative, yet assertive. 3. Candid, not arrogant. 4. Ready to defend own ideas and listen to others. 5. Enjoys forthright give-and-take. 6. Decisive. 7. Reserves right to challenge the "experts."
Self-realization (Q4)	1. Inquiring, searching, curious, good learner. 2. Willing to take intelligent risks. 3. Likes innovation. 4. Enjoys challenge. 5. Willingly discusses differences. 6. Doesn't mind being proven wrong. 7. Openly shares information. 8. Willing to experiment.

Two Cautions

a. In any one sales call, a customer's behavior may change as different intangible needs come to the fore. A customer who's distant and hard-to-read (Q2) at the start may get belligerent and even abusive (Q1) later. So deal *now* with the behavior you observe *now*; deal *later* with the behavior you observe later. That's Q4 flexibility.

b. A customer may evidence more than one intangible need at a time. For instance, outgoing, agreeable behavior (evidence of Q3 social needs) may appear *together with* readiness to take a chance on an unproven product (evidence of Q4 self-realization need). If that happens, deal with both needs.

THE MYSTERY GUEST

Intangible needs are the "mystery guest" at every sales presentation. Both you and the customer may be unaware of the intangibles, but they *make their presence felt* nevertheless. If you can't identify them, if you can't remove the mystery, you can't deal with them, and they'll be left free to cause mischief. Unmasking the mystery guest, determining that unfilled security or social or esteem or independence or self-realization needs are *there* — across the desk from you — is essential to Q4 selling. More than that, it's essential to *successful* selling. If you doubt this, think back on all the times you've made a sales call, dealt effectively with the customer's *tangible* needs, and still failed to close the sale because you didn't deal effectively with the intangible needs. In spite of your hard work, the mystery guest "vetoed" the deal. From now on, that's something you can *prevent* — by following *all three* pathways to the sale.

SUMMARY

1. Q4 sales behavior is motivating behavior. It motivates by proving to the customer she'll be better off if she buys because her needs, tangible and intangible, will thereby be filled, and it does this in a way that gratifies her intangible needs here and now — during the presentation.

2. You have two tools for filling any customer's needs: your product or service and your method of presentation. When you use these tools to the fullest extent, you have three pathways to the sale. Your product or service can be used to fill both tangible and intangible needs; your presentation method can be used to fill intangible needs. When both sets of needs are filled, the customer should be motivated to buy.

3. Tangible needs are always for something objective, something "out there" — not in the customer's mind. Intangible needs are always for something subjective, something that exists in "the customer's head" — a feeling, emotion, or frame of mind.

4. Tangible needs cannot be enumerated because they're limitless. Intangible needs can be enumerated. One widely-accepted scheme for doing so is the Maslow Pyramid of Needs.

5. The intangible needs you're most likely to encounter in customers are security, social, esteem, independence, and self-realization needs.

6. People buy when they have what they consider a good reason to buy. The reason may be rational or emotional or both, but in every case it leads the customer to think, "This purchase will produce a plus for me or my organization or both." The best way to deliver the plus is to follow the three pathways to the sale.

7. You can't fill any needs if you don't know what they are. In the case of tangible needs, the customer may volunteer them; if not, you can ask about them. Tangible needs are easily discussed.

8. Intangible needs aren't usually discussible because they aren't apparent; they're buried beneath behavior—what the customer says and does. To discern a customer's intangible needs, you must therefore observe her behavior, analyze it, and infer the needs.

9. Generally, customer behavior correlates with the intangible needs on the pyramid. Q1 behavior usually implies strong unfilled needs for esteem and independence. Q2 usually implies a need for security. Q3 usually implies social needs, and, to a lesser degree, esteem and security needs. Q4 usually implies self-realization and independence needs.

10. In any one sales call, the customer's behavior may change; to cope with such change, you must deal now with the behavior you're confronting now. Furthermore, the customer may evidence more than one intangible need at a time. If she does, deal with both needs.

7

Motivating Customers

Chapter 6 was an "insight" chapter, not a "skill" chapter. It explained why people buy, but not how to get them to buy. It explained what motivation is, but now how to do it. *This* is a "skill" chapter. It zeroes in on techniques for filling needs, turning minuses into pluses, and convincing people they'll be better off if they buy. These are *Q4* skills; their object is not to pressure the customer (Q1), rely on luck (Q2), or lean on friendship (Q3). Their object is to *persuade.*

THE MOTIVATION PROCESS

Fully motivating a customer—making him feel *committed* to the purchase instead of just lukewarm—requires three things:

1. **Crystallizing the customer's needs**—getting him to see he lacks something which could make him better off. He may or may not already know this; either way, it's your job to make sure he does.

2. **Satisfying the customer's needs**—showing that your product or service would fill his needs—tangible and intangible—and thereby make him better off (as we've seen, you can do this by following the three pathways to the sale).

3. **Proving net gain**—showing that your product or service will make the customer not merely better off but better off than *any other* need satisfier, that it will provide *more* benefit than competitive products or services or anything else. You want to demonstrate that what *you're* selling will provide a *bigger* plus than he can get from any other source—so that if he buys from you, he'll not only be better off, he'll be *best* off.

If you do these three things, you'll provide a virtually irresistible reason to buy. Let's see *how* they're done.

1. Crystallizing Needs

As we saw in Chapter 6, crystallizing customer needs may be easy or hard. Some needs are self-evident, some are obscure. Some customers are willing to discuss their needs, some are reluctant. Some needs are simple, some are complex. Still and all, we can make two safe generalizations:

A. To crystallize *tangible* needs, you'll usually have to *probe*—ask questions and draw out thoughtful, thorough answers. Probing requires a chapter in itself (Chapter 9), so we won't get into it now. We'll only say this: except in those instances when the customer volunteers them, you cannot uncover tangible needs without mastery—not just superficial acquaintance, but real mastery—of probing.

B. To crystallize *intangible* needs, you'll usually have to probe, listen carefully to everything the customer says, watch his expressions, gestures, and body language, and then, from all of this, *infer* the needs. Almost always, intangible needs must be inferred—deduced from indirect evidence. That's because most customers haven't thought much about their intangible needs, and therefore can't be explicit about them. Nevertheless, they unwittingly *reveal* those needs by the way they behave: the content and manner of their speech, their facial expressions, gestures, movements, and so on. If you know which clues to look for (we listed most of the common ones in Figure 16 in the last chapter), you can study them and reach fairly safe conclusions about the customer's intangible needs.

2. Satisfying Customer Needs

We said in Chapter 6 that you have two tools for satisfying customer needs: your product or service and your method of presentation. In this chapter, we'll talk about only one of the tools: your product or service—and how to use it as you move along Pathway 1 and Pathway 2. Our discussion of presentation methods—and Pathway 3—will make more sense later (Chapter 11), after we've discussed some other skills.

BENEFIT STATEMENTS

We've said that people buy—as a rule—when they're convinced buying will make them better off. *Benefit statements* do the convincing. They *prove* that the product or service *will* fill the customer's needs and make the customer better off. Benefit statements, in effect, are *proof statements.* They provide evidence that the customer—the particular customer in front of you here and now—will indeed *realize* a *plus* if he buys from you.*

Probably the most widely-used method for developing benefit statements is one called FAB. FAB stands for *feature, advantage, benefit:*

- Every product or service has a number of *features*—traits that make it what it is. Take a simple product like a felt-tip pen; some of its features might be: an easy-grip plastic barrel, a snug-fitting plastic cap, a rust-proof clip, a plastic-coated point, and so on. These features, or characteristics, make the pen the pen that it is.

- Every feature has one or more *advantage* or function. That is, the feature is put there in the first place because it serves a purpose—*it does something.* In the case of the felt-tip pen, the easy-grip plastic barrel (a feature) makes it possible to *hold the pen under all conditions without slipping* (an advantage); the snug-fitting plastic cap (F) insures that, *when closed, the pen will neither dry out nor smear* (A); the rust-proof clip (F) assures that *the pen can be kept*

---

*Our use of the word "proof" goes beyond what's found in much sales-training literature. Traditionally, proof is the use of evidence to show that a product or service makes people *in general* better off. "Tests show that six out of seven users prefer Product X" is a typical proof statement of the traditional type; it uses external authority ("Tests show ...") to make a point about customers *in general* (... "six out of seven users ... "). It does not zero in on a *particular* customer and his *particular* needs. In this book, we mean something different by *proof.* We mean the *linking* of evidence about a product or service with the *particular* needs of a *particular* customer, so as to show that *this* product or service will satisfy *these particular* needs. When we refer to proof statements, we're referring to *individualized,* not generalized, statements—statements that answer the question "What's in it for *me?*" One possible response to a traditional proof statement ("Tests how that six out of seven users prefer Product X") is: "So what? Why should *I* care?" But an *individualized* proof statement doesn't allow such a response, because it already contains the answer to the question: "So what?".

shiny-looking and secure in a pocket (A); and the plastic-coated point (F) *keeps the point tapered and capable of writing a fine line* (A). The *advantage*, in other words, is the reason the feature was included in the product. (Some people maintain, with good reason, that *A* should stand for *action* – because it always describes the action or function performed by the feature.)

- Finally, the advantages of a product or service produce *benefits* for people who *need* whatever the product or service does. Take a copywriter in an ad agency who spends hours each day writing, revising, and editing, and who feels he works best with a pen instead of a typewriter. He needs a pen he can grip firmly even in humid weather; a pen he can rely on because it won't dry out quickly or leak; a pen he can carry in his pocket without its dropping out or leaving rust marks on his shirt; and a pen he knows will write a clear, easily-readable line. The pen we've described will provide *all* these pluses; for *this* copywriter, all the advantages we've listed can be converted into *benefits.* (This wouldn't be true for a copywriter who uses only a typewriter, never a pen. A benefit fills a need; where there is *no* need, there can be *no* benefit.)

Figure 17 should make the connection between features, advantages (or actions), and benefits clearer. Obviously, the benefits shown in Figure 17 wouldn't be benefits for *everyone* – only for investors who need spendable income, a sure return, the ability to do some long-range financial planning, and a quick source of additional funds in case of emergency. *Other* investors – with other needs, might think that the features and advantages we've listed don't produce any benefit at all.

What the FAB method prescribes is this:

1. Crystallize the customer's needs. Find out what he *lacks* – his *minuses.*

2. Describes the *pertinent* features and advantages of your product or service. Explain those characteristics which are relevant to *his* needs, and what those characteristics do.

3. Then link those features and advantages to his needs so he sees the *benefit* – what's in it for him. Prove that your product or service will convert the minuses into *pluses.*

Why is FAB so important? Because it reminds us of something that's easily overlooked: an effective sales presentation should focus *not* on the product or service – but on the *customer.* FAB begins by

Figure 17. An Example of FAB.

	Service: Municipal Bond	
Features (characteristics of service)	Advantages (what those characteristics do)	Benefits (what's in it for an individual investor with $10,000 to invest)
Tax free 9% return	Pays guaranteed rate of interest which is not liable to federal income tax.	Customer can depend on sure return, and can keep it, so entire return becomes spendable income.
10-year maturity	Makes full amount of principle available to bondholder in ten years.	Customer, knowing exactly how much money will be available, and when, can make long-range plans for spending it.
AAA rating	Guarantees bond will be considered good collateral for cash loans.	Customer can use bond to borrow money against in case of emergency, while investment would remain intact.

talking about the *customer* and his needs. Then it discusses the product or service—its features and advantages. And then it returns to the *customer* and what *he'll* get out of the product or service. The importance of FAB is that it reminds us of this circularity: any discussion of the product or service must revolve around *the customer.*

The following discussion, on *benefit statements* and how to *phrase* them, is based on the FAB idea. But we've simplified the process, boiling it down to only two steps. That's because, on actual calls, many salespeople ignore the distinction between F and A, and simply telescope them. *There's nothing wrong with this.* Features and advantages *are* so intertwined that the distinction between them sometimes seems artificial. From the customer's viewpoint, what matters is not the mechanical distinction between F and A, but what F and A mean to *him.* Customers are interested in features and advantages, but *not in the abstract*; they're interested in them in the light of one question: "What's in it for *me?*"

So our discussion of benefit statements reflects what actually happens in many sales calls; it treats features and advantages as a simple *unit*—as *evidence* that buying will make the customer better off.

HOW TO PHRASE BENEFIT STATEMENTS

To *phrase* a benefit statement, do two things:

1. State the customer's needs — tangible or intangible.
2. Prove (by citing pertinent features and advantages) that your product or service will fill the needs.

We'll call this *NB* (need–benefit) selling. Here are a few examples:

- Ted Bryan is a sales representative for a luggage manufacturer; he sells sample cases to companies whose salespeople must carry samples from call to call. In Step 2 of a presentation (Exploring Customer Needs), Ted learns the following from his customer:

  > Our salespeople carry a lot of heavy metal samples around. We need sample cases that can handle the weight, so we don't have to spend a fortune replacing them every 6 months.

As a result, in Step 3 (Presenting the Product), Ted makes the following benefit statement:

> You expressed concern about replacement costs. That's something you won't have to worry about with our case. There's a steel gridwork inside each outer wall, and tests show each wall will take up to 1,000 pounds of pressure. With this case, your replacement problems are over—no matter how many samples your people stuff into them.

Let's analyze this exchange:

The need expressed by the customer was for cases that can *handle heavy weight* and *don't need to be replaced often.* Ted linked a *feature* (steel gridwork inside each outer wall) and its *advantage* (will take up to 1,000 pounds of pressure) to this need and thereby proved the *benefit* — the saving in money to the customer ("Your replacement problems are over—no matter how many samples your people stuff into them").

- Here's another example of *NB selling.* Janet Howell sells printing inks. Yesterday, while exploring customer needs during a presentation, she heard the following:

  > Our signboards are taking a terrible beating from the weather. We've got to find an ink that'll stand up in bad rainstorms, or our costs for re-surfacing each billboard are going to zoom.

When presenting her product, Janet made this benefit statement:

> You're bothered by the high cost of re-surfacing billboards defaced by bad weather. Our K-12 ink has a polyethylene base that makes it impervious to moisture of any kind—rain, snow, you name it. Allen Corporation in St. Paul has used it the last three winters, and never had to replace a signboard. You can expect the same results—and the same kind of savings.

Here the *need* is for ink that'll *stand up* in *bad storms* so *costs can be kept down*. Janet linked a *feature* (a polyethylene base) and its *advantage* (impervious to moisture of any kind) to produce a *benefit*—again the saving in money to the customer ("You can expect the same results—and the same kind of savings"). It's worth noting that, in this example, Janet *strengthened* her proof by citing the experience of another user.

- Our last two examples were about *tangible* needs. Let's look at one on *intangible* needs. Stacy Fitzgerald runs a small travel agency. This morning, a woman dropped in to talk about a European tour; she was curt, argued about minor points, and made it plain she had a low opinion of travel agents. From all of this, Stacy inferred a strong *Q1 independence need*; she told herself, "This woman has a mind of her own. She thinks she knows all the answers, and she hates to hear advice." Here, then, is Stacy's benefit statement:

> You're obviously independent-minded, and you like to think for yourself. Our special "Freedom Tour" will let you do just that. Once the plane touches down in Madrid, you'll be on your own for ten straight days—with no obligations to the rest of the group. You can literally design your own tour while getting the price advantage of group travel.

Here, the intangible *need* (for independence) was met by a *feature* ("Freedom Tour") and *advantage* (on your own for ten days with no obligation to the group) which produced a strong *benefit* ("design your own tour while getting a price advantage").

All three examples illustrate *NB selling*. They:

1. Clearly state the customer *need*—tangible or intangible.
2. Prove that the product or service will fill the need—provide a *benefit*.

Figures 18 and 19 provide other examples. Figure 18 focuses on tangible needs; Figure 19 on intangibles. In each benefit statement, we've italicized the features and advantages to show the "skeleton"

Figure 18.   Satisfying Tangible Needs.

Product	Customer Need (voiced by customer)	Benefit Statement (features and advantages in italics)
Life insurance	"Now that the twins are here, I need a lot more coverage—fast. But there's no way I can afford a fancy premium."	"You want a sizable increase in coverage, but must hold down premium payments. This *modified term plan* is the perfect answer. *All you pay for are death benefits—no cash values.* This is high payoff, low premium insurance—and the fastest way to give those twins the protection they need."
Security services	"We know we need guards on the premises. But we don't want poorly-trained people who may cause more harm than good."	"You're concerned—rightly—about having high-calibre, dependable security officers. With us, that's no problem. All our security people are *former police officers*—and they've *all been trained in the police academy.* That's a requirement of their employment. When you use our service, you're using professionals."
Word-processing equipment	"We're convinced a word-processing machine is the way to go. But we just can't afford one. All capital expenditures have been ruled out—completely—for the next year."	"You need word-processing equipment but feel you can't afford it. Our *lease-purchase arrangement* was designed for situations like yours. You can *lease our machine for up to three years. Any time* during those three years that *you decide to buy, a percentage of the lease payments will be applied to the purchase price.* You can have your cake and eat it too."
Securities	"I don't have a lot of money to invest, so I need to be sure that whatever I do will give me a maximum net return."	"You're looking for the highest net return you can get. This municipal bond provides a *tax-exempt 12% return.* So *your net is 12%.* Your tax bracket is 50%, so this is comparable to a 24% yield on a taxable investment. This bond seems to be just what you're looking for."

Figure 19. Satisfying Intangible Needs.

Product	Customer Need (inferred from customer's behavior)	Benefit Statement (features and advantages are in italics)
Office furniture	"This customer is trying to come across as a real big shot—bragging continually about how he built his company single-handedly." (Q1 esteem need)	"We've got just the thing for an executive like you who appreciates the symbols of achievement. It's our *VIP Suite*—and it's *available only in a limited edition.* You'll find this furniture in just a few top-executive offices—nowhere else."
Copying machine	"This purchasing agent is unsure of himself. He keeps saying he can't afford to try anything that hasn't already proven itself many times over." (Q2 security need)	"You're obviously looking for dependability. Rest assured, you'll get it with the Model K–2. We've sold more of these machines to more companies than any other we manufacture. *In durability tests, it outperforms any other machine at its price.* In fact, some of our customers call the K–2 'Old Faithful'—because it's so reliable."
Building maintenance services	"This customer wants to please everyone. He keeps saying how unhappy people in his company are when their offices aren't cleaned properly—how bad it is for morale." (Q3 social need)	"I know how important it is to you that your people be satisfied with the condition of their offices. With our *White Glove service*, you know they'll be satisfied. *If anyone in your organization complains* that her office hasn't been properly cleaned, *we guarantee to re-clean it*—that day—at no cost. That should please everyone."
Industrial chemicals	"This buyer's interested in innovation. He's asking lots of questions about new developments. He seems to enjoy being on the cutting edge." (Q4 self-realization need)	"Our *double ion* etching acid is ideal for someone who appreciates technological advance as much as you do. Our lab tests show *it'll bite into plates—copper or steel—in half the time of any other acid on the market.* It does require more careful handling by your platemakers, but the saving in time makes it well worth the challenge."

on which the statement is draped. But, in the field, you'll want to deliver *full* benefit statements, with a *statement of need* followed by *proof*, which should include the feature, advantage, and *any other* supporting evidence – like the experience of other users, testimonials, etc. – followed by a statement of what it all *means* to the customer.

As Figures 18 and 19 show, three guidelines help in phrasing benefit statements:

1. Always begin by stating the customer's need. When stating an intangible need, be careful not to offend. A flat statement like "You have a strong security need" won't sit well with many customers; a more considered statement like "You're obviously interested in dependability" will.

2. Explain how your product or service can fill the need. Don't just say it can; *prove* it. Customer's aren't interested in unsubstantiated claims; they want *evidence.* Of course, the evidence won't always be short and simple as in our examples; the "right" amount of evidence varies from product to product. What's important is that it be as conclusive as you can make it.

3. Use the word *you* frequently in each benefit statement. Make the statement revolve around the customer. Don't water down your benefit statements by *generalizing* them; *personalize* them with *you.* From the customer's viewpoint, there's a big difference between hearing a general statement – like "We've got just the thing for executives who appreciate the symbols of achievement" – and a personal statement – like "Since you're an executive who appreciates the symbols of achievement, you're sure to appreciate . . ." or "You're obviously an executive who appreciates the symbols of achievement, so let me show you . . ."

3. Proving Net Gain

Sometimes, all it takes to motivate a customer to buy is a simple statement of need followed by proof of benefit. But not always. Very often, a third step is required. That third step is *proving net gain.*

Net gain is what a customer will get from buying your product or service *over and above* what he'd get from buying a competitive product or service or from keeping what he has. Proof of net gain always involves a *comparison* between what *you've* offered as a need satisfier and *other* potential need satisfiers. (A customer with a 150-year-old Persian rug on his living room floor might be convinced of the benefits of buying new carpeting—easier cleaning, greater durability, better soundproofing – and yet decide to keep what he has because, *on balance*, he sees *more* benefit from owning an antique rug than a new one – it's a status symbol, has more aesthetic appeal, is appreciating in value, etc.

The net gain concept is so important you can ignore it only at your peril. When a customer buys from a competitor instead of from you, or when he decides not to buy but to stick with what he already has, it's usually because he thinks or feels (it may be a rational or an emotional decision) that *that's* where the greatest *net gain* lies.

Let's be clear on what *net* means. When people figure the *net* result of anything, they compare it to other things that could produce the same general result, and then they *exclude* all those factors which cancel one another out. The *net* result is what's *left over*; it's the *margin* by which Benefit C *exceeds* Benefit B and Benefit A. Now, in buying situations, people don't always compute net gain as neatly as that, but they *do*, as a rule, buy what they think or feel will give them the *most* benefit. In competition between *more* and *most, most* is likely to win.

What's needed to prove net gain? Two things:

1. A thorough knowledge of the *other options*, competitive or otherwise. The more you know about competitive products or services, the better. If you were selling newsprint, for example, you'd want to know all you could about the newsprint made by competitive paper mills: its quality (tear resistance, ink absorption, smudge control, drying time, etc.); its availability (where it's warehoused or shipped from, whether orders are shipped as soon as received); its cost; warranties; and so on. If you don't know all this in advance, you should be able to get it from the customer during the call – by probing.

2. The ability to make comparisons *without* belittling the other options. *Net gain* selling is *not* "negative selling." Negative selling uses scare tactics; it's more concerned with pointing out the flaws in the competitor's product than the strengths of yours. Negative selling implies: "If you buy Product X, *you'll be sorry.*" Net gain selling is different. It makes factual comparisons and draws factual conclusions; it does not knock the options, or suggest that Product X is a "bad" buy. It merely proves that, between Product X and Product Y, Product Y is a *better* buy.

This is critically important. Very few customers *want* to hear that a product they're considering is a "bad" buy; if you belittle the product, you indirectly belittle *them.* After all, they've been sufficiently impressed with it to give it serious consideration; they're not eager to hear that they've let themselves be misled. Therefore, to make net gain work *for* you, be *positive*.

THE ULTIMATE NET GAIN

In a great many cases, the ultimate net gain—the thing that finally makes one option preferable to the others—is *you*, the salesperson. This may sound like a Q3 pat on the back, but it isn't. It's a sober statement of fact.

It's often very difficult to determine which option will, on balance, prove best for the customer; weighing benefits against one another sometimes leads to inconclusive results. In such cases, *you yourself* can be the factor that tips the balance in your favor. That's because, all else being equal, customers are likely to buy from the salesperson who's *most responsive to their needs*.

Let's take a classic instance: the situation in which there is literally *no* difference between Product A and Product B. Securities are a good example. As far as the *product* is concerned, there's no difference between buying 100 shares of "Ajax preferred" from Broker X or Broker Y. Why, then, when selecting a broker, don't people open the telephone business directory to the section headed "Investment Securities," blindfold themselves, throw a dart at the page, and choose whichever broker the dart hits? After all, all of them sell the *same* product. The answer, obviously, is that people want more than just the product; they want a broker who can provide wise investment counseling, who's concerned about their needs, who inspires confidence and trust, who's strongly committed to their welfare, who conscientiously follows up on transactions. They want a broker with whom they feel "comfortable" and in whom they can confide, a broker who makes them feel confident their investments are in "good hands," a broker who never causes them to worry. In other words, in the securities field, where so much else is equal, the broker very often makes the difference. The broker *is* the net gain.

It would be very wrong, however, to leave the impression that this is true only in the investment securities business. It's true in many businesses. In fact, in many businesses the salesperson is such a strong "plus" that he actually *offsets* a number of "minuses" in his product or service. Everyone in the sales field has heard customers say things like: "Sure, I know we could get it cheaper from Company X, but Company X doesn't have Joe as one of its salespeople" or "Okay, Company Y offers better delivery, but that doesn't compare with the advice I get from Louise at my present supplier" or "I don't care if Company Z does have a better warranty; I feel comfortable with Larry calling on me." *That's* the ultimate net gain.

A Caution

NB selling *won't* work if the customer's not *aware* of his needs. In fact, if he doesn't know which of his needs your features and advantages are supposed to link up with, then—no matter how authoritatively you present those features and advantages—his reaction will probably be: "So what?" And a "So what?" reaction means *you're* in trouble.

To prevent the "So what?" reaction, always do two things:

1. Make the customer's need *explicit.* Never assume he knows what it is. Never take it for granted he knows—without being told—which need you're linking up with. *Tell* him. Spell it out. Don't be "clinical-sounding" about it ("You have a strong esteem need"). Be conversational ("You obviously want to command respect"). It's easy to spell out needs without ever using the word "need." The important thing is to *make them plain* to the customer as well as to yourself.

2. When phrasing a benefit statement, ask *yourself*: "So what?" Ask yourself: "If I were the customer . . . if *I* were sitting on the other side of the desk *listening* to this instead of saying it . . . would I really *care?* Would I clearly understand why it's important to *me* — the customer? Would I realize why it matters to me?" If you can answer *yes* to these questions, fine; your benefit statement is probably on target. If you can't, something's wrong. Either you haven't clearly stated the customer's need, or you haven't shown how your features and advantages link up with the need. Either way, you still have some work to do.

CONCLUSION

Let's recall the diagram we introduced in the last chapter:

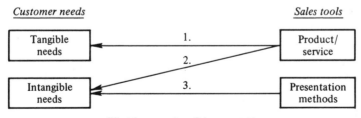

What happens in a Q4 presentation.

In the light of what we've said about NB selling, we can draw two conclusions about the diagram:

1. The only way to travel Pathway 1 successfully is to do NB selling—state the customer's tangible need and then prove, by citing pertinent features and advantages, that your product or service will fill it.

2. The only way to travel Pathway 2 successfully is also to do NB selling—make clear the link between your product or service and the customer's intangible need.

NB selling is the vehicle, so to speak, that will move you along both pathways—smoothly, efficiently, surely.

SUMMARY

1. Fully motivating a customer—making him feel committed to the purchase—requires (a) crystallizing his needs, (b) satisfying them, and (c) proving net gain.

2. To crystallize tangible needs, you'll usually have to probe until the customer discloses them. To crystallize intangible needs you'll have to probe, observe the customer's behavior, and then infer the needs.

3. Benefit statements convince people they'll be better off by buying. They prove a product or service will fill the customer's needs, so they can be called "proof statements."

4. The most widely used method for developing benefit or proof statements is FAB, in which product features—characteristics—and their advantages or actions—their functions—are linked to the customer's needs. This link-up proves "what's in it" for the customer—the benefit.

5. NB selling (need–benefit selling) is a "shorthand" version of FAB. It treats features and their advantages as a unit—as evidence that buying will make the customer better off. In NB selling, this evidence is linked to the customer's needs, tangible and intangible.

6. Three guidelines help in phrasing benefit statements: (a) always state the customer's need first; (b) explain how your product or service can fill it; (c) use the word *you* frequently.

7. Net gain is what a customer will get from buying your product or service over and above what he'd get from buying a competitive product or service or from keeping what he has.

8. Two things are needed to prove net gain: (a) full knowledge of the other options available to the customer; (b) the ability to com-

pare your product or service with the options—without belittling them.

9. In many cases, the ultimate net gain is *you*—the salesperson. Where all else is pretty much equal, you can be a "plus" by proving more responsive to the customer's needs than any competitive salesperson.

10. NB selling won't work if the customer's not aware of his needs. To prevent a "So what?" reaction on his part, make his needs explicit and ask yourself, "So what difference does this benefit make to the customer?"

11. NB selling is the vehicle that can move you smoothly along Pathway 1 and Pathway 2 to the sale.

8

Timing the Presentation

In our last chapter, we called need–benefit selling the "vehicle" that will move you along Pathways 1 and 2 to the sale—smoothly, efficiently, and surely. Like any vehicle, however, it won't get you to your destination smoothly, efficiently, and surely if you use it at the *wrong time*. The finest automobile in the world, for example, may not get you to your destination at all if you drive it when the highway is blocked by a landslide, or when the bridge is washed out, or when the exits are barricaded. And the most skillful NB selling may not get you to your destination, either, if you do it when the customer's distracted, preoccupied, or distraught. *When* you use a vehicle is sometimes just as important as the vehicle itself. In this chapter, we'll look at the *when* of selling—the whole question of *timing*.

Imagine the following situation (which you may well have *experienced*). You're in a sales call, explaining the benefits of your product, and feeling optimistic. You have a strong feeling "everything's going well," and why not? You know just about all there is to know about the product; you've prepared for your presentation; and you're in "good form"—making each of your points colorfully and enthusiastically. All in all, there's good reason, as you see it, to be satisfied.

As you conclude your discussion of benefits, you ask the customer: "Well, how does that sound?" She answers, in a lackluster voice, "I dunno, I'll have to think about it." This catches you off-balance; you'd expected an eager, lively response. You quickly regain your composure and ask: "What are you unsure about?" Again, you get a flat, monotone answer: "I dunno. I just have to think about it. That's all." You try again: "Well, can I clear anything up? Anything you didn't understand?" And again you get a humdrum response: "No. I'll think about it. If I decide to do anything, I'll give you a call." Knowing full well you're getting the brushoff, you make a few more futile attempts to find out what's bothering the customer and finally give up. As you get into your car, you say to yourself: "I don't get it. I did everything right. In fact, I did everything better than usual. And all of a sudden, the whole presentation fizzled out. I sure wish I knew what went wrong."

What probably went wrong was your *timing*. Timing—doing the right thing *at the right time*—is crucial to Q4 selling. In fact, from the Q4 point of view, there's no such thing as doing the right thing at the *wrong* time; if it's done at the wrong time, it's the *wrong thing*.

In selling, the "right" thing is what's effective—what gets results. And what's effective is always, in part, a matter of timing—of when it's done as well as how it's done. Anything done at the wrong time—when conditions aren't ripe—is fairly certain to be *in*effective. And that makes it "wrong."

Let's go back to our example. What happened, apparently, is that while you were explaining benefits, the customer lost interest. This could have happened for many reasons: maybe she began worrying about something, and stopped paying attention to you; maybe she misunderstood something you said, started to fret about it, and ignored the rest of your presentation; maybe you triggered a memory, and she began dwelling on *it* rather than on your presentation; maybe a noise outside distracted her, and she lost track of what you were saying; maybe . . . maybe . . . maybe. Any number of things might have happened, all of which could have had the same result: to cause the customer to *lose interest*. And, *whenever* a customer loses interest, that's the *wrong time* to explain benefits or *anything else* demanding attention and thought. No matter how forceful or eloquent or sensible your explanation may be, it's sure to fall on deaf ears if the customer's lost interest (or never had it). And, in a sales presentation, anything that falls on deaf ears is *badly timed*.

PERSUASION AND TIMING

Selling is a matter of persuasion, and persuasion is a matter of *timing*. If the customer isn't *ready* to listen, your benefit statements (or anything else) will have as much impact as the falling of a tree when nobody's around to hear it. What may strike you as compelling reasons to buy may not strike her *at all.* If your timing's off, the whole presentation may prove futile. Because the timing problem is so common, we'll devote all of this chapter to it.

Let's describe the problem:

1. Any time you start a sales presentation, you're presumably *ready*—psychologically. You're "in the mood"; you're "up" for it. And, presumably, you'll *stay* in the mood. That's part of your job.

2. That's not always true of the customer. In fact, there's a good chance she's *not* as ready as you are. You're prepared to put your heart into the presentation; she may feel half-hearted—or less—about the whole thing.

3. Thus, from your viewpoint, the time *is right* for a sales presentation. But, from the customer's viewpoint, the time may not be right. Even if she's granted you an appointment, even if she's been expecting you she may have other—and, to her, more urgent—things on her mind. As you see it, the presentation is the most important thing you can do; as she sees it, there may be other, more important, things to do. That you're prepared to concentrate on the presentation doesn't mean she is.

4. Still and all, you must go ahead with the presentation. If you wait for every customer to be "in the mood," you may go through entire weeks with no presentations at all. But, in going ahead, you may be talking to a customer who doesn't feel like listening or responding. For all *practical* purposes, you may end up making the presentation to yourself.

This is known as the *receptivity problem*: you may be ready for a presentation when the customer isn't; Sure. the customer may *be there*, physically, and may *appear* to be paying attention. But unless she's *psychologically* ready—prepared to "put herself" into the presentation—you're going to have trouble. Nevertheless, you must go ahead with the presentation. How can you do it without falling on your face? We're about to see.

Receptivity

The receptivity problem confronts every salesperson, so we'd better define *receptivity* carefully:

Receptivity is willingness to listen carefully to someone, consider what's heard, and respond constructively and candidly. Or, in fewer words, it's the desire to make an interaction pay off through give-and-take.

A receptive customer does four things:

1. *Listens carefully.* She pays close attention, without rushing or interrupting you.

2. *Open-mindedly considers your ideas.* She gives you a fair hearing, weighing your ideas before accepting or rejecting them.

3. *Responds constructively.* She gives informative, candid, useful responses.

4. *Asks useful questions.* She seeks clarification and exploration of your ideas.

When these four behaviors are present, that's *high receptivity.* When they're absent, that's *low receptivity.*

Receptivity and Agreement

High receptivity and *agreement* are different things. A highly receptive customer won't necessarily *accept* your ideas, but she will try to *understand* and *consider* them. Once she has understood and considered, she may accept or reject them. This means you can go through a presentation in which the customer's receptivity is consistently high and still not make the sale because you failed to persuade her. A highly receptive customer *gives you a fair chance* to make the sale; whether or not you *do* is up to you.

This leads to a crucial point: a customer who's receptive won't necessarily be persuaded, but a customer who's unreceptive is almost sure *not* to be persuaded. Let's see why:

1. To persuade means to generate understanding and commitment.

2. You can't generate understanding or commitment in someone who doesn't pay close attention, doesn't weigh your ideas with an open mind, doesn't respond informatively, and doesn't ask useful questions. In other words, you can't persuade someone who's not receptive.

This is one reason, maybe the major reason, why so many *good* presentations don't work. By "good," we mean knowledgeable, logical, clear, benefit-oriented presentations. Such presentations "should" produce sales, but frequently don't. As we said before, most salespeople have had the experience of making a good, strong presentation, only to walk away wondering, "What went wrong? Why didn't I get the order?"

The answer may be that, good as your presentation was, the customer didn't really *hear* it. Closed minds—and unreceptive customers have *closed* their minds—*don't* hear in any meaningful sense; they don't give ideas a chance to sink in and make a difference. Either they don't pay attention at all, or, if they do, they immediately reject what they hear. For all practical purposes, when you make a presentation to a closed mind—an unreceptive customer—you're talking to yourself.

Spinning-up Receptivity

The idea that you may be talking to yourself during a presentation is hard to accept. After all, on most sales calls, the customer *seems* attentive; you get the feeling you're talking to someone besides yourself. That's because many unreceptive customers *appear* receptive; they seem to be listening; they nod their heads; they grunt or even encourage you ("Sounds great"); they give every *appearance* of being "with you." The appearance is deceiving. Their minds are actually closed—shut off. That's why, after a while, you begin to feel that you're "talking to a brick wall." You come to realize that the customer's mind seems surrounded by a brick wall which, try as you will, you cannot penetrate.

Let's look at some examples:

Q1 LOW RECEPTIVITY

Low receptivity sometimes takes the form of *Q1* behavior. When it does, the message is always: "I'm not going to give you a chance to get through to me." This message may be delivered in a number of ways:

- **Embarrassment or entrapment.** The customer may try to make you feel awkward ("You're not making sense") or trapped ("You don't expect me to believe *that*, do you?").

- **Flat-out rejection.** She may flatly deny what you've said ("That's utterly ridiculous" or "Don't give me that baloney").

- **Flat assertions.** She may pepper her remarks with unqualifiedly negative comments ("It'll never work," "That product's nothing but a piece of junk," "I wouldn't trust anybody in that organization").

- **Deliberate rudeness.** She may be intentionally impolite (yawning rudely, say, or voicing impatience: "Come on, let's get on with it").
- **Interruptions.** She may deliberately break into one of your sentences, showing no regard for what you've been saying.
- **Sarcasm.** She may make snide or sneering remarks ("Hey, you really think you're quite an expert, don't you?").
- **Belligerence.** She may be openly hostile ("I'm getting sick of you hotshots coming in here and telling me how to run my business").
- **Disparagement.** She may let you know she thinks she's smarter than you are ("Let me tell you: I knew all that stuff when you were still a kid").
- **Negative emotions.** She may shout, slam her fist on the desk, shake a finger at you, or in some other way let you know she doesn't like what you're saying.

Obviously, all these Q1 behaviors make the same points: "I'm not really paying close attention . . . my mind's already made up . . .I'm not going to bother weighing your arguments on a balanced scale . . . I don't need to cooperate with you." In other words: "My receptivity's low . . . my mind is closed."

Q2 LOW RECEPTIVITY

Low receptivity sometimes comes packaged as *Q2* behavior. When it does, it's recognizable by the following:

- **Silence.** The customer may not respond at all. Her mouth may remain shut, and her face an inscrutable mask, giving you the disconcerting feeling you're talking to a "bump on a log."
- **Restlessness.** She may seem uneasy: fidgeting, drumming her fingertips on the desk, looking around distractedly, and so on.
- **Mechanical responses.** She may give terse, non-committal answers to most questions ("I'm not sure," "It's hard to say," "Maybe, maybe not").
- **Apathy.** She may seem bored, indifferent, uninterested, eager to get the presentation over with.

All of this behavior makes one point: "I'm too tense to pay real attention . . . I'm so eager to end this thing that I can't take time to consider your ideas. My receptivity is low . . . and my mind is closed."

Q3 LOW RECEPTIVITY

Where *Q2* low receptivity is mostly silent or terse, *Q3* is mostly talkative. The customer *sounds* receptive—until you examine what she's saying:

- **Capitulation.** The customer goes along with *whatever* you say, never voicing doubt, much less disagreement. She instantly labels your ideas "great" or at least "good." While this is nice to hear, you know—objectively—it's not really merited. Her enthusiasm's too strong and too mechanical to be genuine.

- **Meandering.** She rambles, never settling on one topic long enough to discuss it thoroughly. She treats one subject superficially, moves to another, skims its surface, shifts to yet another, and so on.

- **Selective questioning.** She goes out of her way not to embarrass you. She asks easy questions, drops subjects that threaten to get "out of hand," changes the subject when something awkward comes up, makes excuses for you ("Well, I can appreciate your not having the answer. . . . That's really a tough question"), and even blames herself for your shortcomings ("I shouldn't have asked such a complicated question. . . . That wasn't fair").

- **Excessive socializing.** She's unwilling to settle down to business, spending disproportionate time on irrelevancies ("Before you get into that, let me tell you a true story about somebody I used to work with . . .").

All these behaviors make one point: "I don't really *want* to settle down and concentrate on your proposal . . . or think very hard about it . . . or do anything else that might get in the way of our relationship. As far as your *presentation* is concerned, my receptivity is low . . . my mind is closed."

Many salespeople have trouble dealing with Q3 low receptivity because they have trouble recognizing it. Where Q1 and Q2 low receptivity are readily apparent, Q3 isn't. The customer's behavior is deceptive; it seems to signal that things are going great. As a result, when the customer *doesn't* buy, as she often doesn't, her refusal (which usually takes the form of an apology—"I'd like to buy it, but . . . ") comes as a shock. The best way to avoid this shock is to examine the behavior carefully, looking for signs of the above actions.

HIGH RECEPTIVITY

High receptivity can be recognized by *Q4* behaviors:

- **Qualified responses.** Instead of making dogmatic, know-it-all comments ("You're all wrong," "That completely misses the point," "I've never heard anything so impractical") the customer makes tentative comments ("I'm not sure I go along with that," "That seems somewhat off the mark," "I don't think it's completely practical"). She avoids absolutes ("Unquestionably") in favor of limited responses ("Maybe"); she avoids superlatives ("That's the worst idea I've heard yet") in favor of comparatives ("That doesn't seem as workable as some other ideas I've heard"). She does *not* pretend to have all the answers.

- **Appropriate approval.** When the customer approves of something you've said, her approval fits the circumstances. Instead of the unrestrained enthusiasm typical of Q3 behavior ("Terrific!", "Sensational!", "Absolutely great!"), her enthusiasm is considered and realistic: "That's a pretty fair analysis," "By and large, I like what you've shown me so far," "I think that would work." Q4 approval is *not* the approval of a cheerleader ("Let's say something positive no matter what the circumstances") but the approval of someone who's trying to provide an *objective* assessment.

- **Patience.** The customer gives you a real chance to say what you have to say. She doesn't interrupt or hurry you; she doesn't fidget or dart gazes around the room. She lets you tell your own story in your own way; she looks you in the eye; her face registers interest.

- **Thoughtful questions.** The customer asks questions which show she's thinking; they're designed to inform or to clarify—not to embarrass. They may be tough, and they may put you on your mettle, but they're nevertheless fair.

- **Rational discussion.** The customer's willing to reason things out with you. She may express her views with conviction; she may show emotion; but she's still willing to discuss things in a reasonable, thoughtful way. If she disagrees, she does it without arguing or belittling. She answers questions openly and constructively. Whatever her opinions, she has solid evidence or strong reasons to support them.

- **Candor.** The customer speaks her mind, and she does it constructively. She's not dogmatic (Q1), vacillating (Q2), or apologetic (Q3). She says what she thinks, admitting she could be wrong;

she's firm but not unbudgeable; and she's willing to disagree if she thinks it's called for.

- **Doubts and uncertainties.** If the customer's perplexed or unsure about something you've said, she says so, without hesitation or apology, but also without faultfinding. She expresses doubts and indecision as matters of fact ("I'm still having trouble understanding how that latch operates"), not as matters of blame ("You're just not making that latch operation very clear").

- **Insistence on proof.** The customer's open-minded but not gullible; she accepts things on evidence, not on faith. She expects you to justify your claims, and will probably dismiss any benefit statements that aren't supported by proof. She's fair-minded but hardheaded.

All these behaviors make one point: "I'm willing to listen and cooperate . . . my receptivity is high . . . my mind is *open*."

Figure 20. Recognizing Levels of Receptivity.

	How to Recognize LOW Receptivity
Q1 low receptivity	Customer (1) tries to embarrass or entrap you, (2) makes flat assertions – completely negative statements ("That's absolutely crazy"), (3) shows impatience or boredom, (4) interrupts, (5) treats you sarcastically or belittles you, (6) shows anger, hostility, scorn, (7) is deliberately rude, (8) let's you know she has all the answers ("I don't need you to tell me how to run my business").
Q2 low receptivity	Customer (1) is silent and unresponsive, (2) seems indifferent, (3) stares into space, fidgets, (4) gives non-committal answers ("Maybe," "It's hard to say"), (5) seems worried, tense, ill-at-ease.
Q3 low receptivity	Customer (1) goes along with whatever you say, (2) shows excessive enthusiasm, (3) meanders from subject to subject, (4) asks only easy questions, (5) changes subject when awkward topic comes up, (6) seems reluctant to settle down to business.
	How to Recognize HIGH Receptivity
Q4 high receptivity	Customer (1) qualifies responses ("I'm not sure I agree" instead of "That's completely wrong"), (2) voices appropriate approval, (3) gives you chance to speak your piece, (4) asks fair, thoughtful questions, (5) discusses issues without arguing, (6) voices doubts candidly and without apologizing, (7) wants evidence for all claims.

For convenience, we've summarized the signs of low and high receptivity on Figure 20.

IS THERE A SOLUTION?

We've described low receptivity as a brick wall surrounding the customer's mind. Can the wall be breached? Can closed minds be opened? *Yes.*

Low receptivity is *not* a permanent condition, unless you make it that way. An unreceptive customer *can* be made receptive. Closed minds can be reached. How? By using the *probing skills* (special skills for discovering what a customer knows, thinks, or feels) described in the next chapter. If low receptivity is a brick wall, probing skills are a device for loosening the mortar between the bricks so they can be taken down. Once they are, you can do what you came to do: talk with the *customer* instead of to yourself.

Receptivity and Talk

At this point, you may be thinking:

> Why bother learning a whole new set of skills just to make an unreceptive customer receptive? There's an easier way to get inside a closed mind. *Talk* your way in. If you have plenty of facts at your command, are good with words, and can make a logical case, you can get through to any customer. Selling is basically *talk*. If you're a good talker, and know what you're talking about, you can knock down most brick walls. That's faster and more efficient than taking them down brick by brick.

That's a comforting idea, but it won't work. In fact, given the nature of low receptivity, it *can't* work. An unreceptive customer isn't willing to let your ideas in. You may have plenty of facts at your command, but what good are they if the customer won't pay attention? You may be good with words, but what value do they have if she won't let them sink in? You may have logic on your side, but what difference does it make if she won't follow it? The simple truth is: You'll be *wasting* facts, words, and logic if you use them when the customer's unreceptive. You'll be firing verbal ammunition at a brick wall, only to find that it bounces off. The thing to do is to *raise* the customer's receptivity *first*, and *then* use facts, words, and logic. This point is so important that we'll spell it out:

1. Don't waste your breath on facts, eloquence, or logic when the customer's receptivity is low. (That's when, for all practi-

cal purposes, you're talking to yourself. And talking to yourself *is* a waste of breath.)

2. Save your breath and arguments; *spin up* the receptivity first. (In other words, change the situation so that the customer starts paying attention and cooperating: at that point, you can stop talking to yourself and begin talking with her.)

3. Once you've spun up receptivity, present the facts and logic — the needs–benefit package — as effectively as you can. (At this point, you're no longer wasting your breath; you're *getting through.*)

In effect, spin up receptivity *before* presenting your product or service. To do it, you need *probing skill.* Probing skill is *indispensable* to Q4. Without it, you may not be able to do needs–benefit selling at all. That's why our next chapter is devoted to probes and probing.

The Receptivity Continuum

We've been talking as if there are just two kinds of receptivity, high and low. This is an oversimplification. Actually, a customer's receptivity can be high or low or anywhere between. In one sales call, a customer can display different degrees of receptivity at different times. Figure 21 shows how receptivity ranges along a continuum.

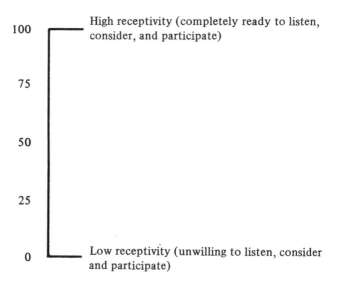

In many sales calls, the customer's mind is neither wide open nor tightly shut. It's partly open and partly closed. What you'd like, of course, is continuous high receptivity (wide open). But *spontaneous* and *continuous* high receptivity is rare. Continuous high receptivity requires continuous effort by you. In every case, keeping receptivity high *takes work*.

Fluctuations in Receptivity

Always expect receptivity to fluctuate. We can't predict what the fluctuations will be, but you'll probably run into some. A customer's receptivity may start out high, drop down, go back up, and so on, like a roller-coaster. Or it may start out low, go up, slide down and level off. The customer may shift from interest to boredom, from attentiveness to daydreaming, from cooperation to resistance. And all this can happen in just minutes. Any number of variations are possible. So:

1. Be alert to these variations. Ask yourself, repeatedly: "Where is the customer's receptivity *now?* What's *happening* to it? Is it level? Going up? Falling?" Never ignore the customer's receptivity. If you do, you may suddenly find the brick wall once again in place.

2. At the first sign of falling receptivity, move quickly to spin it back up. If you don't, if you let it stay down or go lower, you may suddenly find the brick wall higher and thicker – more impenetrable – than ever.

A Caution

We may have left the impression that good probing skills will *always* turn low receptivity into high. If so, that's wrong. No matter how hard you try, sometimes all you can do is make low receptivity a little less low. Figure 22 shows what we mean.

The diagram at the top shows what you'd like to do. You'd *like* to take the customer's low receptivity – which, in this example, is strongly Q2 – and convert it to high – strongly Q4. Chances are you won't succeed, because the move from A to C is a very big move to make during the course of a sales call.

What you're more likely to do is shown in the bottom diagram. With diligent probing, you'll probably move the customer from A to B. Receptivity will still be low, but not *quite* as low. You'll still detect Q2 behavior, but not as intense as before.

Figure 22

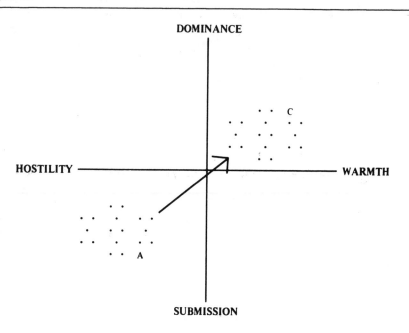

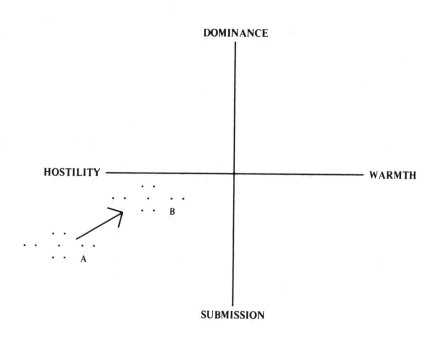

Is moving the customer from A to B worth the effort? Sure it is. The distance between A and B may *look* small, but it's still significant. The difference between a customer who's *very* aloof and one who's *somewhat* aloof could be the difference between not getting and getting the order. It's always worthwhile to spin up receptivity. But don't expect miracles.

AN EXAMPLE

This chapter may strike you as somewhat abstract because we've talked *about* receptivity without illustrating it. If you feel some examples of low and high receptivity would be helpful, and if you'd like to see how "spinning up" receptivity works, we urge you to read Appendix A—"A Q4 Sales Presentation." You'll find plenty of examples there, all clearly labelled.

SUMMARY

1. Need–benefit selling may not work — in fact, probably won't — if it's tried at the wrong time. The question of timing is crucial to Q4 selling.

2. Selling is a matter of persuasion, and persuasion is a matter of timing. If a customer isn't ready to listen, your benefit statements won't do any good. A mis-timed presentation may prove futile.

3. Whenever you begin a sales presentation, you're presumably ready psychologically. But the customer may not be. In spite of this, you must proceed. This is the *receptivity problem.*

4. Receptivity is willingness to listen carefully, consider, and respond constructively and candidly. It's the desire to make an interaction pay off through give-and-take.

5. Low receptivity takes the form of Q1, Q2, or Q3 behavior. Q1 behavior makes the point: "My mind's made up . . . I don't need to cooperate with you."

6. Q2 behavior makes the point: "I'm too tense to pay real attention. . . . Let's just get this over with."

7. Q3 behavior makes the point: "I don't really want to settle down and concentrate . . . I don't want to put our relationship at risk."

8. High receptivity can be recognized by Q4 behavior. The message is: "My mind is open."

9. Low receptivity need not be a permanent condition. An unreceptive customer can be made receptive through the use of probing skills.

10. Facts, eloquence, and logic are usually wasted at low receptivity. Receptivity should be spun up before facts, eloquence, and logic are employed.

11. In one sales call, a customer can display different degrees of receptivity at different times. Her receptivity can fluctuate unpredictably. Continuous high receptivity almost always requires continuous effort by the salesperson.

12. Low receptivity cannot always be converted into high. Sometimes, it can only be made less low.

9

Probing

Let's repeat three big points from the last chapter:

1. To persuade – sell – you must generate understanding and commitment.
2. You can generate understanding and commitment only if the customer's receptivity – willingness to give and take – is up. If it's not, you'll have to spin it up.
3. To spin up receptivity, you must be able to probe.

All of which boils down to seven words: *probing skill is essential to successful selling.* That's why we're spending this entire chapter on it. It's a long chapter – and for good reason. Thousands of salespeople and sales managers who have taken Dimensional Sales and Sales Management Training have attested to the same fact: learning to probe has made a very real difference in their ability to do their jobs. Mastering the contents of this chapter should make a very real difference in *your* ability to do *your* job.

TWO DEFINITIONS

Let's define *probes* and *probing*.

- A *probe* is a communication tool for finding out what a customer (or anyone else) knows, thinks, or feels. Just as surgeons use probes – slender metal tools – to explore wounds, salespeople use probes—verbal tools—to explore minds. Probes generate dialogue; they're the mechanism that gets discussion started and keeps it going. In the process of discussion—verbal give-and-take—you can learn what's in the customer's mind.

- *Probing* is the *use* of probes.

THE FUNCTIONS OF PROBING

Probing helps you do two important things:

1. Learn what's in the customer's mind (so you can detect his needs, tie them to your product or service, and develop meaningful benefit statements).
2. Spin up or keep up receptivity (so the customer gives your benefit statements a fair hearing).

By probing, you can do both things at the same time. You can get the customer to say what he knows, thinks, and feels; in that way, you create give-and-take. And give-and-take—listening, responding, and getting involved—is what receptivity is all about.

Why Bother?

Must you go to all this trouble to raise receptivity? Must you learn a complete set of skills before you can time presentations effectively?
    Strictly speaking, no. There *is* an easier way. You can make receptivity soar by *extravagant promises.* Don't bother to probe; just promise the moon—or something close to it:

- "Take my word for it. Install our System 12X and your profits will jump 25 percent in a month. That's a guarantee."
- "Sign this order, and you'll never . . . not once . . . know what a machine breakdown is. This thing will run for years and years."

    Pledges like these—not mere claims, but *commitments*—are almost sure to make receptivity zoom. There's only one problem: promising miracles, even small ones, is risky business. Once you promise the moon you'd better deliver. If you can't, the only *other* way to raise receptivity is *probing.*

How Probing Spins Up Receptivity

Probing spins up receptivity by filling unfilled intangible needs. Unfilled intangible needs *bother* us. By making us tense, worried, fidgety, they *call attention to themselves.* They *force themselves* on our awareness, making it difficult to concentrate on anything else.

This is the cause of *low receptivity*: When we concentrate on our *unfilled intangible needs*, we can't concentrate on other things. We refuse to listen not because we're "pigheaded," but because we have *other* things on our minds, and they *come first.* Our attention has been "taken over"—monopolized—by our pesty unfilled needs. Our minds are—almost literally—*pre*-occupied.

To spin up receptivity, you must clear away the customer's preoccupation. He must *stop thinking about himself* before he can focus on other things. Probing helps bring him to this point.

How? By helping *fill* his unfilled intangible needs. As they fill, they become less nagging, and the customer's mind is "freed up." He can zero in on something besides *himself*; he can focus on *your presentation.*

Probing does this by relieving the customer's concerns. It lets him talk, get things off his mind. And it reassures; it helps him "untense" and occupy himself with other matters. Figure 23 shows how this happens.

Finding Out What's On The Customer's Mind

Probing not only spins up receptivity; it helps you learn what's on the customer's mind. It does it by:

1. **Involving the customer.** A probe is meant to produce a response, which will usually be verbal, sometimes gestural or facial. Unless the customer ignores the probe, which is unlikely, he must *respond* in some way. In responding, he gets *involved*; he shares information and ideas.

2. **Eliciting information that can't be learned any other way.** If customers always volunteered their ideas, and were always *clear* about them, probing would be less important. But many customers don't spontaneously divulge their thoughts, or they divulge them confusingly. That's another reason for probing; it gets the customer to open up, and it clarifies his ideas.

3. **Making the presentation matter to the customer.** A sales call matters—is important—to you, but it may not matter to the customer. His reaction may be "So what?" or "Who cares?" Probing changes this. It makes the call matter to the customer by including *his* ideas, letting him say what *he* wants to say.

Probing is also a *request* for aid. It says, "Look, I can't make this presentation by myself—I need *your* help." This makes the customer

Figure 23. How Probing Fills Intangible Needs.

If the customer's behavior is:	his major personal concern (unfilled intangible need) is probably:	and your probes should convey this message:
Q1: belligerent, impatient, interruptive, sarcastic, negative, dogmatic	*Esteem*: "I'm not sure I'm going to get the respect I'm entitled to; I don't want to be taken for granted." and *Independence*: "This salesperson is going to crowd me; he'll try to run the show his way, and make me conform to his ideas."	"I *do* respect you; that's why I'm trying to find out what *you* think. Your ideas *matter*. I don't want to shove my ideas down your throat. I want to hear *your* ideas, so any decisions we reach are influenced by *you* as well as me."
Q2: silent, indifferent, inattentive, mechanical, nervous	*Security*: "I don't think I'm going to like this presentation. It could prove risky. I may be pressured or outwitted, and end up buying something I don't need. The whole thing could work to my disadvantage."	"I'm not trying to make trouble or to show you up. I'm giving you a chance to say what *you* want, in your own way and at your own pace. I may guide, but I won't push or manipulate you. I'm *listening*. I want to understand."
Q3: agreeable, meandering, easygoing	*Sociality*: "I want to come across as pleasant and likeable. No matter what the outcome of the presentation, I want to come out of it knowing I'm accepted."	"I'm interested in you as a person. That's why I'm asking questions. If I weren't interested in you, I'd say what's on my mind and call it quits. Instead, I'm talking *with* you—not *at* you—proof of my interest in you as a person."

feel *needed*, and a situation in which the customer feels needed is *important* to him.

4. **Venting interfering emotions.** Troublesome emotions—ranging from anger to sulking to giggling—hinder the presentation. They lower receptivity and impair thinking. Probing eliminates or lessens them. It clears the air so the presentation can proceed in a rational, businesslike way.

5. **Keeping the presentation on track.** Q4 selling aims at Q4 dialogue. Trading chit-chat, gossip, jokes, war stories—all this may

be dialogue, but not *Q4* dialogue. Q4 dialogue sticks to the subject. It's relevant. Probing lets the customer know which topics *are* relevant. Every probe, in effect, says, "Let's talk about *this*—not something else." Probes *channel* the dialogue.

6. **Forcing yourself to listen.** Probes work on you as well as on the customer. When you probe, you must *pay attention* to the response. Why? Because probes usually come in series: first one, then another, and so on, until the topic's covered. But you can't intelligently phrase the second probe in a series unless you understood the response to the *first*; you can't phrase the third probe unless you heard the reaction to the second; and so on. You can't probe and daydream. Once you probe, you must listen—at a *thinking* level.

In these six ways, probing helps you learn what the customer knows, thinks, and feels. If you wait for him to volunteer the information, you may wait a long time. In most cases, you *must* probe.

PROBES AND INTERACTION

Let's recall the five steps to the sale: opening, exploring needs, presenting the product or service, managing objections, and closing. In *all five* steps, you'll usually need to do three things—all of which require probing:

1. Get the customer to *open up*—reveal what's on his mind.
2. Get him to keep talking until you *fully* understand.
3. Make sure you've understood *correctly.*

We can classify the various probes by keeping these three things in mind. There are eight different kinds of probes. You can remember them and what they do by grouping them under one of these three functions:

1. **Probes that open up**
   - *Open-end probes*

2. **Probes that keep the talk going**
   - *Pauses*
   - *Reflective statements*
   - *Neutral probes*
   - *Brief assertions*

3. **Probes that check understanding**
    - *Closed-end questions*
    - *Leading questions*
    - *Summary statements*

We'll discuss the eight probes in the above order. Our discussion will define each probe, give examples, explain the functions of the probe, describe its effect upon the customer, and, where necessary, offer some cautions.

1. PROBES THAT OPEN UP

- *Open-end probes*

a. Definition. An *open-end probe* is a question or request worded so as to produce a broad, wide-ranging response about a single topic. Open-end probes invite *expansive* responses. They usually start with *how, what,* or *why,* or with phrases like *tell me* or *fill me in.* Because of the way they're worded, they *cannot* be answered "Yes," "No," or "Maybe." And it's difficult to answer them with single words or short phrases, like "Two" or "Yesterday, I think." They invite longer, fuller responses.

b. Examples

- How do you expect the strike to affect deliveries?
- Fill me in on the inventory problem at Northridge.
- What do you anticipate from competition?
- Why do you feel you've been treated unfairly?
- Update me on the contract negotiations.

Compare these probes with probes which are *not* open-end:

- Who gave you that information?
- Where was the shipment finally located?
- When do you expect to have the press installed?

These questions can be answered in one or a few words; they don't invite a free-ranging response.

Can you always identify an open-end probe by its first word? No. Some probes which begin with *how, what,* or *why* are *not* open-end.

Even some probes beginning with a phrase like *tell me* are *not* open-end.

If the opening word or phrase doesn't make a probe open-end, what does? Three things:

1. The *overall* wording. The probe *as a whole* invites a free-wheeling response.

2. The *information* asked for. Open-end probes invite *more* than isolated facts; usually, they invite *clusters* of facts plus *opinions* and maybe *feelings*. For example: "Tell me how you think this proposal would affect your market position," invites *facts, opinions,* and *feelings*; it's much less limiting than a probe like "Tell me who will be there."

3. The *function* of the probe in the overall discussion. Open-end probes are used to *open up* discussion, not channel it or pinpoint it.

c. What open-end probes do

- They *draw out* the customer. They tell him which topic you're interested in, and let him fill you in in his own way.

- They let him know his thinking *counts*. They spin up receptivity by saying: "Look . . . I'm not going to force *my* ideas on you. I'm going to shut up while *you* tell me *your* ideas. I'm *interested* in them."

- They help cope with negative emotions. If the customer looks unhappy, you can find out why by asking: "How do you feel about that?" or "What's your reaction?" If the customer's said something negative, you can learn why by asking: "Why do you say that?" or "What makes you feel that way?"

- They help you handle *flat assertions*. Flat assertions are (1) dogmatic and unqualified ("That's the dumbest idea I ever heard"), (2) usually exaggerated (the idea may be "dumb," but is it really *the* dumbest?) and (3) usually contain a nugget of truth (the idea may not be *the* dumbest, but it may not be very smart, either). With open-end probes, you can do two things: (a) give the customer a chance to modify the flat assertion, and (b) isolate the nugget of truth. For example:

CUSTOMER: That's absolutely the wildest thing I ever heard. It'll never work.

YOU: What makes you say that? (Open-end probe)

CUSTOMER: It just won't. We tried something like that once, years ago. What a mess!

YOU: What happened? (Open-end probe)

CUSTOMER: What happened was, we tried a plan almost identical to yours . . . the Omnibus Plan, we called it . . . and it fell flat. Nobody understood it.

YOU: Why not? (Open-end probe)

CUSTOMER: Because nobody bothered to explain it, that's why. We never got any instructions on it. It was a real joke. Believe me, your idea won't work unless you explain it . . . in detail . . . to the people who have to live with it.

In this exchange, the customer stripped away the exaggeration and revealed the nugget of truth inside his original flat assertion. Open-end probes did the job.

d. How open-end probes affect customer behavior

Q1. Use open-end probes to temper Q1 anger or belligerence, and to qualify flat assertions. Invite the customer to talk out his feeling. Clear the air by letting him "get it out of his system."

Example: "What's the trouble?"

Q2. Use open-end probes to loosen tight lips. Encourage amplification.

Example: "Tell me why you say this product can't do the job."

Q3. Go easy on open-end probes with meandering customers, or you may make things worse. Save the open-end probes until you get the dialogue *on track.* Here's an example of the risk involved:

YOU: Ed, how's the new inventory system working?

OTHER: Good question . . . darned good question. The best way I know to answer it is to tell you about an experience we had around here a couple of years ago. This may seem roundabout, but . . . believe me . . . it'll throw a lot of light on the new inventory system. Take it from me, the whole thing is more complicated than anybody ever knew. That's why what I'm about to tell you is so important. If . . . "

Q4. When the customer's receptivity is at the Q4 level—candid and cooperative—he still must know *what* you expect him to talk about. Before he can get on track and stay on track, he must know *which* track. Guide him with an open-end probe.

Example: "Dave, what kind of results are you expecting from the market study?"

e. *Caution*

- Don't contaminate an open-end probe by inserting your own ideas. Here's an example: "I'm sure it'll work. What's your opinion?"

2. PROBES THAT KEEP THE TALK GOING

- *Pauses*

a. Definition. A pause is a deliberate short silence, a planned break which lets the customer collect his thoughts.

b. Examples. We obviously can't give examples of silence. We can say that the typical pause is brief, about five or ten seconds, maybe a few more or less. During the pause, nobody speaks. As soon as someone does, the pause ends.

c. What pauses do

- They give the customer time to mull over your ideas.
- They let him put his thoughts in order so he can decide what to do next.
- They slow things down, so the customer doesn't feel pressured.
- They let *you* order *your* thoughts, so you can plan ahead.
- They encourage silent customers to open up. Pauses create an awkward feeling which can be overcome only by *saying something.* Most of us feel uncomfortable when a dialogue grinds to a half. That's what a pause is: a momentary halt. If the halt continues long enough, both you and the customer will probably feel awkward. The customer will probably end the awkwardness by speaking out, *unless you end it by speaking out first.* To use a pause effectively, *hold* it until the customer speaks. *Don't* (as in this example) be the first to resume talking:

JACK: How about it, Dorothy? Can we draw up the order? (A short pause)

DOROTHY: (No immediate response)

JACK: (Quickly) Well . . . I appreciate your not wanting to commit yourself. That's only normal. So let me ask you: Do you think we ought to trim the quantity a bit . . . maybe shave off a thousand or so units? (A short pause)

DOROTHY: (No immediate response, although there's a thoughtful look on her face)

JACK: (Quickly) Well . . . we can come back to that. I know it's a tough question. Why don't you think about it between now and my next call?

In this example, Jack used two pauses but didn't sustain them. By being impatient, he squelched the customer; if he'd prolonged the pauses a few more seconds, he might well have acquired some useful information and maybe made the sale.

Pauses require *discipline*. They require *staying* quiet as long as it takes the customer to respond.

d. How pauses affect customer behavior

Q1. Use a pause to "count to ten" if provoked by Q1 behavior. If the customer starts annoying you, take time to frame a response you won't later regret. Pause . . . and think.

Q2. Use pauses to cope with uncommunicative Q2 behavior. We've already described how this works.

Q3. Use pauses sparingly with a talkative customer. Like air filling a vacuum, the customer will rush in to fill the pause with his own words.

Q4. Use occasional pauses so the customer can arrange his thoughts and present them effectively.

e. *Caution*

Not every silence is a pause. A pause is *intentional*. Most silences are unintentional; they happen because nobody knows what to say. Real pauses are sometimes called *pregnant* pauses because they're designed to *bring forth* pertinent responses; phony causes aren't designed to do anything – they're simply lapses.

• *Reflective statements*

a. Definition. Reflective statements assert that you're *aware* of and *understand* the customer's feelings, *without* indicating whether you agree or disagree with them. They tell the customer: "Your emotions are getting through to me; I know how you feel." But they never say or imply whether you think the emotions are justified.

Reflective statements reflect the customer's feelings, just as a mirror reflects his face. But they don't *pass judgment* on his feelings, any more than a mirror passes judgment on his face. Mirrors and reflective statements are non-commital.

b. Examples

- I can tell it's bothering you.
- You seem pretty indignant about it.
- You're obviously happy it worked out.
- You're sure enthusiastic about the news.

Note that reflective statements can mirror either positive or negative feelings.

c. What reflective statements do

Reflective statements let the customer *vent*. *Venting* is "letting off steam," expressing suppressed feelings. Suppressed feelings lower receptivity; when we're angry, for example, we think mostly about our anger, not about other things. Our anger monopolizes our attention. Venting dispels suppressed feelings, so we can concentrate on other matters.

Here's an example:

SALESPERSON: Frank, how are deliveries?

CUSTOMER: (Disgustedly) Lousy, that's how. We've been completely out of inventory twice this past month. (His voice rises) I'll tell you, Dave, I'm sick of the whole situation. (Talking rapidly, obviously very agitated) Everybody's blaming me for a rotten mess that's out of my control. Your company's at fault— not me. All I get is alibis instead of merchandise. The trucker lost the shipment . . . there's a wildcat strike at the factory . . . a major piece of equipment broke down. I've had it.

SALESPERSON: This delivery thing's got you pretty frustrated.

CUSTOMER: (Intensely) You're darned right it has. I've got a right to be frustrated. I'm under pressure. Real pressure. And you people are making life miserable for me. (Very angrily) Everybody's screaming at me . . . all because your company can't do its job.

SALESPERSON: I can tell you're exasperated.

CUSTOMER: (A little less angry) Yeah . . . I'll say. Everybody's jumping down my throat lately, Dave. You don't know the half of it.

SALESPERSON: Go ahead, Frank. I'm listening.

Let's analyze this exchange:

1. Suppressed feelings, like suppressed steam, build up force—a "head of steam." So Frank first expressed his feelings with considerable force.

2. Once suppressed feelings *are* expressed, the force usually *builds*. The emotion *intensifies*, just as Frank's anger did. This is called *peaking*. In peaking, emotions rise to a high point. This is normal, even expectable, and should be *permitted*. Peaking may not be fun to listen to, but it is—ultimately—productive.

3. This is where reflective statements come in. They encourage peaking, which *dissipates* the emotions. We all know how tiring it is to keep our emotions at a peak for very long. Once we've "gotten things out of our system," once we've "had our say," our emotions usually subside. And, once they do, we can discuss things reasonably, just as Frank is about to do.

4. Reflective statements do more than encourage peaking; they tell the customer, "You're not alone . . . I know what you're feeling." Without implying either agreement or disagreement, they make it difficult for the customer to feel that "Nobody knows what I'm going through." Reflective statements make it plain that you're an aware, responsive human being—a good person to do business with.

Several other points should be noted:

1. Our example was so brief it's somewhat artificial. Venting frequently requires more time and effort.

2. One of the reflective statements in our illustration is an example of "anchoring"—connecting the emotion to the event that triggered it ("This delivery thing's got you pretty frustrated"). Anchoring can be valuable because it shows the customer that you're aware of both his emotion and the reason—or the alleged reason—behind it. It's another way of convincing the customer that you're someone who "catches on."

3. Use enough reflective statements (which may be combined with other probes) to vent the feelings *fully*. Generally, the *stronger* the feelings, the *more* reflective statements you'll need.

4. As the customer peaks, you may find yourself or your company on the receiving end of a tongue-lashing. If you feel the urge to stifle the customer (and you probably will), resist it. Any attempt to restrain him ("Now, now . . . don't get excited") will only imply that you don't take his feelings *seriously*. That will fuel his anger, not extinguish it. Like it or not, *let him peak*.

5. What will happen if you *don't* let the customer vent? Three things: (a) he'll begin seeing everything in *personal* terms; (b) he'll let *stereotypes* dominate his thinking; (c) he'll have trouble thinking *logically*. If his strong emotions are held back long enough, any customer will begin thinking subjectively, rigidly, and illogically. And that will make persuasion all the more difficult.

d. How reflective statements affect customer behavior

Q1. Use reflective statements to vent the whole spectrum of Q1 emotions: anger, scorn, condescension, sarcasm, and so on.

Example: "You sure have some strong convictions on this issue."

Q2. Use them to vent Q2 tension and anxiety.

Example: "Something I've said has made you uncomfortable."

Q3. Use reflective statements to dispel positive emotions, which can also block the presentation. Gushiness, inability to settle down, irrelevant chatter can all be lessened by reflective statements.

Example: "You really are wound up about it."

Q4. Even customers who mostly Q4 it can get emotionally worked up. If they do, use reflective statements to restore calm.

Example: "I've hit a nerve."

e. *Some cautions*

- Don't *overuse* reflective statements. You don't want to reflect *every* emotion, only the troublesome ones—those that *must* be dispelled if you're going to get back on track.
- Don't *agree* with the customer's sentiments unless you're *sure* you want to. Statements like the following are risky; they imply agreement, and could come back to haunt you:
  - *I can certainly see why* you're upset.
  - *I don't blame you* for being angry.
  - You're sore, and *I think anyone else in your situation would be sore too.*

- *Neutral probes*

a. Definition. A neutral probe is a question or statement that encourages the customer to elaborate *on one aspect* of a topic being discussed. Neutral probes sometimes *sound* like open-end probes. But they have three characteristics which open-end probes lack:

1. They ask for *additional* information. They often (not always) use phrases like:
   - Tell me *more* . . .
   - Explain that *further* . . .
   - Please *expand* on . . .
   - Please *elaborate* . . .

2. They *channel* the discussion (open-end probes start it). They *narrow down* or *funnel.* They *zero in* on part of a subject and request more information. They *restrict* the customer more than open-end probes do.

3. They're used some time *after* the customer opens up. Open-end probes introduce a subject; neutral probes come later. Open-end probes launch a topic; neutral probes keep it afloat on a particular course.

b. Examples

- Fill me in further on why you want to switch models.
- Tell me more about why you feel our credit policy's unrealistic.
- Give me some more details on that packaging problem.

Neutral probes don't *have* to contain words like *further* or *more.* Our examples could be reworded and still be neutral probes:

- Tell me why you want to switch models.
- Explain your remark about our credit policy being unrealistic.
- Give me the details on that packaging problem.

These examples show that, *taken out of context*, it's not always possible to distinguish a neutral probe from an open-end probe. What matters isn't the wording of the probe, but its function. All the examples above, no matter how worded, do one thing: they focus on a *piece* of a subject *already* being discussed, and ask for *more information.* That makes them *neutral* probes.

Sometimes, neutral probes are nothing more than a word-for-word repetition of something the customer's just said. These verbatim restatements serve the same purpose as any other neutral probe: they let the customer know you need more information about what he's just said. Here's an example:

CUSTOMER: I dunno. It doesn't sound bad. But it looks like energy consumption would be a real problem. (Pause)

SALESPERSON: (Pause) It looks like energy consumption would be a real problem.

CUSTOMER: (Slowly) Well . . . yeah. From what I've heard, that thing uses a terrific amount of fuel. In fact, I read somewhere that it burns nearly twice as much as our present model. And that means our costs are gonna jump. Believe me, there are lots of things I like about your machine, but the energy cost worries me.

In this example, "It looks like energy consumption would be a real problem" is a neutral probe. Its *function* is to elicit additional information; it says to the customer, in effect, "Expand on what you just said. Tell me more about it."

c. What neutral probes do

- They help you get the *whole* story instead of just a piece.
- They signal the customer that you're still interested in what he's saying. This keeps receptivity up.

d. How neutral probes affect customer behavior

You can make good use of neutral probes no matter how the customer's behaving. Whenever you need more information or clarification ("Explain that, please . . ."), neutral probes will help.

e. *Caution*

- If you repeat the customer's words verbatim, don't overdo it. A string of such neutral probes will make the customer think you're parroting him. Used occasionally, not repeatedly, exact repetition can be (as in our example) very useful.
- Keep neutral probes *neutral.* Don't use them to pass judgment. For example:

    (Belligerently) "Why in the name of common sense *don't* you think it's a good idea?"
    (Sarcastically) "Whaddya mean . . . you don't think it'll work?"

These aren't really requests for more information or clarification; they're signals that you have your own ideas and don't like being contradicted. Probes like these will probably *block* the flow of information.

- *Brief assertions*

   a. Definition. A brief assertion is a very short statement, question, sound, or gesture to let the customer know you're interested.

   b. Examples

Brief assertions usually contain two, three, or four words:

- I see.
- Keep going.
- I get it.
- That's interesting.
- I'm amazed.

They may be questions:

- Is that right?
- Really?
- No kidding?

Brief assertions may be sounds, not words:

- Hm-m-m-m-m

They may be short exclamations.

- Boy!
- Wow!
- My gosh!

And they may simply be body language:

- (A nod of the head)
- (Raised eyebrows)
- (An appreciative smile)
- (Eye contact)
- (Leaning forward)

c. What brief assertions do

- They encourage the customer to continue talking.
- They bring out additional information.
- They raise or keep up receptivity. The customer is more likely to listen to you when he knows you've been listening to him.

d. How brief assertions affect customer behavior

Brief assertions are useful no matter what the customer's behavior, but especially with Q2 brevity. If the customer discloses information in small and not very instructive packets, use a brief assertion after each packet. This will probably produce fuller disclosure.

e. *Cautions*

- Use brief assertions carefully when dealing with talkative Q3 behavior. Don't open the spigot wider when it should be turned off.
- Of all probes, brief assertions are the easiest to use without thinking; it's very easy to say "I see" and "Go on" without realizing *what* you're saying. This is risky. The customer may think you *do* see when you really don't; he may "go on" when you *don't* want him to. Be careful. Think first.
- Mechanical brief assertions may sound insincere. If you keep repeating automatically, "That's interesting" or "I'll be darned," the customer may get the idea you don't mean it, that you're just making noises. Once again, think first.

3. PROBES THAT CHECK UNDERSTANDING

- *Closed-end questions*

a. **Definition.** A *closed-end* question is any question worded to produce a short, precise response on a restricted topic. There are three kinds:

1. *Fact-finding questions.* These usually start with *who, whom, what, when, where, how much.*
2. *Commitment questions.* These seek a *yes* or *no* answer (although they may elicit a *maybe* or *I don't know*).
3. *Option questions.* These can be answered by selecting one of two or more alternatives.

b. Examples

- *Fact-finding questions*

  · Whom have you been dealing with?
  · What time should I get there?
  · How much should we deliver on Tuesday?
  · When will your new plant start operating?
  · Where should we mail the invoice?

- *Commitment questions*

  · Do you think the idea will work?
  · Should we begin drop-shipments next week?
  · Can we settle on ninety-day billing?

- *Option questions*

  · Should we make it Wednesday afternoon or Thursday morning?
  · Do you want me to wire or call?

Closed-end questions are designed to get short, specific answers, but they don't always work that way. *Any* closed-end question may produce a vague, longwinded answer if the customer is determined to give one.

c. What closed-end questions do

- They establish facts or opinions.
- They test commitment ("Yes," "Okay," "Sure thing").
- They tell you if you're reaching for commitment too soon:

SALESPERSON: How about it, Dan? Can I write up a carload at the present price?

CUSTOMER: Hold on, Fred. Not so fast. I'm still not clear on a couple of things. I want some answers before I commit myself.

An answer like this tells you it's too early to "nail down" a commitment. More dialogue is needed.

- Closed-end questions control Q3 meandering. The technique isn't guaranteed, but it usually helps. For example:

SALESPERSON: Vince, can you take this shipment Monday?

SUBORDINATE: That's a tough one, Kate. I can think of at least six things that could get in the way. On the other hand, we might have no trouble at all. I remember one time in a situation like this . . .

SALESPERSON: Vince, pardon me, but if I don't call the factory in the next few minutes, we won't get the material rolling in time. Shall I tell them to go ahead and schedule it for Monday?

Pointed, closed-end questions might produce a straight answer.

d. How closed-end questions affect customer behavior

Q1.   Inflated claims or commitments are typically Q1. Closed-end questions can bring them down to earth:

- Do you think you might want to scale down this projection a little?
- Is there any chance you're aiming a bit too high?

Q2.   Option questions help overcome indecision. Introduce the question by explaining why you're asking it:

- Harry, it'll help us both if we settle on a figure. Which amount makes more sense: 10% or 12%?
- Alice, I'm still not sure I know your preference. Should we ship rail or truck?

Q3.   As we just said, closed-end questions restrict rambling.

Q4.   A customer whose behavior is Q4 will probably provide details without prodding—if he knows *which* details. Closed-end questions zero in on details.

e. *Cautions*

- Usually, it's best to start a discussion with open-end probes, follow with neutral probes for selected data, and then use closed-end questions sparingly near the end. Don't "machine gun" closed-end questions; a barrage of pointed questions creates the "interrogation effect," which most customers rightly resent ("Why is he giving me the third-degree?"). If you must use a number of closed-end questions close together, explain why. This should neutralize the interrogation effect.
- Use closed-end probes carefully with Q2 or you'll encourage more Q2. In fact, if you ask enough closed-end questions, the customer can breeze through the call with just a few grunts. So, go easy on closed-end questions with close-mouthed customers.

- *Leading questions*

a. **Definition.** A *leading question* allows only one reasonable answer. That's because the answer is built in. While the question may *seem* to allow a choice, it actually leads the customer to the answer *you* want.

Leading questions can be used in a Q4 or a Q1 way. Q1 leading questions are called "entrapping" questions; they're used to snare customers into saying things they might not otherwise say. Naturally, most customers resent this.

Q4 leading questions are a legitimate way to check understanding and move the customer to action. They're useful for getting the customer to say what he obviously believes but hasn't yet said; once he says it, he can move forward and do something about it.

Some people insist that leading questions aren't really questions at all, but *statements* that *sound* like questions. This is a good point. Real questions, after all, not only invite a reply, but allow a choice as to what it will be. Leading questions may or may not invite a reply, but they're not meant to allow a choice.

b. **Examples**

- You don't want your competition to think you're falling behind, do you?
- It's not worth doing if it's going to bankrupt you, is it?
- You're interested in any idea that'll put money in your pocket, aren't you?
- You don't want to damage your credit rating, do you?

c. **What leading questions do**

- They help you learn if the assumption you've built into the question is correct. They should be used only *after* full discussion. If they're used too early, the customer may think you're trying to put words in his mouth.
- Leading questions can be used as veiled threats. As such, they may fortify the customer's resistance and bring the presentation to grief. Here's an example:

SALESPERSON: Lou . . . I'm telling you . . . if you don't sign the order today, there's a good chance the factory won't ship it at all.
This stuff is scarce and getting scarcer. We may have to start
taking orders on a first-come first-serve basis. If you get

your order in late, we may not be able to fill it. You don't want to be left out in the cold, do you?

CUSTOMER: Doesn't worry me. If I can't get it from you, I'll get it from your competition.

SALESPERSON: C'mon, Lou. Those guys are in the same boat as us. They're short of product, too. Believe me . . . you're better off signing right now—and not taking chances. You don't want to find yourself without inventory, do you?

CUSTOMER: Don't threaten me, Joe. I don't like being pushed.

As this shows, leading questions are *supposed* to produce one and only one answer, but they don't always work that way. Leading questions, improperly used, may produce unwanted responses.

d. How leading questions affect customer behavior

Q1. Q1 behavior usually implies strong needs for *esteem* and *independence*. You can't fill these needs if you lead the customer by the nose. Be careful; he may consider *any* leading question an attempt to "crowd" him. In fact, leading questions often push the customer into a dependent role; seeking an opportunity to assert himself, he finds himself maneuvered into following *your* lead instead. With Q1 (or Q4) behavior, this can be very risky.

Q2. After some discussion, leading questions can help overcome Q2 indecision.

Q3. Q3, like Q2, often vacillates. Again, leading questions can help pin down a decision.

Q4. Chances are that with Q4, you'll use leading questions mostly to sum up what's already been agreed on.

e. *Cautions*

- Don't use leading questions too early in the call.
- Don't use many leading questions. Of all probes, they're the most likely to be resented. After all, you won't find many customers who enjoy playing "dummy" while you play "ventriloquist."

• *Summary statements*

a. Definition.   A summary statement recaps information received from the customer. It paraphrases and condenses what you understood the customer to say.

Four points are worth noting:

1. Summary statements *differ* from reflective statements. Reflective statements mirror feelings and emotions; they deal with moods or states of mind. Summary statements repeat, briefly and usually in different words, an argument or train of thought; they're not concerned with feelings, but with information, ideas, facts, opinions, and logic.

2. Summary statements aren't always accurate. When you summarize, the best you can do is state the customer's ideas *as you understood them.* If you understood wrong, your summary will be wrong, too.

3. Summary statements are the longest of all probes. Other probes usually take a sentence or less. Summary statements may take several sentences.

4. Summary statements don't *evaluate*, and they don't imply *agreement.* The fact that you're restating the customer's ideas doesn't mean you go along with them. In this *one* respect, summary statements and reflective statements are alike:

- "Joe, you're really troubled about it" (reflective statement) doesn't mean you feel Joe *should* be troubled. You may or may not.

- "As I get it, you don't think the Model J is worth the extra money, because it won't reduce your down-time" (summary statement) doesn't mean you *agree.* You may or may not.

In effect, a summary statement says: "This is the information you're trying to get across to me, as I understand it." That's *all* it says. In effect, a reflective statement says: "This is the way you feel, as I perceive it." That's *all* it says.

b. Examples

- "As I get it, Barbara, you think you'd be better off junking the whole purchase arrangement, and going out on the open market."

- "If I hear you right, Charlie, you're saying we've got to get our bid in by Tuesday, and there's no way you can give us an extension."

- "So, you're saying you shouldn't be asked to pay full price for a shipment that arrived a week late, even if our company wasn't at fault."

c. What summary statements do

- They show that you're trying to understand the customer – that you've been listening *actively* (if you haven't, you can't phrase a good summary statement). In effect, this is a compliment to the customer, and it helps keep up receptivity.

- They evidence your interest in, and concern for, the customer. They say, in effect, "I've been paying attention to you. I've been following your words closely. I'm interested in what you've been saying." This is a powerful message.

- They let you know if you've understood or interpreted correctly. If you haven't, they signal the customer that he's not getting through. Either way, they confirm whether or not you're hearing the same thing the customer's saying.

- They bring crucial points into focus. They zero in on important points and ignore unimportant ones. Summary statements separate the wheat from the chaff.

d. How summary statements affect customer behavior

Q1. If the customer's Q1ing it, expect a barrage of objections. Summarize them, then deal with them one by one. The summary will help you organize the objections so you can handle them in a logical sequence. It will also gratify the customer's esteem needs by showing you've been paying attention:

> Let's see if I've got this straight, Jane. You say our billing system is messed up . . . our customer-service department is giving you the runaround . . . and I haven't been returning your calls fast enough. Is that right?
>   It sure is.
>   Okay. Let's talk about each point, starting with the first.

Q2. Q2 seldom provides enough information to require more than very brief summaries.

Q3. It's sometimes hard to keep up with Q3 meandering. Summary statements help. By summarizing *only* what's worth summarizing, and ignoring the rest, you can usually restrain the customer and get him to focus on what counts:

> Ben, let me try to boil this down to essentials. As I understand it . . .

Q4. Even when the customer's cooperative and candid, you can't be *sure* you understand him unless you periodically summarize. If he confirms your summary, fine. If not, you can find out what he *really* means.

e. *Cautions*

- Don't turn a summary into a speech, and don't use it to take over the dialogue. Be concise.

- Keep your own ideas *out.* Concentrate on what you think the *customer* said. Don't editorialize. Don't stack the deck by summarizing only those points you agree with. If you do, your summary may backfire.

- Try not to parrot the customer by using his exact words. He may think you're mimicking him—which isn't likely to make you popular. If you can (and you usually can), *rephrase* his ideas.

- **PROBING STYLES**

Each pattern of sales behavior—Q1, Q2, Q3, and Q4—has a characteristic probing style. The authors have seen these styles again and again in Dimensional Sales and Sales Management Training seminars, where salespeople and sales managers role-play situations in which probing would be useful. The role plays are videotaped; when played back, they provide excellent information on probing styles. Generally, here's what's seen:

Behavior	*Probing style*
Q1	Mainly closed-end and leading questions, and brief assertions.
Q2	Very few probes at all. Some brief assertions, or other superficial probes.
Q3	Mainly brief assertions and leading questions designed to produce positive responses.
Q4	The full range of probes.

Two points are important:

1. Every salesperson and sales manager has a distinctive probing style, a characteristic way of soliciting information and stimulating give-and-take. This style usually does much to explain the *quality* of information and the *degree* of involvement obtained.

2. Evidence from DST and DSM seminars indicates that many salespeople and sales managers have poorly developed probing skills. In fact, four of the most useful probes—open-end, reflective, summary, and pauses—are actually used the least. What this means is that

most salespeople and sales managers could dramatically increase their effectiveness by learning how to use—and *using*—the *full range* of probes. People who have taken the DST or DSM course often make remarks like:

> The most important thing I learned was how to probe, I never knew there was so much to probing, I didn't realize how much I could accomplish by using a mixture of probes.

The sad fact is that many salespeople and sales managers seldom use most of the eight probes. Some of their most helpful tools lie at the bottom of the tool box, unnoticed and untouched.

- **The Frequency of Probes**

Dimensional Sales Training seminars reveal a sobering fact: before they're trained to probe, 90 percent of the salespeople in DST never use open-end probes during role plays; 98 percent never use reflective or summary statements; and 99 percent never use pauses (although there are plenty of awkward silences). These are startling figures, because they probably reflect what happens *on the job* as well as in role plays. For all eight probes, the rough usage figures look like this:

Probe	*Percentage of salespeople who use the probe*
Open-end	10%
Reflective	2%
Summary	2%
Pause	1%
Neutral	50% or more
Brief assertion	50% or more
Leading question	50% or more
Closed-end	50% or more

The conclusion is clear: reflective statements, which are so helpful in handling emotions; summary statements, which are so useful in communicating interest and understanding; pauses, which are vital for dealing with Q2 behavior; open-end probes, which are almost indispensable for getting customers to open up—are ignored most of the time by most salespeople.

You can, of course, ignore probes if you want to. But you *cannot* ignore probes and practice *Q4* selling. The two are inseparable. In fact, the appropriate use of *all eight* probes is part of the definition of Q4. Take that away and whatever's left isn't Q4.

Figure 24. Probes and Probing.

Function	Probe	Definition	Characteristics	Useful in Dealing With:	Cautions
1. Getting customer to open up	Open-end probes	Questions or requests that get wide-ranging response on a broad subject	Usually begin with *what, why, how, how, tell me.* Involve customer by letting him tell what he knows or thinks.	*Q2 silence:* combined with pause, open up silent customer. *Q1 negative emotions:* combined with reflective statements, vent anger and hostility.	Don't use with Q3 meandering; customer will only meander further.
2. Getting the customer to keep on talking	Pauses	Short silences that let customer mull over and respond to what he's heard	Relax pace so customer doesn't feel pressured. Let you collect thoughts and plan ahead. Excellent for tightlipped customers.	*Q2 silence:* encourage silent customers to respond.	Don't end pause prematurely; let customer break the silence.
	Reflective statements	Statements that show you know how customer feels (without implying you agree)	Clear the air so customer can think clearly. Vent overly negative or positive emotions.	*Q1 anger:* vent bad feelings. *Q2 silence:* help customer acknowledge tension and become more responsive. *Q3 exuberance:* vent high spirits.	Voice understanding of how customer feels, but don't voice agreement unless you're sure you want to.
	Neutral probes	Questions or statements that get customer to expand on topic being discussed	More focused than open-end probes. Tell customer what *further* information you need.	Useful across the board. Help acquire more information and show you're listening.	Zero in on significant aspects of topic. Don't encourage talk about trivia.

3. Making sure you understand	Brief assertions	Short statements that encourage customer to keep talking	Maintain good rapport. Usually produce additional information.	*Q2 terseness*: encourage customer to amplify brief responses.	Too many of these sound mechanical or absent-minded.
	Closed-end questions	Questions worded to produce short, precise answers	Excellent for getting final commitment and gathering details.	*Q3 meandering*: focus on specifics and control roaming. *All others*: help you learn details and fill in gaps.	Watch out for "interrogation effect."
	Leading questions	Questions that suggest own answers	Excellent for getting customer to commit. Check your understanding by telling you whether assumption built into question is correct.	*Q2 and Q3 indecision*: use late in discussion to guide and move customer to action.	Use sparingly, or customer will think you're trying to trap him.
	Summary statements	Statements that summarize information obtained from customer	Focus on facts, not emotions. Help customer clarify own thinking by hearing it summed up by you.	*Q1 multiple disagreements*: summarize, then deal with them one by one. Gratify customer's esteem by showing you're listening. *Q3 confusion*: focus on relevant facts. Separate wheat from chaff.	Don't put words in customer's mouth; summarize what you *heard*, not what you *wanted* to hear.

10

Building Trust

Let's recall what happens in a Q4 presentation:

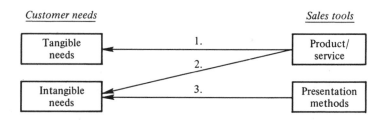

A Q4 presentation is distinguished from any other kind by the fact that it follows *three pathways* to the sale at *one time*. So far, we've concentrated on the skills needed to move along Pathway 1 and Pathway 2:

- We've talked about benefit selling—showing the customer she'll be *better off* if she buys your product or service. That took us into the subject of *motivation skills*.

- We saw that, before you can figure out *what* will make the customer better off, you must crystallize her needs. That took us into *sizing-up skills*.

- Then we saw that, to *convince* the customer she'll be better off, you must make sure her receptivity is high. That took us into *timing* skills.

- Finally, we found that you can't very well crystallize needs or raise receptivity if you can't *probe.* That took us into *probing skills.*

If need–benefit selling is the vehicle that will move you along Pathways 1 and 2, these four sets of skills—motivation skills, sizing-up skills, timing skills, and probing skills—are the mechanisms that propel the vehicle. They're like the ignition, fuel line, cylinders, and drive shaft in an automobile; without them, the vehicle cannot move forward.

In this chapter, we'll see that these *same* skills are equally important for moving forward along Pathway *3*—the pathway that's frequently strewn with more obstacles and barriers than the other two. The Q4 skills we've just listed—motivation, sizing-up, timing, and probing skills—can be used to remove or get around the barriers that so often stand between the salesperson and the close. These barriers— skepticism, doubt, uncertainty, indecision—can all be grouped under one label: *lack of trust.* Q4 presentation methods—employing the four skills we've listed—can be used to *build trust.* In this chapter we'll see how.

PERSUASION AND TRUST

Trust is the conviction—held by the customer—that you *want* to make her *better off.* It's the feeling that "You're on my side . . . so I know you won't take advantage of me, or mislead me. Whatever you say or do is in *my* best interest. Of course, it's in *your* best interest too—but I'm confident you won't advance your interest at my expense. If you win, I win too."

Trust hinges on *honesty.* That's obvious. But the sad fact is that many completely honest salespeople don't *convey* trustworthiness; they *deserve* trust, but they don't *inspire* trust. Many highly competent salespeople never realize their full potential because they don't *come across* as trustworthy. There's a huge amount of psychological evidence that proves what we all feel: *believability depends upon trust.* The more people trust you, the more readily they'll believe you. The more readily they believe you, the more easily you'll generate *understanding* and *commitment*—which is what persuasion is all about. Where there's little or no trust, your chance of persuading

the customer is very poor. This simple fact has enormous consequences: in selling, it's not good enough to *be* honest and trustworthy; you must *come across as* honest and trustworthy. You must
make what you are *apparent — obvious —* to the *customer.* If you can't
do that, if you can't convince *her* that you're reliable, dependable,
deserving of trust, you'll have a very hard time closing the sale with
the understanding and commitment so essential to repeat business.

The best way to demonstrate trustworthiness is *Q4* behavior. Q4
evokes trust because:

a. It's *responsive.* It manifests interest in and concern for the
   customer's needs, ideas, feelings.

b. It's *attentive.* It puts the *customer* at the center of the presentation, and makes everything else revolve around her needs.

c. It's constructively *candid.* It speaks out without blame, editing,
   or censoring; it tells the *whole* story.

Thus, the basic message of Q4 selling is: "I'm on *your* side. I'm here
to make *you* better off." That's not usually the message delivered by
Q1, Q2, or Q3. To test this statement, think back on your own
experience.

Q1. You've no doubt dealt with "hot shot" salespeople who make
high-sounding, unsubstantiated claims, insist they have all the answers, seldom bother to ask questions, and pressure hard for an
order. What's your reaction been? Chances are you felt suspicious
("Why is she pushing so hard?") and guarded ("I don't like being
rushed like this . . . I'd better be careful"). *Even though these salespeople may be completely trustworthy,* they generate *mistrust.* That
often happens with Q1.

Q2. You've probably known salespeople who go through the motions — lackluster performers who don't have their hearts in what
they're doing. What was your reaction? You probably felt uncomfortable ("She's so distant . . . I wonder if she's hiding something")
and guarded ("I don't see any reason to buy . . . so why should I?").
These salespeople may be *completely trustworthy,* but they generate
doubts.

Q3. Finally, you've probably dealt from time to time with easygoing salespeople — genial, talkative, consistently positive. How did you
react? Chances are you felt skeptical ("Things can't possibly be as
great as she says") and maybe uneasy ("I've got some real doubts —

because I'm getting only one side of the story"). "Nice" sales-people may be *completely trustworthy*, but they very often generate *apprehension.*

Mistrust, doubt, apprehension—all these diminish the salesperson's reliability *in the eyes of the customer.* And when a salesperson does-n't seem wholly reliable—when the customer's not sure she can be trusted—understanding and commitment are badly impaired. None of this, it must be emphasized, has anything to do with *intention.* A salesperson who *deserves* trust may not be trusted—not because her *intentions* are bad but because her *behavior* doesn't convey the mes-sage: "I'm reliable . . . you can depend on me to act in *your best interest.*" After all, customers have no way of knowing a salesper-son's intentions; all they know is what they see and hear.

PRESENTATION BARRIERS

A *presentation barrier* is something a customer says or does that slows down, sidetracks, or permanently stops the presentation. To say that customers *always* erect barriers as a *reaction* to something the *salesperson* says or does would be an exaggeration. A customer may erect a barrier for reasons that have nothing to do with the salesperson; she may, for instance, *come into* a presentation so pre-occupied that she barely hears what the salesperson says; the pre-occupation—a barrier—can't be considered the salesperson's fault. Nevertheless, a great many barriers *are* reactions to something the *salesperson* says or does that triggers *mistrust, doubt,* or *apprehen-sion.* They're responses to Q1, Q2, or Q3 sales behavior. Let's see how this happens.

Barriers Raised by Q1 Selling

The basic message of Q1 selling is either: "*I* know what's best for you . . . and I'll prove it to you—or make you buy it anyway" or "I don't really *care* what's best for you . . . but I do care about mak-ing the sale—and I'm willing to overpower you to do it." Either mes-sage is conveyed by characteristic Q1 behavior: high pressuring . . . arguing. . . knocking competitors . . . interrogating . . . pushing ahead when receptivity is low . . . belittling the customer's ideas . . . boast-ing . . . making unsupported claims . . . interrupting . . . sermonizing . . . demanding.

As a result, the customer frequently sets up barriers to stop the attack, and maybe even force a retreat:

- *Open antagonism.* The customer may meet the salesperson's claims with undisguised Q1 hostility ("Baloney!" "Don't give me that stuff," "Watch yourself . . . I don't like being pushed").

- *Withdrawal.* The customer may Q2 it—freeze up, grunt, refuse to cooperate.

- *Suspicion.* At the very least, she's likely to become skeptical and wary ("I've got a feeling I shouldn't believe what I'm being told.").

- *Capitulation.* Of course, the customer may give in; the bulldozer may flatten her into submission. But, if that happens, the sale will conclude on a sorry note. Understanding will be low; commitment may be even lower. And *that* means a barrier will already be in place for the *next* call. *Repeat* business may prove impossible.

All these barriers are evidence of *mistrust.* They're erected for one reason: the customer doesn't dare repose confidence in the salesperson; she's unwilling either to confide in her or believe her. She's mistrustful.

Barriers Raised by Q2 Selling

The basic message of Q2 selling is: "I'm not strong enough to influence you . . . so I won't try. When you're ready to buy, you'll buy— and I hope I'm around to pick up the order—but I certainly can't persuade you. I can only explain my product to you and hope for the best." The message is conveyed by characteristic Q2 behavior: the salesperson goes through the paces . . . fails to confront objections . . . seems detached . . . evades touchy questions . . . wavers when asked for a firm commitment . . . doesn't bother with benefit statements . . . and makes a generally lackluster presentation. All of this leads to the building of customer barriers:

- *Uncertainty.* The customer starts feeling uneasy ("If this salesperson's so unenthusiastic about her product, why should *I* be enthusiastic?").

- *Disrespect.* She may look down on the salesperson ("I'm dealing with someone weak and ineffective").

- *Annoyance.* The customer may feel irritated because the presentation is so perfunctory ("I'm busy, and here's this salesperson— wasting my time going through a bunch of motions").

- *Lack of understanding.* The worst barrier of all may be that the customer doesn't see any *reason* to buy ("I don't get it. Why should I spend money on *that?*"). This isn't strange, since the salesperson hasn't crystallized her needs or made any attempt to do N-B selling. Naturally, the customer's ultimate reaction is: "So what?'"

All these barriers are evidence of *doubt.* They're erected for one reason: the salesperson seems so unsure and so unconvinced that the *customer* feels unsure and unconvinced. The customer may not be openly mistrustful or disbelieving, but she is *doubtful.*

Barriers Raised by Q3 Selling

The basic message of Q3 selling is: "Let's relax . . . get to know one another . . . be friends. Once we establish a good personal relationship, we can get around to talking about other things – like my product or service. Once we're friends, you'll probably want to buy something from me. After all, what could be more natural than doing business with a friend?" This message is conveyed by characteristic Q3 behavior; the salesperson fails to mention, much less come to grips with, touchy business problems . . . takes an upbeat approach to everything, even if it's unrealistic to do so . . . digresses frequently to keep the presentation on "cheerful" topics (and avoid troubling ones) . . . compromises quickly to prevent "arguments" . . . and sometimes even "gives away the store." All of this leads to the raising of customer barriers:

- *Disrespect.* The customer gets the impression the salesperson's "soft" – unable to stand up for herself.
- *Skepticism.* As the salesperson dodges or glosses over one sticky topic after another, the customer wonders: "Am I getting the whole story? Is she holding something back?"
- *Seizure of control.* Vexed by the salesperson's slow-moving, rambling tactics, the customer may "take over" the presentation ("It's time to get this show on the road").
- *Lack of understanding.* Because her needs haven't been thoroughly probed, the customer can't fully understand "what's in it for me."

A Q3 presentation is long on generalities but short on details; the customer's expected to buy on faith, not evidence. As a result, she's not really sure *why* she should buy – and she's certainly not committed to the idea.

All these barriers are evidence of *apprehension*. The presentation is so loose, so one-sided, so unbusinesslike, that the customer is bound to feel apprehensive. She may not be openly mistrustful, but she does have *misgivings*.

Barriers, then, are *behavioral roadblocks* put up by the customer. They impede, or even halt, the presentation by substituting mistrust, doubt, or apprehension for openness and high receptivity.

Are these barriers inevitable? Certainly not. The salesperson can behave so that the customer has no reason to put up barriers. That's one thing that distinguishes Q4 from other sales behaviors: it gives the customer *no reason* to be mistrustful, doubtful, or apprehensive. If the customer *does* put up barriers during a Q4 presentation, it's not because of anything the salesperson's done.

Q4 Sales Behavior

Can Q4 sales behavior be defined in one fairly simple sentence? We think so: "Q4 sales behavior is a system of behaviors and skills for working trustfully with customers, to the ultimate benefit of everyone concerned: the customer, the customer's organization, the salesperson, and the salesperson's company." Or, in simpler language, "Q4 sales behavior is trustworthy sales behavior that produces a net gain for the customer, the salesperson, and their companies."

To do this—sell in a Q4 way—you must give the customer *no reason* to raise barriers; if they're raised anyway, you must *overcome* them. If you can keep obstacles from arising in the first place, or if, once they've arisen, you can remove them, you stand a good chance of producing (1) trust, (2) understanding, and (3) commitment.

How can you use Q4 behavior to *demonstrate* trustworthiness—so you can then go on to generate understanding and commitment? By combining the skills we discussed earlier: sizing-up, timing, probing, and motivation skills. In the rest of this chapter, we'll discuss sixteen guidelines for doing it—for combining Q4 skills to build trust. All of them are ways to keep customers from raising barriers—or to overcome barriers once they are raised. We'll list the guidelines first, then discuss them.

THE GUIDELINES

To build trust:

1. Become aware of your behavior.
2. Search out feedback.
3. Make every call a trust-builder.

4. Listen at a thinking level.
5. Maintain two-way involvement.
6. Demonstrate interest and understanding.
7. Prove you're open-minded.
8. Create a problem-solving climate.
9. Create an advice-seeking climate.
10. Keep receptivity high.
11. Face up to objections and troublesome emotions.
12. Try to close only at high receptivity.
13. Manifest respect at every point.
14. Discuss facts, not personalities.
15. Sell net gain, not net loss.
16. Create a win–win situation.

1. *Become aware of your behavior*

Before anything else, try to discover what you're doing *now* that might undermine trust. To begin, ask yourself:

- On sales calls, do I Q1 it – blame, judge, threaten, warn, demand, moralize, counterargue, deride, or interrogate?
- Do I Q2 it – deny or evade hard issues, go through the paces mechanically, show indifference, or withdraw?
- Do I Q3 it – smooth over differences, deprecate myself, digress, or compromise quickly?

Don't give glib answers. Think back on your experience; look closely at your behavior on recent calls; examine the *evidence.* Then answer the questions as candidly and objectively as you can. See if you're doing anything now which might create mistrust, and which should therefore be *changed.*

2. *Search out feedback*

Even with the best efforts, you may not be able to answer these three questions candidly. Like most of us, you probably judge yourself by your *intentions*, while your customers judge you by your *actions.* And your actions may be Q1, Q2, or Q3 even though you don't intend them as such. That's why feedback from others is often so important in gaining self-awareness (and why DST seminars lean so heavily on feedback). If you can, search out feedback from your co-workers; ask your boss, or fellow salespeople whose candor and judgment you respect, how *they'd* answer the three questions about you. This is worth doing, because you *need* the answers. If, say, you persistently smooth things over instead of confronting them, and if you don't realize you're doing it, you *should.*

Once you know it, you can correct it. Until you know it, you can't. (In DST seminars, feedback is provided by a *team*, which bases its feedback on careful observation of role plays *and* on equally careful observation of video tapes of the role plays. On the job, you're not likely to get feedback this thorough or systematic, but you can still get candid, balanced feedback that should prove of real help.)

3. *Make every call a trust-builder*

To do it, show concern for the customer's needs, ideas, and feelings on every call—no matter what its purpose. Whether it's a sales call, a follow-up call, a call to discuss a complaint or handle a problem, probe to uncover any needs you might fill. If the customer's called you with a complaint, for example, don't walk in and immediately tell her how you intend to handle it. *Investigate* the complaint first. Make sure you fully understand it. See if there are any other needs or problems you might help out with. Use *every* call, for whatever purpose, to build your image as a problem-solver—someone who's there in the *customer's* best interest.

A remarkable number of salespeople *don't* do this. They "drop in" just to chat or to "drop off our new catalog." But, aside from questions like "How are you?" and "What's new?", they don't do any serious, business-oriented *probing.* They don't attempt to uncover or anticipate needs. They not only fail to prove their concern for the customer, they sometimes gain a reputation as "time-wasters" or "pests." That's hardly the way to build trust.

4. *Listen at a thinking level*

You can't build trust unless you *pay attention* to the customer. She's unlikely to think you have *her* best interests at heart if you think only your own thoughts—and ignore or twist hers to your own purposes. Trust requires listening at a *thinking* level, to hear what the customer really thinks and feels. To listen at a thinking level, ask yourself: "Do I really get what she's saying? Do I know why she's saying it . . . why she considers it important? Do I understand how this ties in with everything else she's said? Am I getting the point?" Never *assume* the answer to these questions is "yes."

Test your understanding by probing. Two probes will help:

a. **Summary statements.** Restate what you think she's said, then see if she agrees. If she does, fine; let her continue. If she doesn't, probe to find out why.

b. *Reflective statements.* If she's expressed strong feelings, reflect them. Her reaction will tell whether you're right.

If you've listened closely and still *don't* understand, tell her so and then probe. Summary statements combined with neutral probes will help. For example: "I'm not sure I understand, Alice. As I get it, you say you've got the budget for this order, but you still can't afford it. Tell me more about that."

"Ken, I'm confused. A few minutes ago, you said our price increase was justified. Now you say it's unfair. Help me out."

Caution: If you don't understand, don't blame the customer. Let her know you're confused—but don't accuse her of confusing you:

Wrong way. "Diane, you've lost me. You're just not making your point."

Right way. "Diane, I'm not following you. Programming's complicated . . . and I guess I don't know enough about it. So, let me ask you . . . "

5. *Maintain two-way involvement*

It's hard to trust anyone who does all the talking. Any monologue — any attempt to exclude the customer from the discussion—is likely to create *mis*trust. After all, a monologue usually dwells on *your* interests, which means *neglecting* the *customer's.* And if you seem neglectful of her interests, why should she trust you?

This may strike you as unrealistic. You may object: "When I talk to a customer, there are certain things I must talk about—whether she's interested or not. If I have to talk about warehousing, then I have to talk about warehousing—even if she'd rather talk about something else. That's just the way it is." This is valid. It points up why you must do two things:

a. Start the discussion with a *benefit* statement. If you must talk about warehousing, that's that. But first get the customer to understand that it's to her advantage to talk about warehousing, that *she'll* get something from it.

b. Probe *throughout.* This is the surest way to create and maintain two-way involvement. And it's the only way to make certain you're getting through. Probes provide feedback — reactions—which tell you whether you're talking to yourself or the customer.

There's another good way to maintain involvement: *reward* the customer psychologically for staying involved. Psychological "payoffs" stimulate further involvement. You can make these payoffs in several ways:

- Express appreciation and – if you can – approval of the customer's ideas ("Fine," "I understand perfectly," "Good idea").
- Show interest. An occasional nod of the head can help. So can brief assertions ("Keep going," "Uh–huh"). Keep your eyes on the customer. If you *look* distracted, she'll assume you *are*.
- Ask her opinions. From her viewpoint, exchanging views is psychologically rewarding; it proves you're interested.
- Use reflective and summary statements. These show understanding, and that's rewarding.

Psychological payoffs are important. Without them, the customer may sooner or later get the idea you're not interested. If you're not, you can't have her interests at heart – and there's no reason to trust you.

6. *Demonstrate interest and understanding*

We've just made a key point: why *should* a customer trust you if you don't seem interested in her and don't understand her? The answer, of course, is that she has no good reason to do so. That's why *demonstrating* interest and understanding is so important. Interest and understanding are *not* the same thing. *Interest* demonstrates curiosity or concern. It shows that you want to know what something *means* to the customer either intellectually or emotionally. *Understanding* demonstrates that your interest has *paid off* – that you *do* know what something means to the customer. Put differently, interest *tries* to grasp meaning; understanding *grasps* it. To demonstrate either, probe.

- Five probes are especially useful for demonstrating *interest*: open-end probes, pauses, neutral probes, brief assertions, and closed-end questions.
- Two probes are especially useful for demonstrating *understanding*: reflective statements and summary statements.

Remember: to build trust, it isn't good enough to be interested and to understand. You must *show* your interest and understanding. Once you do, you *yourself* will become a benefit to the customer. That's the ultimate Q4 achievement.

7. *Prove you're open-minded*

Another way to say this is: don't *Q1* it. Don't come into the presentation committed to a line of thought; don't take for granted you know what the customer needs; don't assume you know what's best for her. As we've seen, a customer confronted with Q1 dogmatism and rigidity is almost certain to raise barriers: open antagonism, withdrawal, suspicion.

One way to show that your mind is open is to probe. But not just any kind of probing will do. Superficial Q2 probing, which skims the surface ("How's your inventory today?") but refuses to dig into serious problems, is no sign of openmindedness. Neither is irrelevant Q3 probing, which may ask dozens of questions, but only on "safe" or extraneous subjects ("How're your kids?"). When we say probing demonstrates open-mindedness, we mean, of course, *Q4* probing— which zeroes in on pertinent topics, whether pleasant or unpleasant, probes them in depth, and then draws conclusions.

Even Q4 probing, however, may not be enough to convince the customer you're open-minded. What may be required is a *change of mind.* If you probe skillfully, uncover evidence which disproves your original point, and still insist on sticking to that point, the customer will probably think the probing was nothing more than an elaborate "game." Unless you change or modify your thinking in the light of contrary evidence, you'll come across as "glib" but "closed-minded."

8. *Create a problem-solving climate*

A customer with an unfilled need obviously has a problem. Since Q4 selling fills unfilled needs, it might be called *problem-solving.* Solving a customer's problem is one of the surest ways to build trust. It's also very difficult to do if you don't first create the right *climate*, one in which the customer:

   a. admits she *has* a problem—an unfilled need; and
   b. seeks *your* help in solving it.

Admitting the problem must come first. If you Q1 it—*tell* the customer she has a problem, and then tell her how to solve it—she'll probably reject your advice. She may even deny the problem exists. And she may be right. After all, how do *you* know she has a problem unless you've probed thoroughly? And, if you've probed thoroughly, she'll probably admit she has a problem *without* your telling her. So, if you have to tell her, it probably means you haven't probed thoroughly—that you're only *guessing.*

How can you get the customer to admit the existence of a problem—an unfilled need? By raising her receptivity, probing, and then analyzing her needs as described in Chapter 6. Once that's done, she'll probably acknowledge the problem and *seek your help*. Why will she seek it? Because she'll *trust* you; once you've crystallized her needs, she'll probably think: "This salesperson's concerned about *me*; she's just proven it by helping me understand my own problems. She's been interested, patient, constructive. She can be trusted."

So, our recommendation is: Don't tell the customer she has a problem; help her see it for herself. Bring her to the point where she realizes and acknowledges it. That'll produce a trusting, problem-solving climate—in which you can do some Q4 benefit-selling.

9. *Create an advice-seeking climate*

If telling the customer she has a problem is likely to promote mistrust, so is giving her advice when her receptivity is down.

Unsolicited advice—advice offered at low receptivity—usually suffers the fate of anything else offered at low receptivity. It's unlikely to be considered, understood, or accepted, *even* if the customer nods her head and says, "Great idea." When you offer advice to an unreceptive customer, you're wasting your breath. Spin *up* receptivity first. Bring the customer's awareness that she *needs* advice to the point where she *requests* it. Then give it. Keep three guidelines in mind:

  a. Don't advise at low receptivity. The customer either won't pay attention or will reject the advice outright (although she may Q3 it by feigning acceptance).

  b. Probe. Get her to think and talk about her uncertainty. Once she admits she's not *sure*, she'll find it easier to seek advice. Probing should help her realize she *is* unsure.

  c. When advising (at high receptivity), make certain the customer understands *what's in it for her.* If she doesn't see the benefit, why follow the advice?

10. *Keep receptivity high*

We've said this so often it must sound like an echo. But most of your trust-building efforts will prove futile if you don't work to keep receptivity up. And we stress the word "work." *Never assume high receptivity will stay high.* Receptivity fluctuates; attention can easily deteriorate into boredom. Usually, receptivity will stay high only if you work at it. Stay alert to signs – Q1, Q2, or Q3 – that receptivity is drooping. If it is, probe to spin it back up. Remember: the customer's low receptivity may be a sign that you yourself have lapsed into Q1, Q2, or Q3 behavior. One good way to keep your behavior Q4 is to be alert to signals that the *customer's* receptivity is declining.

In working to keep receptivity up, always keep one thing in mind: N-B selling – if properly done – can do much to maintain receptivity. As long as the customer's aware of her needs and sees the connection between them and whatever's happening in the presentation, it's not very likely her receptivity will decline much. As long as she can say to herself, "I'm getting something out of this presentation . . . what's being said is beneficial to me . . . I can see some real value in all this," her receptivity shouldn't sag a great deal. It's when she tells herself, "I don't see what this has to do with me . . . I can't see any payoff from what's happening now," that you'll run into trouble. At that point, it's a safe bet her receptivity *will* sag and sag badly.

11. *Face up to objections and troublesome emotions*

This is one of the most difficult of all Q4 practices. We've seen that *evasion* – refusing to face harsh facts – is one way to create mistrust. But we also know that evasion is a very tempting way to "get through" a sales call. From time to time, every salesperson is tempted to ignore an objection, or disregard an embarrassing question, or smooth over an angry outburst. From time to time, every salesperson would like to change the subject, pretend she didn't hear, pass off an objection with a joke, or "shush up" a customer. All we can say is: *Don't do it.*

Why not? Because, if you neglect a customer's concern (and objections and troublesome emotions are clear evidence of concern) you convey one of two messages: "I don't care about your concern" or "I'm too weak to do anything about it." Either way, you sow the seeds of doubt or mistrust. In Chapter 9, when we discussed reflective statements, we explained how to deal with troublesome emotions. In Chapter 13, we'll explain how to handle objections. The only point we'll make here is that, if you're going to build trust, you must face up to objections and troublesome emotions. If you dodge them (or even minimize them), you do so at your peril.

12. *Try to close only at high receptivity*

Chapter 14 deals with closing techniques, so we won't get into them here. We will, however, make this important point: rushing the close – trying to "lock up" the order when the customer's receptivity is down—is a very common cause of mistrust. It reinforces these Q1 and Q2 stereotypes:

"Salespeople only look out for their own good. They'll do anything to get an order."

"When you talk to a salesperson, watch out! . . . or you'll get stuck with something you don't need."

We're not saying sales can't be made at low receptivity. Sure they can. High-pressure tactics do work—sometimes. People do make purchases without full understanding and commitment—sometimes. We're saying something quite different: attempting to close at low receptivity—even if it works—is *no way* to build trust. You may get the order—this time—but you may not even get your foot in the door next time. If you're interested in building trust for the long haul, try to close only at high receptivity.

13. *Manifest respect at every point*

Respect and *trust* are two sides of one coin. All of us tend to trust people who respect us, and to mistrust people who don't. That's obvious. What isn't so obvious is that people whose behavior is heavily Q2 or Q3 can easily provoke us into showing *dis*respect—without our realizing we're doing it.

That's because, when you deal with strong security needs (Q2) or strong social needs (Q3), it's very easy to score points at the customer's expense. Sarcasm and put-downs ("C'mon, now . . . you're not afraid to make a simple decision, are you?") may make *you* feel superior but can only offend the customer—and drive down her receptivity. Of course, you can justify your behavior by telling her, "I'm saying this for your own good." But she's not likely to see anything "good" in being belittled.

The point is this: *all* of us, even if we have strong security or social needs, want respect. And all of us find it difficult to trust someone who talks down to us—makes us feel "small" or "foolish" or "inadequate."

It's also easy—and risky—to score points off someone with strong Q1 esteem needs ("Tom, you've got a real romance going with yourself"). But the consequences are different. Customers with Q2 or Q3 needs don't usually answer back; they sit and "take it"—and suppress their resentment. This suppressed resentment may come back to haunt you, either as subtle sabotage or as heightened apathy. People with Q1 needs, however, usually answer back—*then and there*. If they do, you may have a struggle on your hands.

You can be sure of one thing: scoring points at the customer's expense *will* drive down receptivity, build mistrust, and make persuasion much harder.

14. *Discuss facts, not personalities*

Very few customers appreciate having their personalities discussed by a salesperson. Needs, yes. Problems, yes. But *personalities*—their traits, quirks, idiosyncracies, all the special and individual characteristics that make them what they are—*no*. And any salesperson who undertakes to discuss personal traits runs a very serious risk of generating mistrust. Why? Because most customers consider their personal characteristics none of the salesperson's business, and anyone who "sticks her nose" into things that are none of her business is likely to be seen as meddlesome, intrusive, impertinent—in short, not to be trusted.

One good way to avoid personalities (and stay zeroed-in on what really counts: the customer's needs and problems) is to steer clear of *diagnostic language.*

Diagnostic language focuses on the customer's mental state (or what the salesperson *thinks* is her mental state). For example:

"I wouldn't feel so sorry for myself if I were you."

"Boy! You're really convinced everybody's out to get you, aren't you?"

"You sure are anxious to get even with him."

We'd better make two quick points:

a. We're *not* contradicting our earlier advice to size up the customer's needs before trying to motivate her. Sizing up is a form of diagnosis. We're saying: diagnose *behavior*, not *motives*. Behavior can be seen and heard; motives can't. Behavior can be *observed*; motives can only be *inferred*—and there's no way to know for sure if your inference is correct. Leave psychological diagnosis to the psychologists.

b. We are *not* saying, "Don't use reflective statements." Reflective statements reflect *observed behavior*. They don't draw any conclusions about the psychological *reasons* for that behavior. "You're really concerned" is a simple statement of observed fact; it merely implies, "I've been paying attention to you, and I've noticed you're concerned." But saying, "You're really sore. I guess you're one of those people who can't stand criticism," is not a simple statement of fact. It's a statement of fact ("You're really sore") coupled to a statement of inference ("I guess you're one of those people . . ."). And the customer would have every right to respond with "Who asked *you*?" or "I don't think that's any of your business."

To build trust, use your sizing-up skills and use reflective statements. But *don't* use diagnostic language. If you *do* draw conclusions about the customer's motives, keep them to yourself.

15. *Sell net gain, not net loss*

A net-gain presentation focuses on the *superiority* of *your* product or service; a net-loss presentation focuses on the *inferiority* of a *competitor's* product or service. A net-gain presentation draws factual comparisons between your solution to the customer's problem and other potential solutions; a net-loss presentation "knocks" the other solutions. As many salespeople have learned to their regret, knocking the competition is a good way to build *mis*trust.

Why? Because, if you concentrate on knocking the competition instead of discussing your own product, the customer's likely to wonder *why*. "Why is this salesperson working so hard to discredit somebody else? Why is she neglecting her own product? Has she got something to hide?" Many customers consider knocking "unprofessional," "small," "petty" or "undignified." It may be tempting to do, but it's very risky.

Factual, restrained comparisons between products are likely to generate *trust*. Attacks on competitors are likely to generate distrust. It's that simple.

16. *Create a win-win situation*

Win-lose struggles (in which one person's gain is always at the other's expense) are obviously no way to build trust. Once a customer discovers that it's you vs. her, she'll consider you an adversary, and it's very difficult to trust an adversary.

There's another problem with win-lose struggles. They generate high emotion, which makes it hard to think rationally. It's basic human psychology that the more emotional we get, the less clearly we think. Clear thinking requires making sound inferences, and drawing sound conclusions from them. This is very difficult when we're angry. Anger usually produces unwarrantable inferences, and unjustifiable conclusions. In fact, anger makes it difficult to think logically;

when we're "worked up," we have trouble going from a to b to c; we jump from k to z to a. The general rule is: the more intense the anger, the more jumbled the thinking.

We're *not* cautioning against Q4 discussion—spirited give-and-take in which you and the customer explore alternatives, find flaws in each, and try to pick the best one. Q4 discussion is *problem-oriented,* and that's good.

We're cautioning against Q1 quarrels, which are *ego*-oriented, degenerating into personal attacks. Barbed remarks, sarcasm, bad temper—the hallmarks of quarrels—make it very difficult to build trust.

Why? Let's go back to our definition: trust is the customer's conviction that you're trying to *help.* But a win–lose struggle conveys the message that you're trying to *defeat* the customer. Why should she trust someone who's bent on winning at *her* expense?

Q1 belligerence often wins the battle only to lose the war. Q4 discussion creates a win–win climate. How? By crystallizing and satisfying the customer's *needs.* When that happens everybody wins.

SUMMARY

1. Four sets of Q4 skills—motivation, sizing-up, timing, and probing skills—are essential for moving along the three pathways to the sale. Of the three pathways, Pathway 3 is usually strewn with more barriers than the others. These barriers can be grouped under one label: lack of trust. The four sets of Q4 skills are vital for overcoming lack of trust.

2. Trust hinges on honesty. But many honest salespeople aren't trusted because they don't demonstrate trustworthiness. Q4 sales behavior is distinguished from all other types by coming across as trustworthy. Thus, only it raises no barriers to the sale; Q1, Q2, and Q3 behavior do raise barriers.

3. Q1 sales behavior often generates open antagonism, withdrawal, suspicion, or capitulation.

4. Q2 sales behavior often generates uncertainty, disrespect, annoyance, or lack of understanding.

5. Q3 sales behavior often generates disrespect, skepticism, seizure of control, and lack of understanding.

6. Sixteen guidelines—all examples of Q4—are especially useful in building trust: (a) become aware of your behavior, (b) search out feedback, (c) make every call a trust-builder, (d) listen at a thinking level, (e) maintain two-way involvement, (f) demonstrate interest

and understanding, (g) prove you're open-minded, (h) create a prob-lem-solving climate, (i) create an advice-seeking climate, (j) keep re-ceptivity high, (k) face up to objections and troublesome emotions, (l) try to close only at high receptivity, (m) manifest respect at every point, (n) discuss facts, not personalities, (o) sell net gain, not net loss, (p) create a win–win situation.

11

Building Understanding and Commitment

We saw in our last chapter that you cannot move forward on Pathway 3 to the sale without building trust. But trust alone isn't enough. If you're going to make your method of presentation fit the customer's needs, you must build more than trust—you must build understanding and commitment. You must get the customer to see "what's in it for me if I buy," and you must convince him that "what's in it" is really worth having—so much so, in fact, that he's ready and willing to buy it.

Trust, of course, is fundamental; without it, there's not much chance of closing a sale with understanding and commitment. That's because credibility—believability—is so dependent upon trust. As we've seen, a customer who doesn't consider you trustworthy isn't likely to believe you, and if he doesn't believe you—doesn't accept your analysis of his needs and your benefit statements—he won't see much reason to buy. Trust is vital.

This doesn't mean, however, that where there's trust, understanding and commitment will follow automatically. A customer may trust you completely, and have a need for your product or service, but still not understand why he should buy from you. This can happen for many reasons: because your presentation is poorly organized, your arguments illogical, your language unclear, your explanations too technical . . . and on and on.

Trust *is* vital, but it isn't sufficient. Once you've built it, there are *other* things you must do to build understanding and commitment. Like the guidelines for building trust, these "other things" utilize the four basic sets of Q4 skills: sizing-up, timing, probing, and motivation skills. We'll discuss the guidelines for building understanding and commitment in this chapter.

THE GUIDELINES

1. Fit your words to the customer
2. Say what you mean
3. Space your ideas
4. Be alert to differences in interpretation
5. Use first-person statements
6. Use process checks when necessary

1. Fit Your Words to the Customer

Few things will sink receptivity faster than the *wrong* word or words. And when receptivity sinks, understanding and commitment sink with it. Beware of three kinds of "wrong" words, words that aren't suitable for the customer you're talking to:

a. Words that conflict with his intangible needs
b. Negatively-loaded words
c. Inappropriate words

a. Words that conflict with the customer's intangible needs. Words can create adverse reactions when they clash with a customer's intangible needs. For example, a customer with strong esteem and independence needs (Q1), may be irked to hear:

• Just follow my instructions to the letter and you won't go wrong.

• You'll be the second man in town who's tried the idea.

• Before committing yourself, maybe you'd better run it by your boss.

These statements sound harmless enough. But they collide with *this* customer's needs. After all, he wants to be number-one, not number-two. So, any statement that emphasizes *following* rather than *leading* is likely to lower his receptivity.

Statements like the following could well trouble a customer with strong security needs (Q2):

- Here's a real challenge — a chance to do something nobody's tried before.
- If you want people to sit up and take notice, here's my suggestion.
- Sure it's a risk, but if it works, you'll be a hero.

There's nothing wrong with these remarks *as such*. But they're not likely to appeal to a customer who wants serenity, not excitement — who'd rather merge into the background than make people "sit up and take notice."

Here are some statements that will probably unsettle a customer with strong social needs (Q3):

- This decision may not win you any friends, but, believe me, it makes sense anyway.
- So what if you do get a few complaints from your employees? You'll still be saving money.
- Sometimes you just have to do what's right, even if it makes people unhappy.

Imagine saying these things to a customer who's especially eager to be *accepted*. The best rule is: don't say anything that will clash with the customer's strongest intangible needs. With a little effort, all our examples could be rephrased so the *idea* is retained but the *threat* is removed. It's well worth the effort.

b. Negatively-loaded words. Some words carry such a heavy emotional overload that they'll probably offend anybody. *You* may think a customer is *pig-headed, closed-minded,* and *opinionated.* But *saying* so will almost surely drive down his receptivity. If you must talk about his stubbornness, use less loaded terms.

Bertrand Russell, the philosopher, once devised a game that anyone who's in selling should know about. The point of the game is to find three ways to say the same thing: one flattering, one insulting, and one in-between. Russell wanted to show that we usually reserve the most flattering expression for ourselves, use less flattering language to describe the person we're talking to, and save the most insulting terms for people who are nowhere nearby.

- He's thick-headed, you're stubborn, I'm principled.
- She's spineless, you vacillate, I'm flexible.
- He's a neurotic workaholic, you're a bit of a drudge, I'm dedicated to my job.
- She's a loudmouth, you're boisterous at times, I'm goodnatured and outgoing.

As the game shows, almost anything you say about people can be said in different ways. Almost any reference to an individual or his behavior can be made negative or positive by the way it's *phrased*. We're *not* advising that you always pick the most flattering phrase, only that you *eliminate* strongly negative phrases.

c. **Inappropriate words.** An inappropriate word is any word that makes the customer feel uncomfortable. Here are some guidelines for making sure you speak the customer's language.

DON'T USE HIGHFALUTIN WORDS

We don't mean "talk down" to the customer. Talking down oversimplifies; it's condescending and likely to be resented. You don't want to patronize the customer but you do want to use words he readily understands. Good, understandable substitutes can usually be found for highfalutin words. For example, most people who have trouble with the words on the left have no trouble with those on the right, which mean the same:

configuration	pattern
paradigm	model
nugatory	worthless
fortuitous	accidental
postulate	assume

The best rule is: always use the more common word unless you *know* the customer feels "at home" with the less common one. Otherwise, you'll wind up talking to yourself.

DON'T USE OFFENSIVE LANGUAGE

This is sure to torpedo receptivity. Obscenities, very new slang, buzzwords – use these with caution. If you don't know the customer well, and aren't sure whether the word or phrase will offend, don't use it. Keep three things in mind:

- What offends one customer may be fine to another. The best rule is: If you think a word *may* offend, find a better one. Why run a risk?

- Be careful about brand-new slang. If you're not sure it's suitable, avoid it. A little caution can save trouble.

- Buzzwords—words that suddenly gain popularity and then suddenly fade—annoy some customers who consider them unnecessary substitutes for plain English. At the time of this writing, *infrastructure, prioritize,* and *escalate* are buzzwords. There's *nothing wrong* with them as long as *customers* don't object to them. If you have doubts about using buzzwords, use standard synonyms instead, like *foundation* for *infrastructure, rank* for *prioritize,* and *increase* for *escalate.*

2. Say What You Mean

You can't disguise your ideas and expect customers to recognize them. Most of us do disguise our ideas occasionally, because we *don't* want them recognized. We Q2 or Q3 our ideas in four ways: (a) by soft words, (b) by analogy, (c) by abstraction, and (d) by weasel words.

a. Soft words. "Soft" words—also called *euphemisms*—cushion the impact of "hard" words. Some time ago, for example, many organizations began *terminating* people instead of *firing* them, because *terminate* sounded gentler than *fire.* Lately, some organizations have stopped terminating people; they now *select-out,* or, in some instances, *de-hire;* presumably, being de-hired feels better than being terminated.

Soft words are so common we're often unaware of them. *Trash cans* become *ecological receptacles; used* or *second-hand* items are *reconditioned* or *previously-owned. Flattery* becomes *stroking; snooping* turns into *surveillance; saloons* are transformed into *cocktail lounges.*

Obviously, soft words can be useful. Most of us sometimes feel it's kinder to say someone *passed away* instead of *died,* or is *disadvantaged* instead of *poor,* or *portly* instead of *fat.* But when soft words dilute meaning so much that the message gets lost, they've outlived their usefulness.

Thus, soft words can get in the way of Q4 candor. Q4 candor leaves *no doubt.* It's not *destructive* (Q1), but it is direct, pointed, and clear. If you soften your language to the point where it's not direct, pointed, and clear, it may be Q2 or Q3, but it cannot be Q4.

b. Analogies. It's hard to go through a presentation without using analogies. Most of us analogize—compare one thing to another—almost without realizing it. We tell a customer who's just been made president of his company, "Congratulations on winning the World Series." Or we tell a prospect who's been transferred unexpectedly to another job, "I hear they dropped a bomb on you."

There's nothing wrong with this; analogies add color. But they shouldn't be used to *water down* touchy issues. When this happens, analogizing becomes Q2, or more often Q3, behavior. Here's an example:

> Dennis, this reminds me of somebody I knew in college. This guy pitched for our college baseball team, and he had a mean fast ball—one of the fastest—but he lost a lot of games because he couldn't keep runners from stealing bases. As soon as somebody got on first base, this pitcher forgot all about him and concentrated on the next batter. First thing you knew, the runner stole second base.

Anybody would have a hard time getting the point of this. What the salesperson *meant*, and should have *said*, is this:

> Dennis, our factory seems to have trouble doing two things at the same time. If they make the correct shipment, they foul up the billing. If they get the billing right, they foul up the shipment. Your complaint is justified, and I'll take it up with our sales manager as soon as I get back to the office.

This is candid. And clear. Analogies are fine, but don't let them obscure your meaning.

c. Abstractions. The trouble with abstractions is that they don't let you control the *pictures* in the customer's mind. If you say *packaging*, the customer can picture any kind of package, in any material and any design. But if you say *plain brown corrugated carton*, he has almost no choice but to picture a plain brown corrugated carton. The rule is: the more *abstract* your language, the *less* your control over the customer's mental imagery—and understanding; the more *concrete* your language, the *more* control. Put differently, the *broader* or more *general* your language, the less certain its effect. The *narrower* or more *specific*, the more certain its effect. *Details*, of course, make language specific. So do *numbers*. When you can, use them. "Our 25,000-square-foot warehouse, with palletized storage all on one floor" gives you more control over the customer's mental imagery than "Our big, modern warehouse." "We pounded this girder with a 1,000 pound headache ball . . . sixty blows an hour for twelve straight hours . . . before putting it on the market" gives you far more control than "We tested this girder extensively before putting it on the market."

d. Weasel words. Weasels can suck the contents of an egg without damaging the shell. Weasel words—common in Q2 and Q3 behavior—

are used to say things without doing "damage." We all use terms like *perhaps, maybe, on the other hand,* and *I'm not sure but,* to make statements that don't really attack the issue, just as the weasel eats an egg without attacking the shell. Weasel words make it difficult for the customer to know exactly what you mean (just as it's difficult to tell whether an egg has or hasn't been eaten by a weasel). What, for example, do the following phrases *really* mean?

- Maybe you ought to place your July order early.
- On the one hand, there's talk of a price increase, but, on the other hand, it might not happen.
- It's possible you'd be better off buying in carload lots.

Language like this serves one purpose: it *equivocates.* It lets you be on both sides of the fence at one time. And it gives you a perfect "out" if you need it ("Well, I never said you *should* place your order early. I only said maybe").

Weasel words are common in Q2 and Q3 selling. ("You never know where he stands," "She talks out of both sides of her mouth" are common customer reactions to both Q2 and Q3.)

We're not saying you should never use qualifiers like *perhaps* or *could be.* We're simply saying: use them when justified—not to Q2 or Q3 a situation.

3. Space Your Ideas

When you want to explain a complex subject or get across a large amount of information, do it in *small clusters*: (a) convey a little information, (b) check to see if it's understood, (c) clarify or amplify if necessary, (d) get the customer's reaction, (e) discuss it if necessary, (f) convey a little more information, (g) repeat the cycle until you've covered the whole topic. *Spacing* ideas is important for two reasons:

- Ideas are easier to digest a few at a time. When you bunch ideas, the customer is expected to absorb them all at once. But that's difficult; we all have trouble soaking up large doses of information at one time.
- Many customers, especially those with strong security needs (Q2), feel *threatened* by a barrage of ideas ("Why am I being bombarded like this? Is he trying to overwhelm . . . confuse me . . . put one over on me?"). These fears drive down receptivity.

The best rule is: Present your ideas *continually* —not *continuously.* Contin*uous* activity goes on and on without let-up. But contin*ual* activity is spaced out; it pauses, resumes, pauses, resumes, and so on. By presenting information with pauses in-between, you'll stand a better chance of being understood.

4. Be Alert to Differences in Interpretation

What you *want* the customer to hear and what the customer *does* hear are frequently two different things. One reason for this is that the customer may (a) *inflate* what you tell him, (b) *deflate* it, (c) *fail to record* it or (d) *erase* it.

a. Inflation. Customers with strong needs for esteem (Q1), security (Q2), or acceptance (Q3) may inflate what they hear by making it more emphatic or more definite than you intended. Here are some examples:

What salesperson said	*What customer heard*
That's not a bad idea.	That's a darned good idea.
I'm not sure the company would go along with that.	No.
The performance record was so so.	The performance record was terrible.
I kinda like the notion.	That's terrific.

You can cut down on this by probing. Ask the customer to *summarize* what he's heard. That'll tell you whether he's inflating it or not. If he is, you can repeat your *original* message.

b. Deflation. When deflating, the customer makes your ideas *less* emphatic or less definite than you intended. For example:

What salesperson said	*What customer heard*
This is the best model on the market.	This is a pretty good model.
Prices are sure to rise in September.	Prices may rise in September.

You can detect deflation as well as inflation by probing.

c. Failure to record. This happens when the customer tunes you out, which may occur if he's bored or preoccupied. It's literally true that someone can sit through an entire presentation, *appear* to be listening, and yet, minutes later, be unable to repeat what you said.

How can you know if a customer is listening? By probing. Interrupt yourself from time to time and use open-end probes ("What's your reaction?"). *Don't* use closed-end questions. If you ask, "Does that make sense?", the customer can answer "Yes," even if he doesn't know what you're talking about.

d. Erasure. The customer may hear you but feel so uncomfortable that he wipes out the message. He may not remember hearing it at all, or he may convince himself he heard it wrong. For example, if you tell a customer with strong social needs (Q3), "A lot of people are going to be very unhappy to hear what you just said," he may become upset and assure himself that you didn't "really" say what he "thought" he heard; after repeating this a few times, he may believe it. For all practical purposes, your words will be erased. The same could happen if you tell a customer with strong esteem needs (Q1), "You really made a very bad buy . . . in fact, I think somebody put one over on you."

Obviously, if a customer chooses to erase your words, you can't stop it. But, during the presentation, you *can* ask him to summarize what you've said, so you're at least sure he heard it. He'll find it harder to forget something he's repeated out loud.

It's equally obvious that while you want to be candid with the customer, you don't want to be brutally blunt, because brutal bluntness may be so threatening that it'll *force* erasure. For example, telling a customer with strong security needs (Q2) that "I wouldn't do that if I were you—you might get fired" may honestly express what you think, but it's certainly not what the customer wants to hear. If you want to warn such a customer against a certain course of action, get *him* to express the warning for himself. You can do this by probing:

YOU: Under the circumstances, Ned, do you think that's wise?

CUSTOMER: I dunno. Why wouldn't it be?

YOU: Well . . . I was just thinking about what might happen if the market drops in a few months. What do you think management would say then?

CUSTOMER: I guess they'd be kinda unhappy. We might be stuck with a lot of inventory at the old price.

YOU: Right. And remember . . . much as we'd like to do it, we can't protect your floor stock against a price decline.

CUSTOMER: Yeah. I'd forgotten that. So I might be in hot water, huh?

YOU: What do you think?

CUSTOMER: I think I'd better cut back on the order.

The point to keep in mind, *always*, is that *you* don't have to say everything that needs saying. By skillful—and patient—*probing*, you can get the *customer* to say many of these things.

5. Use First-Person Statements*

Q4 selling is marked by willingness to confront touchy or sticky problems—and to resolve them to the satisfaction of both customer and salesperson. Obviously, this is seldom easy. After all, many of the touchiest problems involve the *customer*, and pointing a finger at him will usually make the problem worse. How, then, can you confront a problem—meet it head-on, openly and candidly—*without* antagonizing or upsetting the customer? By using *first-person* statements.

A first-person statement says, in effect, that the *speaker* is implicated in a problem along with the listener. To make that point clear—to demonstrate the speaker's involvement—the statement begins by focusing on the speaker. The focus may later shift, but initially it's on the speaker, who thereby says, in effect, "Look, I'm right in the middle of this thing." Some typical first-person openings are:

"I'm worried about . . . "
"Something puzzles me . . ."
"I'm having trouble understanding . . ."
"I seem to be overlooking something . . ."

Contrast these with *second-person statements*, which focus on "you"—the listener—not "I" or "me"—the speaker. Second-person statements say, in effect: "*You*—the listener—are implicated in a problem" without hinting that the speaker may also be implicated. Some typical second-person openings are:

- You shouldn't say things like that.
- You'd be better off if . . .
- Why do you insist . . .
- Won't you please stop . . .
- You ought to . . .

*A good discussion of this subject, using terminology different from ours, can be found in Dr. Thomas Gordon's *Leadership Effectiveness Training* (Wyden Books, 1977).

All second-person statements:

- Say or imply that something about the customer or his behavior is *wrong* or *undesirable* or, at the very least, *needs improvement.* They're *faultfinding* statements.

- Zero in on the *customer.* The word "you" makes it plain that, as far as the salesperson is concerned, the fault is the customer's. *He's* the culprit.

There are two ways to look at second-person statements, from the *customer's* viewpoint, and from *yours.*

- From the *customer's* viewpoint, second-person statements are *unpleasant.* Nobody enjoys being on the receiving end of blame or criticism: nobody likes being told: "You're at fault." Second-person statements nearly always trigger defensiveness, tension, or anger; they nearly always *lower* receptivity.

- From *your* viewpoint, however, fault-finding is sometimes necessary. Q4 candor, after all, *requires* that you make the customer aware of your concerns, that you tell the *whole* story, the bad news as well as the good.

These two viewpoints are at odds. Can they be brought together? *Yes.* By using *first*-person statements instead of second-person. A first-person statement implies: "Something about your behavior troubles *me*; that creates a situation in which we're *both* involved." First-person statements emphasize *your reaction* to a situation for which you think the customer bears some responsibility.

First-person statements share four traits (not necessarily in the order listed):

- They describe the customer behavior that you—the salesperson—are in some way concerned or troubled about. But they don't *pass judgment* on it; they merely say what it *is.*

- They describe your feelings about the behavior—still without passing judgment.

- They describe the consequences—or possible consequences—of the behavior.

- They ask for the customer's help in solving the problem.

Let's look at the differences between second- and first-person statements.

Second-person	*First-person*
Your bookkeeping department is running late on payments.	I'm worried about your payments running late, because our Credit Department might start insisting on C.O.D. shipments. That means I won't be able to give you the kind of service you deserve. What can we do to stop that?
You didn't keep your word.	I'm in an embarrassing spot. I expected your order in July, so I told my boss it was a sure thing. Now he feels I misled him. Can you tell me what happened so I won't make the same mistake again?
You're driving our shipping department crazy.	I got some worrisome news yesterday. Our shipping department is unhappy because three straight deliveries have been turned back at your receiving dock because of lack of space. So they say that if it happens again, they'll tack on a fifty-dollar re-shipment fee—and that'll run your costs up. Got any ideas how we can prevent that?

Obviously, each of the second-person statements does one thing and one thing only: it points the finger of blame or disapproval at the customer. On the other hand, each of the first-person statements does *three* things:

- It acknowledges the existence of a problem. It confronts a touchy issue without Q2 equivocation or Q3 editing.
- It says, in effect: "Look . . . we're in this together. We're *both* involved in this problem.'"
- It looks for solutions. Instead of dwelling on the problem (what good will that do?), it targets on the *answer.*

First-person statements open up a *Q4* approach to problem-solving. They keep communication open, minimize defensive or retaliatory behavior by the customer, and make him part of the problem-solving process. Thus, they pave the way for a pooling of resources— yours and the customer's—and that pooling should produce a better solution. In fact, it may be the only way to reach *any* solution.

Are customers more receptive to first-person statements than to second? Generally, yes. They may not *enjoy* hearing first-person statements, but they're more likely to be *receptive* to them than to accusatory second-person statements. So, when confronted by thorny problems that must be solved, use first-person—problem-solving—statements.

6. Use Process Checks When Necessary

Every salesperson knows the helpless feeling that comes from being stymied—completely thwarted—during a presentation. Every sales-person has probably at some time (or, more likely, times) thought to himself: "We're going around in circles" or "This is hopeless—I just can't get this customer to settle down and talk business" or "I may as well call it quits—*nothing* I say seems to satisfy this guy." This can happen even if you follow *all* the guidelines we've laid out so far. People being people, there are *sure* to be times when, in spite of your Q4 efforts, you cannot spin up receptivity or get the cus-tomer involved and cooperating. When this happens, a *process check* can be very effective.

A process check is a special type of first-person statement. It does three things:

- It summarizes—without judging—the problem you're having.
- It uses the first-person ("I" or "we").
- It requests the customer's help in solving the problem. It does this with an *open-end* probe.

Here are some examples:

"Cora, we seem to be fighting an undeclared war. What can we do to declare a truce and start working on the same side?"

"We seem to be taking off in different directions, Jeff. How can we get on track and stay there?"

"Joe, tell me what I might have done that's made you reluctant to discuss this."

"I have a feeling, Donna, that we're on different wave-lengths. What can we do to start getting through to each other?"

Let's examine these statements:

- They're called *process checks* because they say, in effect, "Some-thing seems wrong with the *process*—the way we're interacting. Let's see what we can do about it."
- They implicate *both* people in the problem. This makes sense; after all, it takes two to interact. If the interaction isn't going well, both people share responsibility.
- They do *not* blame the customer. A statement like, "Ray, you're doing everything you can to sidetrack this discussion, and I think it's time to stop it," is *not* a process check. A process check ad-

mits that you're *both* involved. It doesn't assign blame; it asks for *help* in solving the problem but it doesn't put the whole burden on the customer.

Do process checks always work? No, but they work more often than you might think. They work because (1) they focus attention on the interactional breakdown and (2) they enlist the customer's help in repairing it. They're a "classic" form of Q4 behavior because they're assertive and constructive, candid and solution-oriented.

SUMMARY

1. To move forward toward a Q4 close, you must first build trust, then create understanding and commitment. To do the latter, you'll find six guidelines useful: (a) fit your words to the customer, (b) say what you mean, (c) space your ideas, (d) be alert to differences in interpretation, (e) use first-person statements, (e) use process checks where necessary.

2. To fit your words to the customer, beware of words that clash with his intangible needs, negatively-loaded words, and any words that might make him uncomfortable.

3. To say what you mean, be careful of: soft words, analogies, abstractions, and weasel words.

4. Space your ideas by conveying information in small packets, each followed by probing to make sure it's understood.

5. Differences in interpretation can be due to inflation of content, deflation, failure to record, or erasure. Be alert to all of these.

6. First-person statements describe a problem you're concerned about, explain your feelings about it, describe the consequences of the problem, and ask the customer's help in solving it — all without passing judgment. Thus, they enlist the customer's cooperation without making him feel blamed for the problem.

7. Process checks summarize an interactional problem you're currently experiencing with the customer, use "I" or "we" in doing it, and then use an open-end probe to enlist the customer's help in solving it.

12

The Five-Step Format

In Chapter 5, we sketched out the five steps that are part of every Q4 presentation. In this chapter, we'll explain them in detail. We can do this now because we've covered the *skills* and *guidelines* needed to make the five steps work: the sizing-up skills, motivation skills, timing skills, probing skills, and guidelines for generating trust, understanding, and commitment. We'll now explain how Q4 selling brings all these together for better results.

This chapter and the two that follow explain the Five-Step Format in *general* terms. Then Chapter 15 explains how the format can be *tailored* to fit Q1, Q2, Q3, and Q4 customer behavior. Thus, we'll describe the *basic* Q4 sales format first, then the *customized* formats. When we're finished, you should have a good idea of what we meant when we said that Q4 selling moves along all *three* pathways to the sale at *one* time..

AN OVERVIEW

Let's recap the format first:

    Step 1: Open the sales call
    Step 2: Explore the customer's needs
    Step 3: Present your product or service
    Step 4: Manage objections
    Step 5: Close the sales call

By "sales call," we mean *any* call made on a prospect or customer to *advance a sale* – either now or in the future. A sales call might be a fact-finding or prospecting call (to explore customer needs in preparation for a presentation at a later date), or a presentation call (to confirm what was learned on the fact-finding call, present the product, and close the sale), or a post-sale call (to provide follow-up service) or a complaint-handling call (to settle a sales-related problem) or a call-back call (to correct an earlier failure). In Q4 selling, all sales calls follow (with some modifications) the same five steps.

Step 1: Open the Sales Call

- *The purpose*: Every Q4 opening tries to:

    a. *Set the right tone* – make the customer feel confident and at ease.

    b. *Arouse interest and attention* – explain the purpose of the call and persuade the customer that it's worth her while to concentrate on it.

    c. *Get the customer involved* – set a pattern of active participation (with the customer speaking up and contributing) instead of passive participation (with the customer merely sitting back and listening).

    d. *Check the customer's receptivity* – find out if she's ready to cooperate in making the call pay off for both of you.

- *How it's done:* (a) extend a Q4 greeting, (b) be suitably sociable, (c) explain why you're there, (d) explain what the customer stands to gain, and (e) probe receptivity.

    a. Extend a Q4 greeting. A Q4 greeting is *confident* (if you don't feel confident about what you're doing, why should the customer?) and *cordial* (friendly but businesslike). A firm handshake, a clear statement of identification (your name, title, and company) and a "social probe" ("How are you?") will usually do it – *provided* you get the *customer's* name right. This is so important that it's worth a little research; if you can, check the pronunciation of the customer's name *before* the call.

    b. Be suitably sociable. The key word is *suitably*. Obviously, you want to establish rapport with the customer, but you want to do it without wasting time or annoying her. This means you must find the right "sociability level" for *this* customer. If she's inclined to Q3 it, you'll have to loosen up a bit and engage in a little extra small talk. If she's inclined to Q2 it, you can cut down on the small talk. And if she's inclined to Q1 or Q4 it by getting down to business quickly, you'll obviously want to get down to business quickly. It's impossible to generalize about how much sociability is the "right" amount; it all depends on the customer—and on your ability to *size up* her behavior.

c. **Explain why you're there.** Once past the small talk, tell the customer what your purpose is—and be explicit: "I was in the neighborhood and just thought I'd drop by" is *not* a statement of purpose; it's a way of saying you have *no* purpose. The customer's entitled to know what the call is all about. Spell it out.

d. **Explain what the customer stands to gain.** As soon as you explain why you're there, she's likely to wonder: "So what? Why should *I* care about that? Why should I give up some of my valuable time for that purpose?" To head off these questions—and to raise receptivity—*couple* your statement of purpose with a *tentative benefit statement.* Tell her why you're there (purpose) and what she's likely to get out of it (tentative benefit). At this early stage, before you've explored the customer's needs, the benefit can only be tentative; you can't be sure of it yet. But you can tell her what she *might* get from the call—and why it might *pay* her to listen and get involved:

> Mr. Kent, I'm here to demonstrate our new fastening machine (purpose). There's a good chance you can use it to eliminate one whole step from your assembly operation, and cut down on your assembly costs (benefit).

> Miss Davis, I'd like to get some financial information from you. Once I've got it, there's a strong possibility we can set up an estate plan that'll give you tax advantages you don't now expect.

> I think we can find a way to solve that absenteeism problem you've been plagued with. That's why I'm here to explain our new employee-incentive program

The statement of purpose can come before the benefit statement or, as in our last example, the benefit statement can come before the statement of purpose. The important thing is that the two be *linked*, so the customer knows why you're there and why she should *care*.

e. **Probe receptivity.** The opening is supposed to lead into the exploration of needs. But how do you know the customer's *ready* to work with you in exploring her needs? You don't—unless you *ask*. So, right after explaining your purpose and the tentative benefit, *probe* her receptivity. An open-end probe will usually do the job ("How does that sound?"). If you get a positive answer, fine. Go on to the next step. If you get a negative answer ("I don't really think I'm interested"), probe to find out why, and then try to raise receptivity before going on. One thing is sure: there's no point in going forward to Step 2 unless the customer's willing to go with you. Otherwise, exploring needs will be like exploring a "dry hole" for oil—a costly waste of time.

Step 2: Explore the Customer's Needs

- *The purpose:* Q4 exploration of needs tries to:

  a. **Confirm (or disprove) your existing ideas**—the assumptions about the customer's needs that you started out with.

  b. **Uncover new needs**—needs you know nothing about, and may not even suspect.

  c. **Get the customer to acknowledge her needs**—say out loud that they exist and that she's aware of them.

  d. **Establish your expertise**—prove, by skillful, intelligent probing, that you know what you're doing.

In a word, the purpose of this second step is to give you the information and the credibility you'll need to develop *benefit* statements that will pay off.

- *How it's done:* (a) probe the customer's needs, (b) summarize them, and (c) probe receptivity before going on.

  a. **Probe the customer's needs.** Six probes are especially useful:

- **Open-end.** These are ideal for starting the customer talking about her needs ("What are you presently doing to provide retirement benefits for your administrative people?").

- **Pause.** If the customer Q2s it, you'll probably have to use several open-end probes, each followed by a pause. Remember: *hold* the pause until the *customer* says something.

- **Neutral.** Once the customer gets started, keep her going with neutral probes so you get *full*—not superficial—insight into her needs ("Fill me in on that profit-sharing feature").

- **Reflective.** If the discussion gets sticky—and discussion of needs *can* get sticky—clear the air with reflective statements ("You're obviously not very happy with the treatment you got").

- **Summary**. Whatever the customer tells you, summarize it from time to time to make sure you've got it right ("As I understand it, you now have a partly-contributory retirement plan . . .").

- **Closed-end**. You'll need some closed-end probes to pin down details. But use them sparingly; otherwise, you may choke off discussion ("How many years of employment are needed to get full-vested rights?").

b, Summarize the customer's needs. When you think you've learned all that's necessary, sum up your overall understanding of the customer's needs, and ask her to confirm or reject your summary ("Let me play back my understanding of your situation. As I see it, you don't think your present program is working well, and you'd like . . . Have I got it right?").

c. Probe the customer's receptivity before going on. At this point, you're almost ready for the "heart" of the presentation, in which you prove that your product or service will satisfy the customer's needs and deliver net gain. The crucial question is: Is the *customer* ready? Will she listen carefully, thoughtfully, open-mindedly? If not, you're in for some rough sailing. So, before setting out, test the water. Use an open-end probe to determine whether the customer's ready for Step 3:

"Fine. Now . . . how do you feel about taking a look at our Senior-Years Program, to see how you can overcome the defects in your present program at no extra cost?"

The *phrasing* of the open-end question is important. If you can, weave in a *benefit* statement (". . . you can overcome the defects in your present program at no extra cost"). This way, you remind the customer that *she* stands to gain something by moving into Step 3 *with* you.

Step 3: Present Your Product or Service

- *The purpose:* This is the "proof" step—in which you demonstrate that your product or service will fill the customer's needs—make her better off—and deliver net gain. Every Q4 presentation tries to:

  a. *Generate understanding*—get the customer to see *how* and *why* your product or service will fill her needs. You want her to accept this on *evidence*—not "faith."

    b. *Generate tentative commitment* —get the customer thinking: "Since this product will fill my need, *maybe* I ought to buy it."

Don't expect much more than *tentative* commitment at this point. While the customer thinks "maybe I ought to buy," she's probably also thinking "maybe there are reasons I *shouldn't.*" This is only normal. The vast majority of customers are guided by *enlightened* self-interest. They're likely to buy once they're convinced buying is in their self-interest. But they're likely to think carefully *before* buying, to weigh the pros and cons. After all, a little skepticism is also in their self-interest.

• *How it's done:* (a) deliver a benefit statement, (b) probe for the customer's acceptance, (c) check her receptivity, (d) deliver another benefit statement—and so on until you've *fully proven* what your product or service can do for the customer, (e) summarize the benefits and check for omissions, (f) prove net gain, (g) check receptivity.

    a. Deliver a benefit statement. We saw how this is done in Chapter 7. To recap: restate the customer's need, prove that your product or service can fill it, and personalize the benefit by focusing on the word *you* —the customer. If the proof is long or complicated, space it out—don't bunch it together. Follow the guidelines in Chapters 10 and 11 for building trust, understanding, and commitment.

    b. Probe for the customer's acceptance. Don't move to the next benefit until she understands and accepts the first one. Try an open-end probe ("How does that strike you?", "What's your reaction?"). If her answer shows she doesn't understand ("Well, I'm still not clear on how that prepayment feature works") or accept ("I don't see how that's going to help me"), go back and straighten things out.

    c. Check the customer's receptivity. Before going on to the next benefit, make sure the customer's ready: "Can we move on to the cash-reserve feature . . . and see how it'll cut your costs?" If she's reluctant, probe to find out why, and straighten it out.

    d. Deliver another benefit statement. Once the customer's ready for the next benefit, repeat the cycle. Keep on until you've completely proven all the benefits your product or service can deliver to *her.* Don't waste time on product information that has nothing to do with her needs. She's *not* interested in what your product might do for other people; she's interested only in what it will do for *her.*

Make your "benefit" statements about *real* benefits: ways the product or service will pay off for *this* customer.

e. Summarize the benefits and check for omissions. Once you've told the *whole* story, summarize the benefits ("Okay, let me recap what this plan will do for you . . ."). Then, check to see if you've omitted anything the customer wants to know ("Have I overlooked any of your requirements?").

f. Prove net gain. Now that you've told the benefit story, you still have a big job on your hands: to prove *net gain.* Remember: you want to generate understanding and *commitment*, and, while the customer may understand you perfectly, her commitment may be weak or non-existent if she thinks: "Sounds like a good deal . . . but not nearly as good as what I can get from Company X." Or, "That's an impressive list of benefits, but it still doesn't add up to what I've already got." Or, "I like the idea, but I wonder if I wouldn't be even better off by going with Company Z." So, now is the time to do some *comparison selling*; stack up *your* benefits against those she's considering getting elsewhere. Show that your *total* package of benefits will deliver more satisfaction—more need fulfillment—than any other package of benefits.

g. Check receptivity. Once you know you haven't overlooked any of the customer's needs, check to see if she's ready to move into Step 4—Managing Objections ("Can we get your reaction to all this?" "What's your evaluation of the plan?").

Don't assume that everything's great and that she must be happy with your presentation. Let her speak her mind—*even if you don't like what you hear.* If you're going to close the call (Step 5) with understanding and *commitment*, you must first let the customer voice her objections and get them cleared up. That's what Step 4 is all about.

Step 4: Manage Objections

Objections can arise at *any* time—not just in Step 4. All we're saying is that they're most *likely* to arise now—after you've presented your product or service. If they don't arise spontaneously, if the customer doesn't bring them up on her own, then now is the time to probe for them. If you don't, if you take for granted that silence means agreement, you may be in for a shock when you try to close and the

customer refuses to buy. Step 4 is the logical place to deal with objections, but the techniques outlined below can be used *any time* an
objection surfaces — from opening to close.

- *The purpose:* Q4 management of objections does three things:

    a. ***Shows you're willing to face up to objections.*** This is impor-
    tant. It bolsters your standing with the customer by saying:
    "I'm confident of my product and my ability to explain it. I
    have nothing to hide, nothing I'm unwilling to talk about. Feel
    free to say anything; whatever you say, I'll discuss it to your
    satisfaction." This is what's meant by Q4 openness, assertive-
    ness, and responsiveness.

    b. ***Uncovers the real objection.*** Many so-called "objections"
    cover up real objections the customer would rather not talk
    about. Time spent on these phony objections is time wasted.
    Only the *real* objection is worth managing.

    c. ***Generates commitment.*** Objections either prevent or dilute
    commitment. Commitment means: "I'm *fully* convinced." An
    objection means "I'm *not* fully convinced." Obviously, the
    only way to get commitment is to get rid of the objection.

- *How it's done:* (a) acknowledge the objection voiced by the customer, (b) probe until you understand the real objection, (c) answer
the real objection, (d) probe for confirmation of the answer.

a. Acknowledge the objection voiced by the customer. Don't
"interpret" the objection at this point. Don't re-word it to make it
say what you *think* the customer means. Simply restate the objection
as you heard it. A summary statement is all that's needed: "Paul, as
I understand it, you think our first-year cost will run higher than
your own in-company plan." Usually, it's a good idea to follow the
summary by commenting that the objection is important: "That's
an important concern . . . no doubt about it." Don't *minimize* the
objection ("In the light of all the benefits I've presented, I don't
think *that* should bother you"). Treat it, whatever it is, as *worthy
of serious discussion.*

b. Probe until you understand the real objection. The objection
voiced by the customer may be genuine or it may be a stall. A genuine objection usually deals with outside factors (cost, delivery, availability, credit, installation, warranties, maintenance, and so on). A
stall is ˉusually phrased in *personal* terms ("I'm just not sure,"

"I'll have to check with my partner," "Let me think about it").
Underneath the stall ("I'll have to check with my partner") may be
a genuine objection that the customer's unwilling to reveal ("I don't
think your warranty is fair, but you're a nice guy and I don't want
to hurt your feelings by saying so"). To get at the real reason for the
customer's resistance, you'll have to *probe.* A variety of probes used
in sequence will usually isolate the real objection:

CUSTOMER: Sounds clear to me. When my partner gets back in town, I'll
                    check with him.

SALESPERSON: I see. You can't move ahead until you check with your part-
                    ner. I can appreciate your wanting his commitment. Why
                    don't we arrange to talk to him together?

CUSTOMER: Hey, it's nice of you to offer . . . but I don't want to put you
                    to all that trouble. I can handle it.

SALESPERSON: Well . . . in that case . . . I'd better make sure I've addressed
                    all *your* concerns. What have I left hanging?

CUSTOMER: Nothing, really. Like I said, I think I understand it.

SALESPERSON: Good. That's essential. But it's also essential that you be
                    committed to the idea. Do I have your commitment?

CUSTOMER: Well . . .

SALESPERSON: You sound a little unsure.

CUSTOMER: Well . . . maybe a little.

SALESPERSON: Fill me in.

CUSTOMER: Well . . . I do understand the program. I'm just not sure
                    about the warranty . . .

SALESPERSON: Go ahead . . .

It's not easy to get the real objection from a customer who Q2s it or
Q3s it. But it *is* vital.

   c. **Answer the real objection.** Once you've uncovered what seems
to be the real objection, summarize it, answer it, and, if possible,
convert your answer into a *benefit statement:*

> Okay . . . as I get it, you're concerned because the permanently-sealed drive
> unit is the only part warrantied for five years . . . while the other parts are
> covered for only a year. You're right . . . but actually that's a plus for you.
> You've said your number-one need is low initial cost . . . equipment for the
> lowest possible capital outlay. That's what you'll get with this model. One
> way we've managed to price this machine below anybody else is by trimming
> back our warranty. Let me show you some figures on the life-expectancy of

the parts in this machine. What you'll see is that your chances of getting hurt by this warranty are very small . . . while your savings on initial outlay are very large. It's a good trade-off.

d. Probe for confirmation of your answer. Never assume that because you've answered the objection to *your* satisfaction, you've answered it to the customer's. Instead, use an open-end probe or closed-end question to see if she's satisfied ("How do you feel about the warranty now?", "Does that set your mind to rest?"). If she's not, go back over your answer.

Objection management is, of course, one of the most important topics in all sales training. For that reason, we'll consider it in much fuller detail in the next chapter. For the moment, this discussion should show how objection management, which is almost sure to be necessary in Step 4 but which may also be necessary at other points, fits into the Five-Step Format.

Step 5: Close the Sales Call

We've said a sales call is *any* call on a prospect or customer for the purpose of advancing a sale — now or in the future. A successful *close* is any conclusion to a sales call that does what the call was intended to do — *advance a sale.*

- *The purpose:* Every Q4 close tries to do two things:

  a. **Confirm the customer's understanding** — get her to acknowledge that she's clear on what the call was all about.

  b. **Confirm the customer's commitment** — get her to take whatever action the call was intended to stimulate.

- *How it's done:* (a) summarize the benefits and the net gain, (b) ask for a commitment, (c) manage the customer's response, (d) work out an action plan and conclude the call.

a. Summarize the benefits and the net gain. By now, the customer should know "what's in it for me." Still and all, it's best to repeat (or get her to repeat) the benefits — and the net gain, the fact that "what's in it" is *more* than "what's in anything else." Spelling this out one final time should reinforce the customer's feeling that "this proposal is not only good for me — it's *best* for me." If you can, have the customer do the spelling out; you can frequently get her to do so with a simple open-end probe ("Janet, before we wrap this up, let me ask you, what do you see in all this as the real payoff for you and your company?"). If you can't get her to spell out the benefits, do it yourself.

b. Ask for a commitment. This is the point at which a great many sales calls break down. After doing a good job up to now, many sales-people Q2 it ("I'll leave our catalog and let you think about it") or Q3 it ("Well . . . I just wanted to drop by and fill you in. I'll be in touch"). Obviously, what's required now is *Q4 assertiveness*: let the customer know you want the order by *asking* for it. (She may save you the trouble by *telling* you she's ready to buy. But in most cases you'll have to ask for a commitment.) There are two ways to do it: by *forced choice* or by *direct request.*

A forced-choice close asks the customer to choose between two or more buying actions: "Now that we've covered the benefits of both models, which one fits your requirements best: the Technoplus or the Ultratec?" The direct-request close is even simpler. It asks for the order point-blank: "How about it, Ted? Shall I write up the order?" Whichever approach you use, *pause* afterward. Give the customer *time.*

c. Manage the customer's response. You'll get one of four re-sponses:

- *A firm yes.*
- *A qualified yes* – usually a "yes, but" statement ("Yes, but be-fore you write up the order . . ." or "Yes, but I'm still not sure about one thing . . ."). Most qualified yeses either ask for more information or offer a minor objection.
- *An objection* – indicating you still haven't resolved the customer's doubts ("I don't know. I'm still bothered by that tax liability").
- *A flat no.*

If you get a *firm yes*, move on to the next part of the close (working out an action plan). If you get a *qualified yes*, summarize the qualifi-cation, ask the customer to confirm the summary, handle the prob-lem, and then ask for a commitment again. If you get an *objection*, acknowledge it, probe it, answer it, get your answer confirmed, and then ask for a commitment again. If you get a *flat no*, probe the rea-sons and handle them. Don't give up without a try.

d. Work out an action plan and conclude the call. Once you have the customer's commitment, work out the details (quantity, date of delivery, terms, etc.), pave the way for the next call ("I'll phone next week to set up a follow-up. That way, we can iron out any installation problems right away"). Thank the customer and move on to your next call.

Like managing objections, closing is a critically important topic, so we'll expand on it in Chapter 14. When we do, we'll have a chance to look at some of the subtleties that this chapter has ignored.

SOME MODIFICATIONS

Do *all* Q4 sales calls follow the Five-Step Format? Yes. But some steps may be emphasized more on some calls than on others. On a fact-finding call, for instance, Step 2 (Explore the Customer's Needs) will be emphasized. Step 3 (Present the Product or Service) will probably shrink to a mere statement of future action ("I'll be back Tuesday morning with a proposal"), and Step 4 (Manage Objections) may shrink to almost nothing. *But it won't be neglected.* The salesperson will at least give the customer a *chance* to voice objections ("Can you see any flaws in the way we're operating so far?"). In Q4 selling, *each* of the five steps is at least *started*, although in some cases it may not be *developed.*

13

Managing Objections

Most salespeople, if asked "Which part of the presentation do you find toughest to handle?", would probably answer, "Managing objections" or "Closing" or both. In fact, some salespeople readily admit that "I dread objections" or "I feel comfortable all the way through a presentation, until I have to tackle objections." And some find closing so intimidating that they sidestep it entirely; they work hard up to the close, and then undo their own efforts by saying something like, "Well, give it some thought and then call me to let me know." With that, they avoid the whole issue, and reduce the whole presentation to futility.

Obviously, then, both subjects—managing objections and closing— deserve more attention than they received in the last chapter. They'll get it now. This chapter will zero in on managing objections, the next on closing.

MANAGING OBJECTIONS

Three Types

In Chapter 12, we distinguished between *real* and *phony* objections. Another classification, which may be even more useful, breaks them down into three types: (1) objective objections, (2) subjective objections, and (3) questions.

171

1. **Objective objections.** These have to do with outside matters: cost, delivery, availability, credit, service, warranties, etc. Objective objections are usually, but not always, real; that is, they usually express *genuine* concerns. When a customer says, "Your price is too high," he probably *means* it, although he could be covering up another objection that he prefers to keep to himself ("I don't trust your company to keep its word"). All objective objections, real or phony, have one thing in common: they're basically concerned with *impersonal* matters. Even when an objective objection is mixed with personal feelings or opinions ("I think your credit policy is unfair"), the *core* of the objection is impersonal; it has to do with something *outside* the customer's mind.

2. **Subjective objections.** These have to do with the customer's intangible needs, emotions, frame of mind, or personal relationships: "I'm just not sure" ... "I don't know why, but I just don't like the idea" ... "I'll have to talk to my wife" ... "I've got a brother-in-law in the business, and I really ought to buy from him." Subjective objections may be either real or phony. A customer who says "I'm just not sure" may be covering up some other objection, but he may also be telling the truth—that he really *isn't* sure, which means *you* haven't provided him with a feeling of certainty. All subjective objections, phony or real, have one thing in common: They revolve around the customer's *feelings.* ("I ought to buy from my brother-in-law" translates into "I'm *afraid* of alienating my brother-in-law by buying from someone else"; "I'll have to talk to my wife" translates into "I'm *unwilling* to take the initiative"; and so on. Subjective objections can always be translated into statements that express feelings.)

3. **Questions.** Obviously, not all questions are objections; many are genuine requests for information. But some questions are not requests for information—they're disguised objections. Here are a few examples:

"Isn't it true your product's got a reputation for breaking down in sub-freezing weather?"

"How come you've lost so many customers in the past year?"

"What's this stuff I read in the papers about your advertising being investigated?"

There's no *sure* way to distinguish an information-seeking question from an objection in question form. Generally however, objections in question form have some or all of these characteristics:

- They contain an *embarrassing* allegation ("... breaking down in sub-freezing weather," "... lost so many customers," "... your advertising being investigated").

- Whether true or false, the allegation's designed to put you on the *defensive.*

- The question is *sarcastic* or *ironic* (as when a customer, who's angry because his last three deliveries have been late, asks, "Why don't they give your company an award for on-time delivery?").

- The question cannot be answered *at all* as it's presently worded (like the classic question, "Have you stopped beating your wife?", asked of a man who has *never* beaten his wife). Imagine a customer saying, "Tell me—yes or no—have you guys finally stopped watering down that chemical?", when the fact is that the chemical has never been watered down.

- The question may be impossible to answer in any form. Suppose a customer asks, "How come your competitor always undersells you by at least a dollar a case?" No salesperson could answer this accurately without having "inside" information about his competitor's production techniques, pricing policies, marketing strategy, and so on—or without making a lucky guess. It's a safe bet that a customer who asks this kind of question *knows* that the salesperson can't answer it; the question isn't really a question—it's an objection.

Why bother to categorize objections in these three ways? Because each kind of objection requires somewhat *different* handling. The general guidelines laid down in the last chapter still apply, but, as we'll see, they may have to be modified, depending upon the *kind* of objection.

When Should Objections Be Answered?

Should all objections be answered *on the spot*—as they occur? No. Whether to answer now or later depends upon three things:

1. The type of objection. If the customer raises an objective objection, and if you plan on providing the answer later in your presentation, you *may* want to delay the answer until then:

CUSTOMER: I still don't understand how that deferred-payment option you've been advertising works.

SALESPERSON: It is pretty complicated. That's why I plan on explaining it in detail just a little later—once I'm done explaining the warehousing options. Okay?

CUSTOMER: Sure. Keep going.

Subjective objections may be tougher to deal with, because they require a "judgment call" on your part. Before deciding how to handle them, you have to decide whether they're real or phony (you can never be sure). If you decide the objection's real, manage it—on the spot—by following the four guidelines laid out in the last chapter: (a) acknowledge the objection, (b) probe for clarification, (c) answer, (d) probe for confirmation of your answer.

On the other hand, if you decide the objection's phony, you may not have to manage it at all. If you can defer it till later, and continue with your planned approach, it may disappear:

CUSTOMER: I really don't know if I oughta be talking to you at all. Y'know, I've got a cousin in the business, and if I'm gonna buy from anyone, I guess I oughta buy from him.

SALESPERSON: I appreciate your feeling that way. But before you make up your mind, you owe it to yourself to see what Apex can do for you. As I just said, there's an excellent chance we can eliminate that leakage at lower cost than anyone else. Can we go ahead, and come back to your cousin later?

CUSTOMER: Yeah . . . I guess you're right. I owe that much to myself.

If your presentation's good enough, you may never hear of the cousin again. If the subject re-surfaces, you can always handle it later. So you *may* want to delay answering a subjective objection. In fact, answering it on the spot (which would probably prove quite difficult before you've developed your benefit statements) might prove futile.

If the customer raises an objection in the form of a *question*, you may also want to delay your answer. For example:

SALESPERSON: I'll show you how the Model X can bring down those costs.

CUSTOMER: Wait a minute. Let me ask you something first. I hear you've stuck the highest price in the industry on that machine. How come? Why are you people so expensive?

SALESPERSON: Fair question. I'm going to explain our whole pricing policy . . . in detail. First, though, I'd like to show you how our Model X can make a big dent in your production costs. How's that sound?

CUSTOMER: Fine . . . if you can really do it. But, before you get out of here, I still wanna know why you've got such a steep price tag on that thing.

SALESPERSON: You will. That's a promise. First . . .

2. The timing of the objection. *When* the objection is raised usually affects when it should be *answered.* It may be extremely difficult to answer certain objections early in the presentation because the answers depend upon information the customer won't receive until later; if so, you'll probably want to defer the answer.

For example, let's assume that the following exchange occurs in Step 2 (Exploring Customer Needs), *before* you've had a chance to present your product:

CUSTOMER: Y'know, your ads say the Model 720 uses microchips that don't contain silicon. I've been in electrical engineering twenty years, and, believe me, that doesn't sound right. I don't care what anybody says . . . I don't think it'll work.

YOU: I can appreciate your being skeptical. It is an innovation. But once I've explained our new technology for printing circuits, I think you'll see why we don't need silicon. Can we get into it then?

CUSTOMER: Sure. You call the shots. I wasn't trying to rush you.

Objective objections, especially technical ones, are often answerable only *after* certain facts have been established. If these objections arise earlier, you'll probably want to table the answer for a while.

3. The customer's receptivity. If the customer's engrossed in an objection, so preoccupied that he can't concentrate on anything else, then you may have no choice but to deal with it then and there. After all, there's no point in expecting the customer to wait for an answer if, while he's waiting, his receptivity is so low you can't get through. You can usually tell that he is engrossed if he *repeats* the objection. If, say, he agrees to let you defer your answer, and then, a few seconds later, raises the objection again, and then again, you can safely assume you're "stuck," and you'll have to clear away the objection before you can proceed.

With these guidelines in mind, let's see how each of the three types of objections should be handled—once you've decided to go ahead and handle them.

Managing Objective Objections

As we've seen, objective objections are usually *real.* In most cases, the customer really believes what he's saying—that your price *is* too high or your warranty *is* defective or whatever. He may, of course, be right. If he's not, it's up to you to show him *why.* An objective objection is *not* something to duck; it is *not* a threat. It's a chance for you to set the record straight—to tell the customer something he doesn't know or to clear up something he doesn't understand. Most of the time, a customer who voices an objective objection is really saying—without being aware of it—"I don't get it." If he doesn't get it, that's probably because *you* haven't completely explained it. Now's your chance.

Put another way, an objective objection is usually a request by the customer for more information. It may not *sound* like a request, but it is. As such, it's nothing to fear—and the anxiety many salespeople feel when they hear an objective objection is usually unwarranted.

To manage an objective objection:

1. Acknowledge it and show that you take it *seriously.* ("I appreciate your point of view," "That's an interesting angle," "I can see why you're worried"). Don't disparage it ("I wouldn't worry about that").

2. Probe until you're confident you fully understand the objection. ("Let me see if I've got this right . . ."). Then summarize it. (If the objection's phony, you'll probably discover that while probing. You should then be able to uncover the *real* objection.)

3. Answer the objection. If you can, do it by developing a *proof* statement. Don't rely on claims and counter-claims; cite *evidence.*

4. Get the customer to confirm his understanding of your answer. An open-end or closed-end probe should do it ("How does that strike you?", "Does that clear up your doubts?").

Let's look at an example:

CUSTOMER: I hear what you're saying . . . and it sounds good—in the abstract. But I don't think it'll work here. What our people like most about our plan is that it's non-contributory—they don't pay a cent. Switching from that to a contributory plan—well, that'd make them very unhappy. Very unhappy. I've heard a lot of them say so.

SALESPERSON: I appreciate your concern. The last thing in the world you'd want to do . . . and the last thing I'd urge you to do . . . is demoralize your workforce. But let me ask you something: a little while ago, you said some of your people were grumbling about room benefits. What exactly is their complaint?

CUSTOMER: Well . . . you know . . . hospital room rates have zoomed lately—and our coverage just hasn't kept up. Most of the complaints have been about dependent coverage—room payments for spouses and kids.

SALESPERSON: Go on.

CUSTOMER: Well . . . there's not much to tell. It's the old story. A kid goes into the hospital to get her tonsils removed. When the father gets the bill, he finds only 60 percent of the room rate is covered by insurance. So, naturally, he comes back here and complains to the personnel department that our insurance program's no good.

SALESPERSON: Have you looked into increasing the coverage?

CUSTOMER: Yeah. There's no way we could handle the premium.

SALESPERSON: I see. Look . . . let me go over this dependent room-coverage feature one more time. We can provide coverage up to 90 percent of the daily rate . . . and *your* share of the premium won't be any higher than it is now. I think there's a good chance this feature would more than offset any dissatisfaction your people might feel about the contributory requirement. Let me explain . . .

As a rule, objective objections are the easiest of all objections to answer. That's because the customer has little or no *emotional* investment in them. Therefore, you can rely mainly on facts and logic to manage them. Subjective objections, in which the customer does have an emotional investment, are usually tougher.

Managing Subjective Objections

Subjective objections are usually harder to handle than objective, for several reasons:

- It's not easy to tell if they're real or phony, so you'll probably have to do some careful probing. If the objection is phony, the probing may not be easy. After all, if the customer were willing to talk about the *real* objection, he wouldn't have covered it up in the first place.

- If the objection *is* phony, it may cover up another—and perhaps worse—subjective objection ("I'll have to talk to my partner" may conceal an accusatory objection: "I don't think I can rely on your word" or it may cover up an objective objection: "Your price is too high"). Either way, the objection may be the customer's way of Q2ing or Q3ing an awkward situation—and probing for the real objection probably won't be easy.

- In managing a subjective objection, then, your first challenge is to find out if it's real or phony, and, if it is phony, to identify the *real* objection. Sooner or later, if you're going to make progress, you must find out what's really bothering the customer.

Figure 25 shows how to do it:

Figure 25. Managing Subjective Objections.

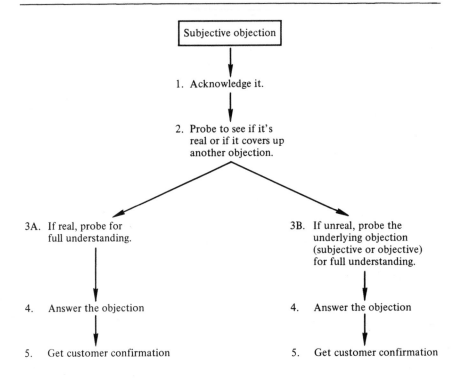

Here's an example in which the subjective objection covers up an objective objection.

CUSTOMER: Sounds good, Al. But I can't do a thing today. Gotta talk to Roy first.

SALESPERSON: Fine, Max, Why not bring him in right now?

CUSTOMER: No way. He's out of town. Extended buying trip. Won't get back for a couple of weeks.

SALESPERSON: I see. Well . . . can we set up a meeting between the three of us when he gets back?

CUSTOMER: Naw. That's not necessary. I can talk to him on my own.

SALESPERSON: Well . . . if you're gonna do that, let me make sure you've got all the information you'll need. What've I failed to make clear?

CUSTOMER: Nothing. Nothing at all. I understand it perfectly.

SALESPERSON: Good. Then what concerns do you have? What doubts?

CUSTOMER: (A bit hesitant) No doubts. No serious doubts anyway.

SALESPERSON: No *serious* doubts. How about minor doubts?

CUSTOMER: Aw . . . just one. No big deal.

SALESPERSON: I'm glad to hear that, Max. Still and all, if you've got any doubts, it's my job to try and clear them up. What's the one doubt that's bothering you?

CUSTOMER: It's not exactly bothering me, Al. I really don't want to make a big thing out of it.

SALESPERSON: Keep going.

CUSTOMER: Look . . . I don't want you to take this personally.

SALESPERSON: Believe me, Max, I won't. Our relationship's strong enough to stand some straight talk. Go ahead.

CUSTOMER: Well . . . it's that letter.

SALESPERSON: What letter?

CUSTOMER: The one from your credit department. About three months ago. That really hurt.

SALESPERSON: What do you mean?

CUSTOMER: Well . . . I explained to your credit manager that I was having some collection problems of my own . . . and that I'd pay the invoice as soon as I could. It seemed to me they should've been willing to trust an old customer. When I got that letter . . . well, it was like being hit in the face with cold water. A real shock.

SALESPERSON: Go on.

CUSTOMER: Collection agency! Imagine . . . threatening to turn my account over to a collection agency. Al, nothing like that's happened to me in twenty-two years of business. Now . . . mind you . . . I'm not blaming you.

SALESPERSON: I understand that. Perfectly. It must've been plenty upsetting. Let me ask you a few questions . . .

The example illustrates the situation we mentioned before: a subjective objection ("I have to talk to my partner") sometimes disguises an objective objection ("Your company's credit policies are unfair"). This happens frequently with customers with strong Q2 and Q3 tendencies.

Here's one more example. In this one, the subjective objection is *real*.

CUSTOMER:	Okay. I've got the picture. Why don't you leave your catalog and a price list? I'll get back to you.
SALESPERSON:	Any questions you'd like to get cleared up first?
CUSTOMER:	No . . . I don't think so.
SALESPERSON:	Well, then, wouldn't it be to your advantage to place the order today, so you can get delivery faster?
CUSTOMER:	No . . . I want to think about it.
SALESPERSON:	You're uncertain.
CUSTOMER:	Yeah . . . I guess I am. It sounds good . . . but . . . I just don't know.
SALESPERSON:	What exactly are you uncertain about?
CUSTOMER:	I'm just not sure it's a better deal than what I'm getting now. I can't point to any flaws in your proposal . . . I just don't feel confident enough to go ahead with it.
SALESPERSON:	You think you might be better off sticking with what you've got.
CUSTOMER:	That's just it. I'm not sure. I wish I was . . . but I'm not.
SALESPERSON:	Okay, then . . . maybe it'll help if we go over this comparative two-year cost projection . . .

In a very large number of cases, subjective objections, *no matter how they're worded*, boil down to one point: "I'm just not *confident* enough to buy now." In other words, the customer's not convinced of the *net gain*; he hasn't been *persuaded.* Remember: the dictionary definition of *persuade* is: to convince someone to *do* something. If a customer's not convinced that he ought to buy, he hasn't been persuaded.

Managing Objections in the Form of Questions

The first problem in managing question-objections is to *recognize* them. Is the question a real question—a request for information? Or is it an objection masquerading as a question? If the question has any of the characteristics listed earlier in this chapter, it's probably an objection, and should be managed as such. The basic technique we've outlined (acknowledge-probe-answer-confirm) will usually work, except that you may have to *clarify* the question before you can intelligently acknowledge it. For example:

CUSTOMER: Everything you've said is all well and good, but let me ask you something. What makes you people think you *belong* in this field?

SALESPERSON: I'm not sure I understand. What are you getting at?

CUSTOMER: Just what I said: What makes you people think you belong in this field? Y'know . . . this is a real high-technology area, and your company's never done any work in it before. Most of your competitors have a ten-year head-start on you. What makes you think you can play in their league?

SALESPERSON: You're saying we don't have the experience to do the job in a field as complex as this one. Right?

CUSTOMER: Right. I think maybe you're out of your class. Precision machine tools . . . that's one thing. But computerization . . . that's something else. I've got some real doubts about your qualifications.

SALESPERSON: I can appreciate that. And you're right to be skeptical. You owe that to yourself. Let me ask you this: how familiar are you with our computerization operation?

CUSTOMER: Well . . . not very. In fact, I didn't even know you *had* one until a couple of months ago.

SALESPERSON: I see. Then let me explain how we made the shift from machine tools to computerization . . . and where our expertise comes from.

As this example shows, objection-questions are sometimes *obscure.* They give you the idea the customer is objecting to *something*, but you can't pinpoint *what*. So, before you can acknowledge the objection, you may have to clarify the question.

SUMMARY

1. Objections can be classified as objective (concerned with external, impersonal matters), subjective (concerned with the customer's feelings or relationships), and questions (which sound like requests for information but aren't).

2. A question is probably an objection if it has any of these traits: it contains an embarrassing allegation, it can't be answered at all as

presently worded, it's sarcastic, it may not be answerable in any form.

3. Whether an objection should be answered as it occurs or answered later depends upon the type of objection, its timing, and the customer's receptivity.

4. All objections can be managed by following four guidelines: acknowledge, probe, answer, confirm. But the guidelines may require some modification depending on the type of objection.

14

Closing

One of the saddest sights in selling (and a common one) is that of the salesperson who works hard and effectively up to the close, and then, in one swoop, sabotages her own efforts by "calling it quits."

- "I'll leave our brochure and get back to you in a few weeks."
- "I'm sure you'll want to think about it. Give me a call when you've decided."
- "I don't want to crowd you. Mull it over, and we'll talk about it on my next call."
- "That's the story. When you're ready to do something, let me know."

These are just a few of the many ways salespeople have devised to Q2 or Q3 the close of a presentation. All of them say the same thing: "I won't even *try* to close. Instead, I'll stop . . . here and now . . . and pass the initiative to *you*—the customer."

Why? Why do so many salespeople shift from *active* to *passive* at this point? Why do they deliberately undermine their own efforts? Why do they back away from doing what they presumably came to do: close the sale?

We'll diagnose this strange situation—and prescribe an antidote—in this chapter.

THREE REASONS

Salespeople falter—or even collapse—at the point of close for three reasons:

1. The close requires more assertiveness than any other step, and many salespeople equate assertiveness with being "pushy" or "unfriendly" or "high-pressure." In other words, they consider closing—wrongly—as *Q1* behavior, something they prefer to shy away from.

2. Many salespeople see the close as a threat to their self-esteem. They're afraid of being turned down or put off; they interpret the word "no" as a personal rejection or as evidence that they haven't done their job.

3. Many salespeople don't know *how* to close. They're assertive enough; they don't worry about being rejected; but they lack the necessary *skills.* Knowing this, and feeling awkward and inept as a result, they prefer to sidestep the close.

THE Q1 WAY

We don't mean to imply that *all* presentations which falter at the close falter because the salesperson Q2s or Q3s it. That's often true, but not always. Many presentations falter because the salesperson *Q1s* it. Here's an example:

SALESPERSON: Well . . . what do you think?

CUSTOMER: I'm just not sure.

SALESPERSON: C'mon, now. Why waste this opportunity? Just say the word and I'll call the factory and tell them to load that truck. We can have it rolling this afternoon.

CUSTOMER: I don't know . . .

SALESPERSON: Listen . . . while we stand here talking, the price could go up. Believe me . . . you've got nothing to worry about. Just give me your signature and I'll pick up that phone and call our plant manager.

CUSTOMER: I gotta have time to think.

SALESPERSON: There's nothing to think about. Take my word for it.

Q1 pressure sometimes works. Some customers do cave in and buy. We don't deny that. But, in a very large number of cases, "the Q1 squeeze" only antagonizes the customer, drives down receptivity, and fumbles away a potential sale.

If Q1 closes are so frequently self-defeating, and if Q2 and Q3 closes (or non-closes) are nearly always self-defeating, what's left is the Q4 close. Before discussing it in detail, however, we'd better talk about a common—and frequently misunderstood—topic: trial closes.

TRIAL CLOSES

The phrase *trial close* is often used as if it describes something special in a sales presentation. Actually, it doesn't. Strictly speaking, *every* attempt to close is a *trial close*; in fact, the word *trial* and *attempt* mean the same thing. Every attempt to close is a *trial* of the customer's intentions; it's an effort to find out if she's ready to buy. If she is, fine; you can proceed with the close—wrap up the sale. If she isn't you obviously can't. But you can't know for sure—one way or the other—until after you conduct the *trial*. So, whether you use the phrase "trial close," "attempt to close," "closing effort" or some other, you're talking about one and the same thing: a *test* of the customer's readiness to buy. Thus, there's nothing "good" about a trial close *as such*. A trial close is "good"—an effective selling tactic—only if it's done at the *right time* and in the *right way*. Let's look at both criteria:

1. *The right time.* We can distinguish between two types of trial closes: *premature* and *timely*. A *premature* trial close (usually Q1) comes *too early* in the presentation—before the customer either understands or feels committed. Here's an example:

SALESPERSON: How y'doing? What can I show you this evening?

CUSTOMER: I'm kinda interested in a sports car.

SALESPERSON: Great! Take a look at this Z37 over here. That's a real beauty, huh? Whaddya say? Should we wrap it up right now?

That's obviously an exaggeration, but it underscores our point. Many closes—especially Q1—are attempted much too early in the presentation, before receptivity has been raised, before needs have been explored, before benefits have been proven. Almost always, premature trial closes are a waste of time.

In fact, Q1 trial closes may be worse than a waste of time; they may actually be dangerous. The danger is that they may push a customer from a "neutral" position to a "no" position; they may arouse active resistance rather than mere apathy. This makes the salesperson's job all the harder; moving a customer from "against" to "for" is always more difficult than moving her from "neutral" to "for."

Timely closes are closes that come at the proper point in the presentation: the point at which you have good reason to believe that the customer understands and feels committed to the purchase. If you *have* good reason to believe this, then, obviously, the next step is to test the belief by finding out if the customer's ready to buy: "In view of everything we've talked about, which model best suits your needs—the Warrior or the Chieftain?"

Is the "proper" point for a trial close *always* Step 5? In virtually all cases, yes. Because only in Step 5, *after* exploring customer needs, *after* proving benefits and net gain, and *after* managing objections, can you have good reason to think that the customer fully understands and is committed. But this doesn't mean you must always wait till Step 5 to close; you *can* do it earlier if the *customer* initiates the close. Suppose, as you're explaining a benefit, the customer breaks in and says: "I'll tell you what: let's just dispense with the rest of this stuff, I've decided to go ahead and buy. Where do I sign?" If that happens, then, by all means, *close* the sale.

The distinction to keep in mind here is between the *close* and a *trial close.* The *close* is the actual conclusion—the wrapping up—of the sale. A *trial close* is an attempt to find out if the customer's ready to *move into* the close. The close can come at *any time* (even Step 1) that the customer indicates a readiness to buy; unless the close is initiated by the customer, however, it's more likely to come as a result of a *trial close*, and *that*, in almost every case, should come in Step 5, when you have good reason to believe the customer understands and is committed to the purchase. Any trial close that comes earlier is likely to be premature.

2. *The right way.* A trial close can be effected in four ways: Q1, Q2, Q3, or Q4.

Q1: high-pressure, coercive: "C'mon, now, you don't want to look like a chump, do you? You don't want to be the only guy in the industry who missed out on this offer."

Q2: weak, pessimistic: "I guess you've already got all the inventory you need, huh?"

Q3: offhanded, personalized: "You know I'd never in a million years put pressure on you. Whatever you decide to do is your business, and I'll understand perfectly. So just do what's best for you. Believe me, our friendship won't be affected one way or the other. Just because we're pals doesn't obligate you to anything."

We'll discuss the fourth way—Q4—in the rest of this chapter. Right now, we'll only say that it's most likely to prove effective because (a) it comes at the right time, (b) it keeps receptivity high, (c) it's assertive but not bulldozing, (d) it's businesslike, not personal.

CUSTOMER-INITIATED CLOSES

In Chapter 12, we laid out a four-part closing format: (a) summarize the benefit and the net gain, (b) ask for a commitment, (c) manage the customer's response, (d) work out an action plan and conclude the call. When the *customer* initiates the close, however, you can usually dispense with (b) and (c). It's still a good idea, though, to (a) summarize the benefit and the net gain (unless you've done such a good job up to this point that the customer does it for you), and, of course, to (d) work out an action plan and conclude the call.

The customer is most likely to initiate a close (and make a trial close unnecessary) when she thinks she knows all she needs to know about the purchase, and when she feels, "This is really best for me—*this* is the way I ought to go." If she's sure of her understanding and sure of her commitment, she may tell you—spontaneously—that she's ready to buy. But don't depend on it. Many customers who are sure of their understanding and commitment still wait for the *salesperson* to initiate the close.

SALESPERSON-INITIATED CLOSES

We said in Chapter 12 that a Q4 close can be initiated in one of two ways. Or, in the language of our present chapter, there are two kinds of Q4 trial closes: forced choice and direct request. Let's take a close look at each.

- **Forced-choice trials.** Obviously, you can use this technique only when there *is* a choice. If what you've presented comes in just *one* version, a forced-choice trial won't work. But, where there is a choice of model or style or color or size or packaging or whatever, the technique can be very useful:

    "Which plan . . . the quarterly payment with straight interest or the annual payment with compound interest . . . meets your needs best?"

The significant thing about forced-choice trials is that they don't make the customer feel *pushed*. If you're dealing with someone who's been Q2ing or Q3ing it throughout the presentation, and don't want her to feel "crowded" or "pressured," a forced-choice trial is your best bet.

- **Direct-response trials.** Most direct-response trials consist of a summary statement followed by a probe, usually closed-end:

    > "Okay, Donna, you've said you must bring rejects down by the end of October. I've shown you that . . . (statement of benefit and net gain). Shall we go ahead and install the system?"

Interestingly, many salespeople find it easier to use forced-choice trials than direct-response trials. That's because the latter is the epitome of Q4 assertiveness. It *asks for the order* in the most direct way.

As we said in Chapter 12, whether you use the forced-choice or the direct-response technique, you'll get (a) a firm yes, (b) a qualified yes, (c) an objection, or (d) a flat no. If you get any of the last three responses, acknowledge it, probe it, manage it, get your answer confirmed, and then try to close again. Do this even with a flat no. A surprisingly large number of flat nos aren't really as "flat" as they sound. For example:

SALESPERSON: Shall we go ahead and install the system?

CUSTOMER: No. We'd better not.

SALESPERSON: Would you tell me why?

CUSTOMER: Because of budget. I do have to bring rejects down by the end of October, but your system's going to put me over budget. It's a good plan, but I just can't afford it.

SALESPERSON: I see. How far over budget would the system put you?

CUSTOMER: About $750. I just don't have that much in this year's budget.

SALESPERSON: When does your budget year end?

CUSTOMER: June 30.

SALESPERSON: What if I were to get billing deferred by one month? That would throw $750 into next year's budget . . . and keep you within budget for this year.

CUSTOMER: That'd be fine. Can you do it?

SALESPERSON: I can sure try. May I use your phone? I want to call the office now. If they approve the deferred billing, we can write up the order now. Okay?

CUSTOMER: Okay.

Obviously, it's not always as easy as that. Nevertheless, our example underscores an important point: flat nos *can*, sometimes, be converted to *yeses*. Don't call it quits without trying.

That last bit of advice may strike some readers as impertinent. After all, if a customer says *no*, shouldn't her decision be respected? Shouldn't the salesperson accept it at face value? The answer to the first question is yes: the decision should be respected. But the answer to the second question is no: it should not be accepted at face value—because, as we've just seen, it may not be a *final* decision.

There's an old adage, popular among salespeople, that "the sale just begins when the customer says no." That's an exaggeration, of course, but it does make an important point: the sale's not necessarily *over* when the customer says no. There are two reasons why this is so: (1) the *no*—as in our example—may not be as final as it sounds, and (2) the customer—in spite of having said no—may actually be *expecting* you to dig in and try to change the no to yes. This isn't always true, of course, but in a surprising number of cases the customer, knowing that it's your job to persuade her, will actually respect a show of tenacity and persistence on your part. The fact is that most people like dealing with salespeople who demonstrate Q4 assertiveness.

A Reminder

We've been talking as if every close should produce a sale. Of course, that isn't so. Many calls aren't made to produce sales; they're made to achieve goals that will lead to sales on later calls. So, in thinking about closing, it's worth remembering three things:

- Every Q4 call has a specific purpose. It may be to set up a presentation, or to handle a complaint, or to follow up a sale, or any of dozens of things. But there's no such thing as a pointless *Q4* call.

- Whatever the purpose, the call should end with a *close*. That is, you should "nail down" whatever you came to do by making sure the customer understands, is committed, and is willing to proceed.

- The closing techniques we've described can be used to close *any* call for *any* purpose.

15

The Q4 Strategies

Back in Chapter 7, when discussing net gain, we made a point so important it deserves to be repeated:

> "In a great many cases, the ultimate net gain—the thing that finally makes one option preferable to the others—is *you*, the salesperson. . . . It's often very difficult to determine which option will, on balance, prove best for the customer; weighing benefits against one another sometimes leads to inconclusive results. In such cases, *you yourself* can be the factor that tips the balance in your favor. That's because, all else being equal, customers are likely to buy from the salesperson who's *most responsive to their needs.*"

In this chapter, we'll explain how you can make yourself the ultimate net gain—how you can prove so responsive to the customer's needs that he considers *you* the benefit that makes the difference. We'll do it by discussing *the Q4 strategies.*

WHAT IS A Q4 STRATEGY?

A Q4 *strategy* is an overall plan for achieving the objectives of a particular sales call. The Q4 *skills* we've described can be thought of as

190

tactics — specific techniques to be used at specific points during the call. A Q4 strategy weaves these tactics into an overall pattern designed for the customer you're actually *dealing* with. It's a configuration of skills individualized for *this* customer on *this* call. Thus, no two Q4 strategies are ever identical. There are basic Q4 strategies for Q1, Q2, Q3, or Q4 customer behavior, but each of these basic strategies is always modified on different calls. If you make five straight calls on customers who Q1 it, you'll want to use the Q4 strategy for Q1 customer behavior, but you'll have to modify it — at least slightly — on each call. Q4 selling is never done by rote; it's always adapted to the needs of *individual* customers.

To clarify this, let's look again at the three pathways to the sale.

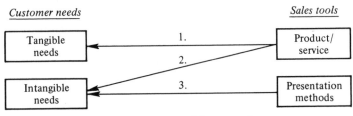

What happens in a Q4 presentation.

As the diagram shows:

- Every qualified prospect has two kinds of needs: tangible and intangible.
- The tangible needs can be filled by your product or service (Pathway 1).
- The intangible needs can be filled by both your product or service (Pathway 2) and your presentation methods (Pathway 3).

The last point is crucial to this chapter. You can fill a customer's intangible needs by both your product or service (Pathway 2) and your presentation methods (Pathway 3) *if* the presentation methods are *right* — that is, if they're *organized* to respond to the needs of this customer on this call. That organization is what we call a *Q4 strategy*. A Q4 strategy is a *structured* plan with one major purpose: to satisfy the customer's intangible needs.

The ability to devise and carry out a Q4 strategy is what enables *you* to become the net gain — the factor that convinces the customer that "I'll be better off buying from *this* salesperson than from anyone else."

PATHWAY 3: SOMETHING SPECIAL

Of the three pathways by which customer needs can be filled, there's something *special* about Pathway 3: it's the only one *completely* under *your* control. That's because Pathways 1 and 2 involve your product or service, and there are a number of things about your product or service you cannot control. For example, if your product's priced higher than your competitor's, or if shipments of your product originate 1,000 miles away, while your competitor ships from a warehouse on the other side of town, or if your company's received some bad publicity about one of its products, you can't do much to change the situation. With few exceptions, you can't affect *what* you sell; control is by and large out of your hands. But you *can* affect *how* you sell; control is *fully* in your hands.

Think about it. Whether or not you spin up receptivity, whether or not you probe, how thoroughly you probe, whether or not you uncover the customer's needs before presenting benefits, the way you handle objections, the skill with which you tailor your presentation to *this* customer—all of this and much more is *up to you.* What happens in Pathways 1 and 2 may be largely determined—or at least influenced—by the home office, the factory, the credit department, the billing department, the shipping department, and so on. But what happens in Pathway 3 is determined by *you*—on the spot. That's why this chapter, which explains how to make Pathway 3 work for you, is so important.

THE Q4 STRATEGIES: AN OVERVIEW

Figure 26 deserves careful reading. It'll acquaint you with each strategy and let you compare them. Note that the strategies stick to the Five-Step Format. Each strategy follows its own general guidelines. A discussion of these guidelines follows.

The Q4 Strategy for Q1 Customer Behavior

GENERAL GUIDELINES

Q1 behavior is generally motivated by strong needs for *esteem* and *independence.* To deal with them, keep these guidelines in mind:

1. Stress benefits that provide *status, importance, prestige, autonomy, control, freedom of action.*

2. Expect anger, belligerence, sarcasm, put-downs, deep-seated skepticism, objection-hopping, flat assertions, impatience, dogmatism.

3. Vent the anger; probe the flat assertions.

4. Stay cool; don't get riled; don't let the customer think he's "getting" to you.

5. Show conviction and strength, *without* sounding pigheaded, cocky, argumentative, or aggressive.

6. Don't argue; probe first, then reason.

7. Rely mainly on open-end probes, summary and reflective statements. Use few or no leading questions.

8. Make sure the customer doesn't lose face.

9. Let the customer take credit for good ideas—even if they're yours.

10. Be ready to shift your strategy if the customer's behavior changes.

Let's take a closer look at these guidelines:

1. Stress benefits that provide status, importance, prestige, autonomy, control, freedom of action. This is fundamental. This customer wants to "look good," "be somebody," "make an impression," "be his own person." If you can, make it plain that your product or service can gratify these needs. More than that, gratify them *yourself*—during the sales call.

Listen with respect. Be interested in his opinions. Seek his advice. Let him boast. If he says something that impresses you, say so. If necessary, bring in high-status people from your own company to meet with him. Above all, be *respectful. Don't* be too familiar or informal—unless you know the customer well and are very sure of what you're doing. *Don't* "kid" the customer—unless, once again, you're very sure of your ground.

2. Expect anger, belligerence, sarcasm, put-downs, deep-seated skepticism, objection-hopping, flat assertions, impatience, dogmatism. This is what Q1 behavior is all about. It's the customer's way of saying "I don't need you" (manifestation of independence need) or "I'm smarter than you" (manifestation of esteem need). If you understand Q1, none of this should surprise you. *Anticipate* it—and be *prepared* for it.

Figure 26. Q4 Strategies For:

Steps to the Sale	Q1 Customer Behavior	Q2 Customer Behavior	Q3 Customer Behavior	Q4 Customer Behavior
1. Open the call	• Set brisk but cordial tone; hold down small talk • Aim benefits at *esteem* and *independence* needs • Expect open resistance	• Set friendly, relaxed tone, but don't Q3 it • Aim benefits at *security* needs • Expect silence, indifference	• Set amiable tone, but don't Q3 it • Aim benefits at *social* needs • Expect meandering and easy yeses	• Set businesslike, helpful tone • Aim benefits at needs for *new* and *better* • Expect high receptivity
2. Explore customer needs	• Expect negative flat assertions • Vent negative emotions (*putdowns, belligerence*) • Use open-end probes; listen carefully; summarize • Do process check	• Expect short, unhelpful answers • Vent negative emotions (*tension, reluctance*) • Listen patiently; use pauses • Use many open-end probes • Do process check	• Expect rambling, positive answers • Vent positive emotions (*optimism, exuberance*) • Control rambling with closed probes • Do process check	• Expect helpful, relevant answers • Use full range of probes, especially open-end, neutral, summary, reflective
3. Present product or service	• Voice strong convictions; no flat assertions • Stress *esteem* and *independence* benefits • Support proof with plenty of organized data; get feedback	• Moderate your pace; pause frequently • Stress *security* benefits • Be factual, but don't machine-gun facts; invite frequent feedback	• Relax pace; allow occasional meandering • Stress *social* benefits • Don't overburden with details • Probe easy yeses	• Voice strong convictions; no flat assertions • Stress *new* and *better* benefits • Be factual; invite feedback

4. Manage objections			
• Encourage customer to sum up objections	• Probe carefully; don't assume silence means approval	• Probe carefully; easy yeses may hide strong objections	• Ask customer to sum up objections
• Vent resistance with reflective statements; no leading questions	• Go easy on closed-end and leading questions	• Go easy on open-end probes and pauses	• Rely mainly on open-end probes and summaries
• Don't expect full agreement	• Don't expect much enthusiasm	• Don't expect full candor	• Expect candor, and, if you do the job, agreement
5. Close the call			
• Encourage customer to sum up benefits	• Be prepared to sum up benefits yourself	• Take the lead in summarizing benefits	• Encourage customer to sum up benefits
• Expect qualified yes, objection, or flat no	• Expect qualified yes or objection	• Expect firm yes, qualified yes, or objection	• Expect firm yes or no backed up by solid reason
• Let customer take lead in working out action plan	• Lead customer in working out action plan	• Lead customer in working out action plan	• Jointly work out action plan

3. Vent the anger: probe the flat assertions. To handle the anger, use reflective statements: "You're really concerned," "I can tell you're bothered," "You don't sound happy with it." If you haven't had much experience using reflective statements, you may feel awkward at first. Don't let that stop you. Once you feel comfortable with them—and you soon will—you'll find them indispensable in Q1 situations.

As far as the flat assertions go, don't ignore them. Remember, many flat assertions contain a *nugget* of truth, and you want to get at the nugget because it could be very important. So probe until you've stripped away the exaggeration and distortion, and found out what's *really* bothering the customer.

4. Stay cool; don't get riled; don't let the customer think he's "getting" to you. This is vital. If he gets the idea he's got you off-balance, he may push his "advantage" (as he sees it) and become even harder to handle. And that'll probably upset *you* even more. Once you paint yourself into this corner, you may have real trouble getting out. The best advice is: *don't get rattled in the first place* — or, if you do, don't let it show. That's easier to say than do, but if you approach the call *realistically*, you should be able to manage it. A realistic approach is one in which you *expect* a "hard time." If you're mentally prepared for this, you should be able to withstand it. Nothing will "tame" a growling customer faster than the realization that he can't irritate you.

5. Show conviction and strength, without sounding pigheaded, cocky, argumentative, or aggressive. To convey strength (which this customer admires), you must convince him that you *know* and *believe in* whatever you're saying. So present your proof of benefits with vigor, assurance, and conviction. But don't go so far as to make flat assertions ("This is the greatest product ever developed," "This will spark a complete revolution in the marketplace"). You'll only arouse disbelief ("Who are you trying to kid? I wasn't born yesterday"). This customer will *respect* you for your conviction and assurance—as long as he doesn't think you're trying to "con" him.

6. Don't argue; probe first, then reason. If the customer contradicts you, offers an objection, or tries to "pick a fight," do two things: probe (to raise receptivity and find out what the resistance is all about), then reason—employ data and logic to make your point. If you probe skillfully enough, you may get the customer to make your point *for* you, which of course, will strengthen your case while bolstering his self-esteem. But—whether he makes the point for you or you make it yourself—*don't argue.* After all, this is the *customer* you're dealing with, and the customer always has the last word. If he's bound and determined *not* to let you win the argument, there's nothing you can do about it. And *this* customer, with his strong needs for esteem and independence, isn't about to let you win. Why knock your head against a brick wall when you can accomplish so much more by probing, then reasoning?

7. **Rely mainly on open-end probes, summary and reflective statements. Use few or no leading questions.** The value of open-end probes is that they tell the customer: "I really do want to hear your views." They make him feel respected and independent. The value of summary and reflective statements is that they tell the customer: "I've been paying close attention—I understand what you're saying." They, too, make him feel respected. The *danger* of leading questions is that they tell the customer; "I have no qualms about putting words in your mouth." They make him feel diminished and dependent. We're not advising that you *never* use leading question with Q1 behavior, only that you use them sparingly and cautiously.

8. **Make sure the customer doesn't lose face.** This is implicit in everything we've said. What might cause this customer to lose face—to feel embarrassed or humiliated? For one thing, going over his head without first telling him. Or making calls without first seeking an appointment. Or failing to send him copies of all correspondence to his company about the sale. Or depreciating one of his achievements ("That's not such a big deal"). Or failing to keep your word. Or forgetting an appointment. And so on. The thing to guard against is the *careless* affront—the *unintentional* insult. Very few salespeople deliberately discomfit customers, but many do so unwittingly. Be careful; with *this* customer, a heedless "slip" could be disastrous.

9. **Let the customer take credit for good ideas—even if they're yours.** After all, you don't really care who gets credit for an idea—as long as *you* get credit for the *sale.* So, if the customer "appropriates" one of your suggestions, fine. Let him. If he insists *he* said something that you know full well *you* said, let it go. And, by all means, if he *does* come up with an idea that's useful, clever, innovative, give him full credit. Never hesitate to pay this customer a deserved compliment.

10. **Be ready to shift your strategy if the customer's behavior shifts.** Once you've sized up the customer's behavior as Q1, don't get *locked into* your diagnosis. Be alert to *changes* in the behavior—

and modify or change your strategy accordingly. After all, the customer's human, which means he's changeable. If his behavior changes, while yours stays in a rut, you may lose control of the call. Stay flexible.

The Q4 Strategy for Q2 Customer Behavior

GENERAL GUIDELINES

Q2 behavior is mostly motivated by strong needs for *security*. To deal with them, keep these guidelines in mind:

1. Stress benefits that provide *stability, low risk, assured outcome, proven value, permanence, durability.*
2. Be patient; slow your pace. Don't rush yourself or the customer. Don't pressure.
3. Show genuine concern; let the customer know you're not there just to advance your own interests.
4. Expect the customer to be remote, uncommunicative, hard-to-read, distrustful, apprehensive.
5. Establish trust. *Use* the trust-building guidelines we've described.
6. Guide firmly but gently. This customer won't take the initiative, so you'll have to. But do it in a low-key, unhurried way.
7. Let the customer keep his self-respect. Don't mock or tease. Don't push.
8. Rely mainly on open-end probes, pauses, brief assertions; go easy on leading and closed-end questions.
9. Be ready to shift your strategy if the customer's behavior changes.

Let's examine each guideline:

1. Stress benefits that provide stability, low risk, assured outcome, proven value, permanence, durability. Tie your proof statements to the customer's desire for assurance ("This program's been used successfully for twenty years") and stability ("Our company's been making these units longer than anyone in the field"). *Don't* stress new or innovative features, *don't* expect the customer to become a "trailblazer" or "pioneer." Make your whole *manner* convey reliability: sound confident but not bombastic, knowledgeable but not pretentious, friendly but not too familiar, helpful but not over-solicitous. Cordial, reassuring, low-key behavior should do it.

In describing benefits, use any sales aids that'll *reassure* the customer: testimonials, references, case studies, independent laboratory reports, surveys, and so on. The best way to prove that your product or service *will* be reliable is to show that it *has* been reliable. Let the customer know that your proposal isn't new or farfetched or untried, but that it's worked *before* for *other* people.

2. Be patient; slow your pace. Don't rush yourself or the customer. Don't pressure. The *tempo* of the presentation is crucial. If you move too fast or throw too much at the customer, he'll feel pressured—and his initial distrust will intensify. Take it easy. Don't "come on strong." Lower your voice. Slow your delivery. Pause often to let him absorb your ideas. Check periodically for his reaction.

Remember: beneath his Q2 behavior this customer probably carries a stereotype of "the salesperson" as a "high-pressure pitchman"; if you push the customer—or even *seem* to—you'll only *confirm* the stereotype. "See," he'll tell himself, "I knew it all along. These salespeople are all alike—they're out to take advantage of you." You want to *extricate* yourself from the stereotype by proving that whatever he may think of "salespeople," you're *different*. To do it, you must adjust the pace of the presentation to *his* needs.

3. Show genuine concern; let the customer know you're not there just to advance your own interests. You can do this by paying close attention to *his* concerns. But this obviously presents a problem, because *this* customer doesn't talk much about his concerns. If anything, Q2 is very *private* behavior; the customer holds back, keeps things to himself. How, then, can you pay attention to his concerns if he doesn't talk about them? Only by getting him to *open up*. And that requires patient, persistent *probing*. If you don't probe tenaciously, follow one probe with another and then another, and give him plenty of time to respond, you're not likely to uncover his concerns, and you won't be able to show your *own* concern. Selling to this customer takes perseverance. It also takes forbearance—the ability to *restrain* yourself, to endure frustration, and to stay cool no matter how tightlipped and uncooperative the customer may be. It isn't easy, but it *can* pay off.

4. Expect the customer to be remote, uncommunicative, hard-to-read, distrustful, apprehensive. You'll find it much easier to be patient and persistent if you *anticipate* the problems we've described.

If you've talked with the customer before, and his earlier behavior has been mostly Q2, you can reasonably assume it'll be mostly Q2 again (that's a likelihood, not a guarantee). So, go *into* the call telling yourself: "This probably won't be fun—but it will be a challenge. I can expect the customer to keep his distance, to make me work for every scrap of information I get, and to maintain a chilly atmosphere. I'd better suppress any feelings of annoyance, and I'd better not push. I don't want to give him the idea I'm squeezing him."

5. Establish trust. Use the trust-building guidelines we've described. All the guidelines (Chapter 10) will help, but the one that may be most important in this case—and most difficult—is: *maintain two-way involvement.* Resisting involvement is, of course, what Q2 is all about. But, unless you draw the customer into the presentation, and make him feel it's "our" discussion, not just "yours," you probably won't build much trust. And that means you won't stand much chance of making the sale.

To maintain two-way involvement, *probe* diligently and persistently, and *listen* patiently. This may prove harder than it sounds, because your impulse may be to stop probing and start *telling* ("This is moving too slowly for my taste; I think I'll skip Step 2 and simply guess at what this customer needs"). If you give in to the impulse, you'll make a mistake. Don't do it. Keep on probing. Don't fidget, don't rush the customer, don't put words in his mouth or finish his sentences for him. *Pause* after each probe. Give him time to tell his story his way. That's the only way you can find out what *his* story is.

6. Guide firmly but gently. This customer won't take the initiative, so you'll have to. But do it in a low-key, unhurried way. Beneath most Q2 behavior is a desire for *guidance.* The customer's really saying, "Look, I don't like making up my mind without help from someone else. I prefer to share that burden with someone who's knowledgeable, competent, and reliable. If you can convince me *you're* knowledgeable, competent, and reliable, then I'll be willing to follow your lead. That way, I'll feel more secure about my purchase than if I made it entirely on my own." In other words, it's a safe assumption that this customer *wants* to lean on you—if he's convinced you're sturdy enough to support him. So, once you've established trust, *take the lead.* Guide the customer (but always remember, *don't push*). Get him to seek your advice; then give it. Manifest unobtrusive *strength.*

7. **Let the customer keep his self-respect. Don't mock or tease. Don't push.** It's easy to belittle Q2 behavior, and usually very costly. The customer may strike you as weak, meek, and indecisive, but he certainly doesn't want to be *told* about it. Seemingly innocent remarks, like "You certainly don't seem very sure of yourself," can easily sound insulting. Intentional barbs, like "What's the matter? Afraid to make up your mind?", will almost surely sound insulting. Be careful. If the customer thinks you're humiliating him (even if that's not your intention), he'll probably *get back* at you by refusing to buy.

For the same reason, pushing or pressuring the customer can be dangerous. He's likely to think: "This salesperson must take me for a weakling—a pushover. That's why he's shoving so hard. Well ... *I'll show him.* He can shove from now till doomsday, but he's not going to sell me *anything.* He'll see how wrong he was to underestimate me." Paradoxically, customers who don't seem very strong (and don't even consider *themselves* very strong), can behave with remarkable strength when their pride is at stake. In the last analysis, a customer who Q2s it may be no more willing to lose face than a customer who Q1s it.

8. **Rely mainly on open-end probes, pauses, brief assertions; go easy on leading and closed-end questions.** Your toughest challenge is to get this customer to *open up.* To do it, you'll have to use open-end probes, followed by pauses (remember: he may be slow to respond). Once he has opened up, use brief assertions (and neutral probes) to keep him talking. Since he'll probably convey information in dribs and drabs, you'll almost surely have to use *a lot* of these probes; one or two won't do. But go easy on closed-end and leading questions. After all, you can't get a customer to open up with closed probes. And you can't build trust with leading questions ("This salesperson's trying to back me into a corner; I don't like that").

9. **Be ready to shift your strategy if the customer's behavior changes.** Once this customer's convinced you can be trusted, he may surprise you. He may relax somewhat, talk more, volunteer information. There's no assurance of this, but it *could* happen. Whatever direction his behavior veers in, be prepared to modify your strategy accordingly.

The Q4 Strategy for Q3 Customer Behavior

GENERAL GUIDELINES

Q3 behavior is mostly motivated by strong *social* needs (joined to fairly strong *security* and *esteem* needs). To deal with them, keep these guidelines in mind:

1. Stress benefits that provide *acceptance, popularity*, a chance to *do something for other people* and come across as a *"good guy."*
2. Be outgoing and friendly but don't get sucked into the Q3 whirlpool, or the whole presentation may drown in a sea of irrelevance.
3. Keep the focus on business, but loosen up enough to allow *some* rambling.
4. Personalize the call; remember the customer's strong interest in people.
5. Guide the customer firmly; make specific suggestions.
6. Don't take his enthusiasm at face value; easy yeses often cover up serious doubts. Suggest he has doubts. Probe.
7. Rely heavily on closed-end probes, summary, and reflective statements. Go easy on open-end probes and pauses.
8. Be ready to shift your strategy if the customer's behavior changes.

Let's look at these guidelines in detail:

1. Stress benefits that provide acceptance, popularity, a chance to do something for other people and come across as a "good guy." This customer wants to be "well liked," a "thoughtful, considerate person" who's "accepted" and "well thought of." Arouse his interest by appealing to these needs. Tie your proof statements to his social needs (and, to a lesser extent, his security and esteem needs): "This program should set well with your people," "This plan's proven popular everywhere it's been tried," "This is a fine opportunity to boost the morale of your employees."

More than that, *be* accepting. Personal relationships are critically important to this customer, so make a particular effort to build rapport.

2. **Be outgoing and friendly but don't get sucked into the Q3 whirlpool, or the whole presentation may drown in a sea of irrelevance.** This can easily happen, so be on your guard. In "building rapport," you may find yourself being lured into subjects that have nothing to do with why you're there, and that you didn't intend to talk about. Once that happens, you may find it difficult to get out of the vortex without "hurting" the customer's feelings. The best thing, obviously, is not to get sucked in in the first place. Be genial, but *not* unbusinesslike.

This may not be easy. In fact, a certain amount of rambling may be unavoidable. This customer's hard to pin down, hard to confine to one subject, and sometimes hard to follow. He's also ready to give instant approval ("Sounds great," "Terrific idea," "That's swell"). Don't let meandering entice you into the whirlpool, or the easy yeses fool you. Deal with both by probing.

What if the presentation does start drowning in an ocean of trivia? Throw out a life-jacket in the form of a *process check*: "Jack, I get the feeling we're heading in four or five different directions, and we're going to find ourselves lost. What do you think we can do to find our way out?"

3. **Keep the focus on business, but loosen up enough to allow some meandering.** Control what's said, but don't control too tightly. If you do, you'll make the customer fidgety—and distracted. If that happens, his receptivity will plunge. So permit a bit of meandering here and there. But only a bit.

The problem is, this customer's longwinded, rambling conversation takes a lot of time but doesn't usually *tell* you very much. Once you've opened up the subject of needs, for example, you'll probably get a whole series of verbose, time-consuming responses, but not much *useful* information. Moreover, the information's apt to be *slanted*, emphasizing positives and ignoring negatives. The customer's especially likely to ignore or downplay any needs caused by *you* or *your company*. So you'll have to do some hard digging to get the whole story.

4. **Personalize the call; remember the customer's strong interest in people.** You'll probably find that this customer is bored by abstractions, technical details, statistics—anything, in fact, *im*personal. To capture and hold his attention, try, when possible, to *personalize* and *humanize* the presentation. Talk about people: their experiences with your product and their reactions to it. Mention *names* that you know are important to the customer. Ask about his family and friends.

In all of this, be careful *not* to downgrade anyone. If you can't say something positive (or at least neutral) about a person, don't mention him at all. You'll make this customer uncomfortable just by *talking* negatively about others.

5. Guide the customer firmly; make specific suggestions. We said before that customers with strong Q2 needs *want* guidance (provided they trust you). The same is true of the typical customer with strong Q3 needs; he, too, wants guidance (and is usually quite ready to trust you). What this customer needs, and appreciates, is guidance on matters of *detail.* His own style is loose and disorganized, so he'll look to you for *structure* and *organization.* Provide it, not by *telling* him what to do, but by *suggesting* it: "Carl, it seems to me, in view of everything we've talked about, that you'll be better off with the Model 270 instead of the 310." As a rule, it's *not* a good idea, when closing, to give this customer options. A forced-choice close, like "Which will it be, Jane, the portable or the permanently-installed model?", may produce a stream of unnecessary conversation. A *guided* close, like "Jane, I think the portable model's best for you; do *you* agree?", should prove more efficient.

6. Don't take his enthusiasm at face value; easy yeses often cover up serious doubts. Suggest he has doubts. Probe. Instant agreement is common Q3 behavior. The trouble is, you can never be sure it's genuine. This customer can say "Terrific" after every sentence you utter, and yet *not* accept a thing you've said. His automatic yeses may be intended not to *reveal* his thoughts but *disguise* them. As you talk, he may be thinking, "This salesperson's a nice guy, and I wouldn't hurt his feelings for the world. Besides, what's to be gained by telling him I think his proposal won't work?" And so, while you present idea after idea that "won't work," he keeps responding, "Terrific, terrific, terrific."

To find out what the customer *really* thinks, do two things: (a) suggest he's not as enthusiastic as he sounds, and (b) probe to find out: "Roger, it's gratifying to hear so much enthusiasm. But usually . . . when people hear this proposal for the first time . . . they've got some serious reservations. After all, it is a pretty unusual approach. How about you? What are your doubts?" It may take several such probes before he admits he's not as enthusiastic as he sounds.

Obviously, if you *don't* test his easy yeses, you may get a rude shock when you try to close. Instead of the "easy" close that would seem to follow naturally from all the easy yeses, you may hear something like this: "I'll tell you, the whole idea's great. Really great. I sure wish we could afford it. It's a darned shame our budget's been cut so drastically. Otherwise, believe me, I'd buy it in a minute. But, as it is . . ."

7. Rely heavily on closed-end probes, summary and reflective statements. Go easy on open-end probes and pauses. If you give this customer a chance to talk at length, he'll take it. So *control* the opportunities; *channel* the talk (closed-end probes), separate the wheat from the chaff (summary statements), and vent interfering positive emotions (reflective statements).

8. Be ready to shift your strategy if the customer's behavior changes. There's no guarantee that nice, easygoing people will stay that way. Even Q3 behavior can change. If it does, be prepared to change with it.

The Q4 Strategy for Q4 Customer Behavior

GENERAL GUIDELINES

Q4 behavior is generally motivated by strong *self-realization* and *independence* needs. To deal with them, keep these guidelines in mind:

1. Stress benefits that provide something *new, creative, innovative, pacesetting, experimental,* or *unusual.*

2. Be pragmatic; tie your product or service to the customer's goals, and prove that it will further their achievement.

3. Be direct and businesslike. Assert authority but *don't* make flat assertions.

4. Expect the customer to be fully involved. Give him every chance.

5. Use whatever probes are called for, but rely on open-end probes and summaries.

6. Keep the customer in a Q4 posture; be careful not to push him into Q1, Q2, or Q3 behavior.

7. Be ready to shift your strategy if the customer's behavior changes.

Let's look at these guidelines in detail:

1. Stress benefits that provide something new, creative, innovative, pacesetting, experimental, or unusual. This customer is receptive to novelty, but not for the sake of novelty. If your proposal is really "different," he'll listen—if he thinks it might *pay off.* It's the payoff—not the novelty as such—that interests him. He's looking for *better* ways to achieve his goals (precisely what he *means* by "better"—more efficient, more economical, etc.—is something you must determine when exploring his needs). If he thinks he can find those better ways by buying something new or untried, he's likely to do it. But he's not about to do anything rash or foolish; he's not about to buy a harebrained scheme just because it's "different." He will take risks, but they'll be *calculated*, with the odds in *his* favor. It's up to you to prove that the odds *are* in his favor.

2. Be pragmatic; tie your product or service to the customer's goals, and prove that it will further their achievement. We're saying that this customer is individualistic *and* practical. He's willing to be unconventional, but only if he stands to *get something* out of it. That's why Q4 customer behavior is *not* easy to deal with. It's demanding and challenging. The customer insists on knowing "What's in it for me." He wants hard proof. He demands high competence on your part. Don't make the mistake of thinking he's a pushover. He's anything but.

We stress this point because many salespeople wrongly assume that Q4 customer behavior poses few or no problems. After all, they wonder, how could anyone have trouble with customers who are reasonable, logical, and willing to listen? But that's the point: such customers can be very hard to deal with *because* they're reasonable, logical, and willing to listen. "Reasonable" means "making decisions on the basis of explanations and justifications." *That* means this customer won't settle for unsupported claims or flimsy generalities; he wants solid reasons—clear-cut explanations—that will justify a decision to buy. "Logical" means "basing decisions on systematic thinking." *That* means this customer won't have much patience with a disorganized or confused presentation; he wants everything laid out a-b-c. "Willing to listen" means "willing to pay attention to something instructive and useful." *That* means this customer isn't interested in wasting time; he expects to *learn something useful* from the presentation. All this adds up to one fact: *this* is a tough customer.

We can go even further: this customer's not only tough, he's *probing.* He's very likely to ask *you* searching questions, to challenge *you* for documentation and comparisons, to prod *you* for details and insights. He's no shrinking violet.

What's the best way to deal with this tough, probing customer? *Pragmatically.* Focus on *results*—on the goals *he* hopes to achieve. Prove that with your product or service, he can reach, or come close to, those goals. Always remember: the question he most wants answered is "So what?". If you tell him, "This is the most innovative idea in a quarter-century," his response (which may or may not be spoken out loud) will be "So what? What does that mean to *me?* Why should *I* care?" So be pragmatic; always tie into *his* goals; give him *practical* reasons to buy. (This advice, of course, applies to *any* customer. But it's especially crucial when the customer's behavior is *Q4*. *Emotional* reasons to buy will carry less weight with this customer than *practical* reasons.)

3. Be direct and businesslike. Assert authority but don't make flat assertions. This customer admires strength. He'll respect you for coming across as someone with convictions who knows his own mind and is willing to stand up and be counted. So assert *authority*; let your technical expertise and your problem-solving ability *show.* But don't go so far as to make flat assertions. Remember, he likes to have things explained and justified. If you say, "No other product in the world can do this," you'd better be prepared to justify that statement. If you can't, if it remains a flat assertion and nothing more, he'll probably dismiss it as exaggeration—and think less of you for exaggerating.

4. Expect the customer to be fully involved. Give him every chance. There's nothing withdrawn or passive about Q4 behavior. This customer *will* listen, but he'll also insist on speaking out. He'll ask questions, comment, disagree if it seems called for. *Encourage this.* If you don't, you may stifle his need for independence, and thereby lower his receptivity.

5. Use whatever probes are called for, but rely on open-end probes and summaries. To encourage involvement, and to keep from "crowding" the customer, make heavy use of open-end probes. To let him know he's getting through, and to check your own understanding, rely on summary statements. But don't overlook the other probes. With this customer, they're *all* likely to prove useful.

6. Keep the customer in a Q4 posture; be careful not to push him into Q1, Q2, or Q3 behavior. It's nice to think this customer will *remain* reasonable, logical, and attentive. But it's not necessarily true. His behavior may change, especially if you provoke the change. A snide or belligerent remark could push him toward Q1 ("I'm not going to let this salesperson come in here and get away with that"); unnecessarily "personal" probing could push him toward Q2 ("I'm darned if I'll answer his questions; that's none of his business"); and too casual a manner could push him toward Q3 ("If he thinks *his* story was funny, wait till he hears *mine*"). One of the most difficult things to do with Q4 behavior is to *keep* it Q4. Yet that's essential if you're going to conduct an *efficient* call. By and large, a Q4–Q4 sales call *is* the most efficient of all calls – the one that achieves the most with the least amount of extra effort. So, to keep him Q4, *stay Q4 yourself.* Any deviation on your part may trigger a deviation on his.

7. **Be ready to shift your strategy if the customer's behavior changes.** If his behavior veers from Q4, make sure yours veers, too. This doesn't mean, of course, that if his behavior becomes Q3, yours should also. It means that if his behavior becomes Q3, you should shift to the *Q4* strategy for *Q3* behavior. The ideal is to keep your behavior Q4 *throughout* the call, adapting it as necessary.

A reminder

Because first-person statements and process checks don't "come naturally" to most of us, it might be a good idea to insert a reminder here: Don't forget to use them no matter which strategy you're employing. They're two of the most helpful communication techniques described in this book.

Both techniques were explained in Chapter 11. A recap of what we said there may be useful:

- *First-person statements* say, in effect, that the speaker is implicated in a problem along with the listener. Thus, they enable a salesperson to deal with a problem involving a customer without attributing the problem *to* the customer.

    Joe, I'm worried about the fact we've had trouble arranging delivery on those last three shipments. It's meant extra cost for your receiving department and for our shipping department. What can we do about it?

    Karen, maybe I got things wrong, because that's not the instruction I gave the factory. That's why you received a duplicate shipment. What do you think we might do to prevent that from happening again?

First-person statements imply: "Something that concerns both of us troubles *me*; *I'm* involved in it along with you." They don't blame or belittle; they merely acknowledge the problem, let the customer know you're "both in it together," and look for a solution. They can be a very useful part of *any* Q4 strategy.

- *Process checks* are first-person statements for dealing with *interactional difficulties.* They describe whatever's happening to impede the interaction, and ask the customer's help in removing the impediment.

Mr. Kelly, we seem to be stuck on this one point. What do you think we ought to do to move beyond it and start considering all the factors together?

Bea, tell me what I might've done to make you insist that you won't answer any questions.

Process checks say, in effect: "The process — the way we're interacting — isn't working. Let's see what we can do about it." They implicate both people — salesperson and customer — and they seek a solution *without* assigning blame. They too can be very useful in *any* Q4 strategy.

AN EXAMPLE

If you'd like to see how one of the Q4 strategies might actually work, you can do so in Appendix A. There you'll find the "transcript" of a fictitious call in which the salesperson's behavior is Q4, the customer's mainly Q1. Because we've labeled all the elements of the call, you'll see how a Q4 strategy brings together all the skills described in this book in a single presentation.

16

Four Ways of Managing Salespeople

If you're a sales manager, you've probably read the earlier chapters with one big question in mind: "How can I *use* all this to help my salespeople?" For the most part, the answer's been self-evident: "If any of my people don't know how to size up a customer's behavior (or spin up receptivity or probe or develop benefit statements or whatever), I can take the pertinent material in this book and teach it to them." *But*—and this is implicit in everything we've said so far— how *well* you can teach any skill to your salespeople depends in large part on how you *interact* with them. If a *sales call* that's mainly Q1–Q1 is almost sure to generate more heat than light, then a *coaching* session that's mainly Q1–Q1 will probably do the same. If a *salesperson* who glosses over unpleasant topics can't expect to produce much understanding or commitment during a sales presentation, then a *sales manager* who glosses over unpleasant topics can't expect to produce much understanding or commitment during a counseling session. And so on. *Sales manager–salesperson interaction is as crucial to explaining a sales manager's success (or lack of success) as salesperson–customer interaction is to explaining a salesperson's.* So, in this chapter, we'll take a close look at sales manager-salesperson interaction. We'll zero in on the four basic patterns of sales management and their consequences.

Does that mean you should skip this chapter if you're a salesperson? Not by a long shot. Your major concern, after all, is to make more sales. That's why, up to now, we've focused on selling skills. However, you'll probably get more out of these skills if you know how to work *with* your sales manager. If you combine your skills and her know-how, the result should be pretty powerful. This chapter will give you some good ideas on how to do it.

THE DIMENSIONAL MODEL OF SALES MANAGEMENT BEHAVIOR

We described this model briefly in Chapter 3. Figure 27 (next page) is a more detailed version. It focuses on planning, organizing, controlling, and leading because they're usually considered the four "classic" functions of management. We'll examine each pattern of management below.

Q1 (Dominant–Hostile) Sales Management

We'll hear first from a sales manager who's a firm believer in Q1:

> Let's not kid ourselves: most salespeople must be *made* to work hard and smart. Without strong prodding, they'll just hang back and coast. So you need sales managers to *push* them into doing the job they're paid to do.

> Let's face it: a sales manager must use *power* to get compliance. Why disguise the fact? Any manager—by virtue of *being* the superior—has clout, and she's foolish not to use it. I exert power openly and unapologetically. My people understand there's a payoff if they do things my way. And a penalty if they don't.

> There are two things I don't let my people forget. First, there's only one boss—and I'm it. I'm paid to make decisions and call the shots. Second, they're *subordinates.* They're paid to do things my way. It's that simple. As long as everyone keeps that basic distinction in mind, as long as everyone remembers who's who, we'll get along fine. If somebody forgets who's in charge, and steps out of line, she's asking for trouble.

Obviously, this "statement of Q1 principles" is a caricature. But *because* it is, it highlights the features that distinguish Q1 sales management. Let's examine them.

1. Q1 can be called "or-else" sales management. The underlying message to salespeople is, "Do it my way—or else." The idea is to use *power* as a basic managerial tool.

Figure 27

DOMINANCE

Quadrant 1

Planning: Rarely involves salespeople ("Why should I? Planning is my prerogative. I make the plans, they carry them out. That's as it should be.")

Organizing: Tight organization. Patterns of relationship emphasize one-to-one interaction ("I make sure everyone knows what to do and how to do it. I call the shots.")

Controlling: Very close supervision ("Any sales manager who isn't vigilant is asking for trouble. Salespeople must know they're being closely scrutinized.")

Leading: Pushes, demands, drives ("Most people want a strong leader to tell them what to do. My people know who's boss.")

Quadrant 4

Planning: Consults salespeople whenever their thinking might help ("I want the best plans possible. That frequently requires ideas from others. I don't have all the answers.")

Organizing: Patterns of relationship designed to stimulate collaboration and interdependence ("I try to get synergism through pooling of resources.")

Controlling: Tries to develop salespeople who control themselves ("Get people committed to their goals and they'll supervise their own efforts.") Provides more structure for those who can't.

Leading: Tries to make salespeople aware of their potential ("Leadership is helping people do what they have it in them to do. A leader develops people.")

HOSTILITY ———————————————————————— **WARMTH**

Quadrant 2

Planning: Relies heavily on own manager ("I prefer to pass along her plans. That way, my people know they'd better follow through.") Or leans heavily on tradition ("It's worked before, it should work again.")

Organizing: Patterns of relationship vague, indefinite. Doesn't encourage interaction ("Just do your own job, and stay out of trouble.")

Controlling: Sees self mainly as a caretaker ("I'm paid to keep things stable. I exert enough control to make sure nobody disrupts routines. There's no point in doing more.")

Leading: Passive, indifferent. Downplays own influence ("Don't kid yourself. No matter how hard you try to lead people, they'll end up doing pretty much as they please.")

Quadrant 3

Planning: More concerned with generalities than details ("If you fence people in with too much planning, you'll demoralize them. I'm flexible; I give my people plenty of leeway.")

Organizing: Patterns of relationship emphasize loosely structured sociability ("If people feel good about their jobs, they'll do their best without lots of regulation. My job is to make sure they feel good.")

Controlling: Relies on high morale to produce hard work ("Control is secondary. What salespeople need most is a good feeling about their jobs.")

Leading: Believes optimism and encouragement get results ("Being a sales manager is like being a cheerleader. You can't let your people get discouraged.")

2. Q1 is usually a solo performance. The manager runs the show *her* way, seeking little help or advice from her salespeople. She makes her own decisions, delegates as little as she must (and, when she does, keeps a close eye on things), and favors one-way communication ("Now, get this . . .").

3. Q1 sales management isn't just a matter of threats, implied or otherwise. It's also a matter of *inducements.* The salesperson gets two simultaneous messages: "If you *don't* do things my way, you'll be in trouble" *and* "If you *do* do things my way, I'll take care of you." The manager seeks a trade-off: the salesperson is to give up autonomy *in exchange for* security. Some salespeople think this is a good bargain, some don't.

4. Q1 management is generous with punishments but stingy with rewards. A salesperson who makes a mistake is almost sure to be blamed or disciplined; one who turns in a good performance may never hear a word about it. This distorts the *development* of sales-people. The frequent use of punishment (what psychologists call negative reinforcement) *does* reduce "ineffective" behavior (ineffec-tive, of course, from the manager's viewpoint). But the *in*frequent use of rewards (positive reinforcement) means that "effective" be-haviors aren't sufficiently encouraged; lacking encouragement, they may languish and finally disappear. Healthy development requires judicious use of both positive and negative reinforcements, rather than the imbalance found in Q1.

5. Q1 management is more concerned with ends than means. What matters are *results*; how they're obtained is less important. To get results, the manager may badger her salespeople, stretch rules, ignore policies. But she *is* results-minded. That's why she's often called a "driver," a "go-getter," and, in some cases, a "winner."

Q2 (Submissive–Hostile) Sales Management

A sales manager who practices Q2 might explain herself this way:

> Too many managers have inflated notions of what they can accomplish. Not me. I know I'm very limited in what I can do to motivate my salespeople. Most managers don't like to admit it, but the truth is that most salespeople are what they are. Some produce, some don't. Either way, there's not much the manager can do about it.

> If a manager can't seriously affect results, what *can* she do? A couple of things. First, see to it that nobody disrupts things. Sales organizations func-tion best without turmoil, so a big part of any manager's job is to keep sales-people from creating turmoil. To do it, you must let them know that the peo-

ple "upstairs" — top management, the big shots — expect certain things done in certain ways. Once they understand that, you shouldn't have much trouble keeping things calm.

The second thing you can do is look out for yourself. Sales organizations are risky places. They're filled with ambitious, competitive people . . . politics . . . traps of every kind. Just staying alive in that sort of environment is pretty much a full-time job. The surest way to stay alive is to stay out of the line of fire: keep a low profile . . . don't volunteer . . . don't be a hero . . . don't call attention to yourself. Flashy managers come and go, but those who know how to fade into the background stay around a long time.

This caricature highlights several features of Q2 sales management:

1. Q2 is pessimistic about people. Its message is: "You can't improve people's work, so why try? In spite of myths to the contrary, managers can't activate or motivate. What they *can* do is (a) look after the *maintenance* of their operation and (b) look after *themselves.*"

2. Q2 is "pipeline" management. The superior is a conduit between the people above and those below. She's a transmission belt, conveying decisions from her own manager to her salespeople, but providing little initiative or personal direction.

3. Q2 usually puts off decisions. The manager feels postponing them is safer ("If I wait long enough, time will take care of it"). She may make a prompt decision if she can get a clear signal as to her own manager's preferences. Otherwise, she'll probably procrastinate.

4. Salespeople in a Q2 operation don't hear much from their manager. She says little, and is regarded as "distant," "reserved," maybe even "unfriendly." Her style of communication can be described as "no-way" ("Don't bother me and I won't bother you").

5. Q2 favors traditional, tried-and-true ways, because the tried-and-true (compared to the new-and-unproven) seem safer. Q2 sales management conservatively prefers "doing things as we've always done them." It dislikes taking risks, even calculated ones.

6. Under Q2, salespeople get very little reinforcement, positive or negative. Undesirable behavior is seldom punished ("What good would it do?"). Desirable behavior is seldom rewarded ("What good would it do?"). The manager fatalistically assumes that people are what they are and will pretty much *stay* that way. This leads to a hands-off policy; instead of punishing or rewarding, she "leaves well enough alone." Indifference breeds indifference: many salespeople become apathetic as a result of this treatment (or non-treatment).

Q3 (Submissive–Warm) Sales Management

Let's hear from a manager who practices Q3.

> The way to improve productivity, it seems to me, is to humanize the company. As companies get bigger, more bureaucratic, more rationalized, there's a real danger they'll ignore the human factor. If that happens, productivity's bound to decline, because there's a strong correlation between productivity and morale, and high morale depends upon treating people with warmth, friendship, and an understanding that we're all human and we all make mistakes.
>
> That's why my most important job as a sales manager is to treat my salespeople amiably, understandingly, leniently. Nothing can be gained—and a lot can be lost—by pushing, blaming, or belittling. I keep my people happy, let them have their way if I can, and let them know I'm in their corner—that I believe in them.
>
> I call this the 'human touch', and it's more important than all the systems and procedures in the world. In fact, without it, the systems and procedures will probably break down. Salespeople only do good work when they're contented—it's that simple."

This caricature points up several features of Q3 sales management:

1. It's easygoing. If a salesperson makes a mistake, the manager tries to overlook or downplay it. If a salesperson's productivity is low, the manager deals with the matter (if at all) by saying something like: "I know you can do better . . . I've got every confidence things will improve." Q3 finds it hard to *confront* unpleasant issues.

2. Q3 is loose, unstructured, poorly organized. Policies, procedures, rules, regulations, systems are all outside the manager's focus. The Q3 philosophy is that the job will get done without structure *if* salespeople are relaxed, happy, content.

3. Q3 makes few demands—because "pushing" people might "demoralize" them. To Q3, *all* demands are "pushy," as if a manager cannot set—and insist upon—high standards *without* seeming unreasonable.

4. The manager dislikes thinking of herself as "the boss." Whereas Q1 maximizes the difference between manager and salespeople ("I'll show them who's in charge"), Q3 minimizes it ("We're one big happy family").

5. Q3 uses indiscriminate positive reinforcement. The manager rarely punishes; in fact, she'd rather not even *talk* about poor performance. If she refers to undesirable behavior at all, she does it so

indirectly that the salesperson may not even realize the behavior *was* undesirable. *Indiscriminate* rewards usually confuse; salespeople lose the ability to distinguish between productive and nonproductive behavior. This either retards or stifles healthy development.

6. Q3 invests much energy in "socializing." Chatting with salespeople about things besides the job—family matters, sports, entertainment, politics, what have you—takes up a disproportionate amount of the manager's time. Q3 considers these conversations worthwhile because they "humanize" the environment and contribute to the "organizational harmony" considered so vital to productivity.

Q4 (Dominant–Warm) Sales Management

Finally, let's hear from a manager who practices Q4.

> My job is to get the best out of my salespeople—and out of *me*, too. To do it, I've got to make two things happen.
>
> First, get my salespeople—each of them—to see what they're really capable of—how good they *could* be. Then, help them develop knowledge, skills, and motivation for tapping their potential, putting it to work. I want to develop salespeople who can produce excellent results by exerting a high degree of autonomy and self-direction, salespeople who don't have to be monitored all day long. That's not easy, and I don't kid myself that *every* salesperson can be that inner-directed. So, in practice, I temper the ideal to fit the person. After all, management is a matter of coming to grips with *individual* realities.
>
> Second, I consider my salespeople resources for strengthening my *own* performance. I don't have all the answers—so I need help to get the job done. Fortunately, there's a reservoir of experience, talent, and ideas I can draw upon: my salespeople. Sometimes, of course, I have to act alone, but, when suitable, I consult my people, check my thinking against theirs, and draw upon their savvy. If I don't, I not only cheat myself of a chance to learn, I cheat them of a chance to grow. The net result is we're *all better off.* My salespeople like *contributing*—and their satisfaction pays off in increased motivation. My own performance improves, too. And the company gains as all of us become more productive.

Let's look closer at Q4 sales management:

1. We're dealing with caricatures, but there *are* sales managers whose behavior approximates the Q4 ideal. They strategically involve their salespeople in decisions, delegate responsibility, encourage critique, encourage two-way communication, and motivate through participation. They may not do these things perfectly (and they sometimes backslide and do other things) but, on the whole, they

try. Close observation of sales managers in virtually any sizable company confirms this.

2. Still and all, some salespeople cannot measure up to the standards of Q4 management. Most sales managers who believe in Q4 are realistic enough to admit this. So, they *adapt* their basic approach to each separate salesperson. Where a salesperson *can* exercise autonomy, she's given the chance; where she *can* contribute to discussions, she's involved in them. But where she cannot do these things, she's subject to close control by her manager. Independence and self-direction are for salespeople who can turn them to good use. Those who can't are closely supervised. Q4 management doesn't let the ideal blot out reality.

3. This leads to one of the Q4's most important features: it's *individualized.* Q4 is based upon the common-sense premise that you can't interact productively with a salesperson unless you *know* her as an individual. You must know what she wants from her work, what her experience is, what her skills are, what her aptitudes and potential are. You must know her characteristic pattern of behavior, her concerns and needs, and whatever else makes her the person she is. Only then can you properly *customize* your interaction with her.

4. Q4 welcomes — or at least appreciates — disagreement. This doesn't mean the sales manager goes around picking arguments. It means she realizes that disagreements are bound to arise, so they may as well be *utilized.* That's what Q4 does: it utilizes disagreement, puts it to work. Q4 gets disagreement out in the open to see what light it throws on things. In Q4 management, *nothing* is beyond discussion; everything can be questioned, debated, challenged. Disagreement, by exposing weaknesses, becomes a way of overcoming organizational inertia.

5. The most basic Q4 idea is that people work best when they have a *reason* to. High productivity depends upon their understanding "what's in it for me." High productivity *cannot* be expected from a salesperson who asks, "Why bother?". Hard, intelligent, efficient work is something people do because they *want* to, and they want to because they'll *get something* out of it. Q4 management therefore sees to it that each salesperson *knows* what she'll get out of being productive. She must *know* "what's in it for me" before she can be expected to work hard and effectively (just as a *customer* must be aware of "what's in it for me" before she can be expected to buy). Making certain each salesperson understands how she'll *benefit* from productive work is a task Q4 takes very seriously.

6. Q4 knows how to develop people. It makes discriminating use of both positive and negative reinforcements, but, when justified, emphasizes positive. While it tries to lessen non-productive behavior, its primary aim is to shape *productive* behavior, because that's the best way to foster growth. Q4 tailors its use of positive and negative reinforcements to fit each particular salesperson.

7. Finally, and most importantly, Q4 sales management is *practical.* Let's see why:

a. It demands *results.* It wants optimal productivity from every salesperson. Anyone who's worked under Q4 management knows it isn't easy. Q4 demands the *best* that people can deliver, and doesn't willingly settle for second-best. It sets tough, exerting goals; it insists upon intelligent, analytic handling of problems; and it never lets anyone forget that *results* are what work is all about.

b. Q4 management is realistic about *people.* It doesn't idealize them or see them in the glow of a halo. But it doesn't settle for negative stereotypes either ("People are no darned good," "You can't rely on anybody these days," "Nobody wants to work hard anymore"). In fact, Q4 doesn't deal with *people* at all; it deals with *persons* – discrete individuals, no two of whom are identical. Instead of dealing with them on the basis of preconceived notions, it gets to know each of them for what he or she *is*, and then deals with them on *that* basis. Nothing could be more practical.

c. The manager who practices Q4 is realistic about herself, too. She knows she's human, limited, flawed, and very much in need of help. So, she *seeks* help from her salespeople and from others in the company. Usually, in seeking help she also *gives* it: most Q4 interactions are an exchange of strengths from which both people gain.

d. Finally, in Q4, the manager is *tough* on herself. She seeks out help when it's needed, but never abdicates her own responsibility. She doesn't "turn over" management to her salespeople, she doesn't let "popular" opinion override her own judgment, she doesn't forget that ultimately she, and only she, is accountable for what happens in her operation. And she doesn't try to lessen her own answerability by dividing it up among her salespeople. In spite of her belief in involvement, she knows that, in the end, she's in charge and nobody else can be. There's an old cliche: "It's lonely at the top." Q4 never forgets it.

A LOOK AT THE REAL WORLD

Let's set our model aside for a minute to ask a question: How common are the four patterns of sales management? There are two ways to answer this:

- First of all, your own experience no doubt confirms that *all* four patterns are very common. Variants of each can be found in virtually every company. You can probably recall many instances in which you've observed, interacted with, or displayed each behavior.
- Our experience in Dimensional Sales Management training strengthens this conclusion. Participants in DSM usually rate their behavior as a mixture of all four patterns, clear evidence that all four are widely used. Our model describes behaviors visible every day in the everyday world.

SALES MANAGEMENT STRATEGIES: A SUMMARY

Let's summarize what we've said about sales management. Figure 28 shows, in a nutshell, the basic attitudes underlying the four patterns, the four basic ways to plan, organize, control and lead, and several other common sales management functions.

WHAT'S THE PAYOFF?

On the whole and over time, Q4 sales management can be expected to *pay off better* than any other. That conclusion comes from three sources: (1) behavioral-science studies like the Ohio State Leadership Studies and those by Rensis Likert and his colleagues at the University of Michigan Survey Research Center, (2) our own experience with managers in Dimensional Sales Management seminars and as consultants to a wide variety of companies, and (3) common sense. This last factor is especially important. We'll explain why.

Our conclusion—while solidly grounded in both research and experience—cannot be proven in the way the boiling point of water can. Real proof is *conclusive*; it closes off debate. In that sense, we can't prove that one kind of management is generally more productive than others. Even after reading this chapter, you may want to

Figure 28. Four Ways of Managing Salespeople.

Management Function	Q1	Q2	Q3	Q4
Basic attitude	Salespeople must be pushed	Salespeople are what they are	Salespeople produce when happy	Salespeople produce when involved and committed
Planning	Does it on own	Transmits from above	Makes popular plans	Strategically involves salespeople
Organizing	Tightly controls operation	Goes by the book; interaction vague, minimal	Permissive, relatively unstructured	Optimal participation, autonomy, and responsibility for everyone
Controlling	Relies on fear and coercion	Leans on routines	Relies on permissive human relations	Fosters self-control through understanding
Leading	Drives and threatens	Indifferent, distant, unresponsive	Eager to please, appeases, smooths over	Aware, assertive, responsive, guiding
Decision-making	Does it on own	Delays or follows custom	Compromises; seeks happy medium	Strategically involves others; seeks optimal decision
Motivating	Negative reinforcement	Neither negative nor positive reinforcement	Indiscriminate positive reinforcement	Appropriate positive and negative reinforcement
Disagreement	Suppresses	Avoids	Smoothes over	Confronts and resolves
Communications	One-way	No-way	Part-way	Two-way

debate our conclusion. But *on the whole*, we think you'll agree that our conclusion meets the test of common sense, and, while common sense doesn't "prove" anything, it's mighty convincing.

Let's see, then, why Q4 *can* be expected to pay off best. We'll examine the seven *end-results* for which sales managers are usually held responsible: (1) sales production, (2) cost of sales, (3) morale, (4) turnover, (5) teamwork, (6) innovation, and (7) development of salespeople. Let's see how each is affected by the various patterns of sales management. (Figure 29 sums up our conclusions.)

1. Sales production. However measured, sales usually improve under Q1, at least initially; this isn't surprising since Q1 *is* hard-driving. Eventually, however, sales may decline because competent salespeople leave and the manager fails to develop and tap potential. Consequently, sales under Q1 are often high in the short run but only average in the long. Under Q2, sales frequently decline or hover below the norm; this is what you'd expect when the manager doesn't really believe in leadership and doesn't make a serious effort to assert it. Under Q3, sales usually stay below the norm because *problems* are ignored or played down; sooner or later, this refusal to confront harsh reality exerts a toll. Under Q4, sales generally go up or stay above the norm.

Figure 29.   Four Ways of Managing: What's the Payoff?*

End-results	Q1	Q2	Q3	Q4
Sales production	High to average over time	Low	Low	High
Cost of sales	High to average	High to average	High	Average to low
Morale	Low	Low	High	High
Turnover	High	Low	Low	Average
Teamwork	Low	Low	Low	High
Innovation	Low	Low	Low	High
Development of salespeople	Low	Low	Low	High

*Our conclusions are based on the assumption that all factors *other than* pattern of management are *equal* and will *remain* equal. Obviously, any of these end-results can be affected by changes in other factors; cost of sales, for instance, can be greatly influenced by inflationary factors over which the sales manager has no control.

2. Cost of sales. Q1 costs usually rise or remain high; the loss of competent salespeople, the squelching of good ideas, and the resentment which Q1 sometimes generates, carry a high price tag. Q2 costs also rise or remain high; bureaucratic procedures may help keep expenditures in line, but the failure to develop new and better ideas tends to drive them up. Q3 costs generally rise; loose organization, unwillingness to say "no," neglect of festering problems – these are expensive. Under Q4, with its emphasis on optimal productivity, full use of resources, and innovation, costs are average to low.

3. Morale. Under Q1, morale is usually low because salespeople resent being stifled or "treated like kids." Under Q2 it's usually low because many salespeople are disspirited by the lack of challenge and excitement; lackluster environments often breed lackluster performance. Under Q3, morale is usually high; many salespeople find Q3 very congenial, although some are put off by the lack of decisive leadership. Under Q4, morale is usually quite high, especially among those with most potential; they like the stimulation and challenge.

4. Turnover. Q1 turnover is generally high; salespeople (frequently the *most capable*) don't like "being pushed around" and often go elsewhere. Q2 turnover is generally low; many people find Q2 "easy" to work under ("The boss doesn't bother me; she just leaves me alone"). Under Q3, the situation is somewhat the same; many salespeople like the atmosphere ("I work for a really nice person"). Moreover, both Q2 and Q3 frequently *retain* ineffective salespeople because the manager "doesn't want the hassle" or "doesn't have the heart" to let them go. Q4 turnover is generally higher than the norm; some salespeople can't measure up to the manager's standards; others can't work for someone who consistently challenges them. Q4 turnover differs from Q1, however; under Q4, turnover is mainly among those who cannot or will not meet the manager's demand for excellence; under Q1, it's mainly among those who *want* to meet a demand for excellence but find themselves stymied by heavy-handed management. Thus, Q4 turns over mostly *weaker* salespeople; Q1 turns over *stronger.*

5. Teamwork. In the strictest sense of the word, there's no such thing as Q1 "teamwork"; either the manager runs the team with an iron hand, dictating conclusions which are obediently ratified, or the team is divided by bickering, backbiting, grandstanding, and gameplaying. Q2 "teamwork" is also a misnomer; lacking strong leadership, the team goes through the motions of teamwork, but that's about all. Q3 "teamwork" is too relaxed, disorganized, and unbusinesslike, with bad results all around. Q4 teamwork is the real thing:

goal-directed, businesslike, collaborative, candid, spirited, and *effective.*

6. Innovation. Q1, Q2, and Q3 management stifle innovation, each in a different way. Q1 discourages it by "tell-and-do" tactics ("When I want your opinion I'll ask for it"). Q2 shies away from anything new or unusual ("Let's stick to what we *know*"). And Q3 pays lip service to new ideas ("Terrific!") but backs away from implementing any that might create conflict or even discomfort. Q4, of course, *seeks out* workable new ideas and tries to put them to use.

7. Development of salespeople. Domineering Q1, fatalistic Q2, and easygoing Q3 all squelch development. If any development occurs, it occurs in spite of, not because of, the Q1, Q2, or Q3 patterns of management. Q4, on the other hand, fosters growth by giving salespeople a chance to perform at their highest level; it helps them discover their own potential, and acquire the skills for fulfilling it.

In considering the points we've just made, keep two things in mind:

1. It's impossible to forecast sales, turnover, costs, and so on, on the basis of managerial behavior alone. Many other factors, some of which have nothing to do with managerial strategies, also affect these outcomes. We've merely made one point: *when other factors are held constant*, managerial behavior does have a discernible influence on end-results.

2. The terms *low, high*, and *average* cannot be precisely defined, and they certainly cannot be quantified. We've used them merely to describe *trends*. In any *single* case, they may not apply.

The classic formula for computing productivity will help us summarize all this:

$$\frac{\text{Value of salesperson's output per hour}}{\text{Value of inputs expended to attain that output}} = \frac{\text{that salesperson's}}{\text{productivity}}$$

Using this formula ($\frac{O}{I}$ = P), it's easy to see why Q4 sales management is, by and large, more productive.

17

Motivating Salespeople

If the authors of this book hear one question over and over again—whenever and wherever sales managers gather—that question is: "How can we do a better job of *motivating* our salespeople?" This isn't surprising. After all, most sales managers realize that a motivated salesperson—who *wants* to meet his sales goals, who *exerts* himself to meet them and who isn't satisfied unless he *does* meet them—is more likely to meet them. So, to a significant degree, the sales *manager's* success depends upon motivating. It's as simple as that.

This chapter focuses on motivating and on another subject inseparable from it—performance standards. It answers a question that perplexes many sales managers: "What can I *do* to make my salespeople eager to reach their sales goals?" Before answering, however, we'd better get one thing on the record: *by themselves*, the skills described in this chapter cannot do the *whole* job of motivating salespeople. To do the whole job, a manager must have other things going for him, like a good sales compensation program, an accurate feedback system, and effective training. When these factors are in place, and the techniques described in this chapter are added, strong motivation should result. But if any of these factors is missing, motivation may be impaired. What ultimately motivates salespeople is the *climate* in which they work—not just a few skills. The skills are necessary, but they can't do the job *alone*.

WHAT IS MOTIVATION?

Motivation is a "drive to achieve a goal." The motivated person *wants* to reach a given objective; he wants it enough to *do* what's necessary to make it happen. He may not succeed (motivation is *not* achievement; it's the urge to achieve) but at least he'll try. Motivation implies effort, striving, exertion.

In fact, if you trace *motivation* back to its Latin root, you find the word *move*. Motivation is inseparable from movement, from activity. The motivated person is always *in motion—on the move.* The movement may or may not be physical, but it's always mental. The mind, the emotions, the imagination are "in motion" even when the body isn't. The motivated person is always *active*, always *doing* things — mental or physical or both—to move him closer to his goal.

When you think about it, this may seem odd. Why should anyone exert himself at all? Why not take things as they come—be passive rather than active? What gives people the drive to achieve goals? What makes them want to move toward a particular goal? And why are they more eager to move toward some goals than others? Because, quite simply, when they reach the goal, they expect to be *better off*—as they see it—than they are now. The goal, once achieved, should provide some *satisfaction* they now lack, or *more* of some satisfaction they're already enjoying. Goals that *don't* promise satisfaction *don't* motivate. Goals that *do*, do.

A *motivating* goal, then, gives a person an *incentive*, a *reason*, to exert himself on the job. There are two different kinds.

Two Kinds of Job Goals

Job goals come in two varieties: *business* and *behavioral*:

- *Business job goals* are the *ends* an employee is expected to attain. They're what he's *paid* to achieve.

- *Behavioral job goals* are *means* to these ends. They're what the employee must do *before* he can attain, or *in order* to attain, his business job goals. ("Before you can reach this year's sales quota [business goal] you must learn how to manage your time [behavioral goal]," "In order to land the Jefferson account [business goal] you'll have to learn how to deal with Mr. Jefferson's Q1 belligerence [behavioral goal].")

A metaphor may help:

- *Business* job goals are the destination at the end of the road the employee is supposed to travel.

- *Behavioral* job goals are paving stones that make the road easier to travel and the destination more accessible.

Here are examples of *business* job goals:

- Utilizing store coupons, introduce Product X to your ten biggest dollar-volume accounts by January 15, without lowering the dollar volume of sales of our other products to these accounts.
- Increase unit sales of Size–1 widgets during the first quarter of the year by 2 percent over unit sales during the last quarter of the past year, while keeping unit sales of all other items constant.

And here are examples of *behavioral* job goals:

- Learn the full range of potential benefits of our Deferred-Payment Plan, so you can get any customer to see "what's in it for him."
- Practice the use of reflective statements for venting negative emotions, so that the next time a customer loses his temper the way Mr. X did, you don't lose control of the call.

These examples illustrate two points:

1. *Business* goals always focus on the *external* environment; *behavioral* goals always focus on the salesperson.
2. Business goals are usually more precise, more easily measured.

Q4 JOB GOALS

A *Q4* job goal is any job objective—business or behavioral—which aims at *optimal* results for everyone concerned: the employee to whom it's assigned, his manager, and their organization. The purpose of a Q4 job goal is to help *everybody win* by an *optimal* score.
    Let's examine the crucial phrase: *optimal results*:

An *optimal result* is the *best* result *under the circumstances.* It's *not* an *ideal* result. An ideal result is what you'd *like* to get, an optimal result is the best you *can* get. Ideal results are *hypothetical*: they're *imagined* results against which you can measure actual results. Optimal results, on the other hand, are *real* results which come *as close* to the ideal as possible.

Every Q4 job goal exemplifies two principles of Q4 management:

1. We're not going to waste time and money chasing dreams. We're going after what's realistically attainable. We intend to

answer one question: in the light of everything we know or can anticipate, what's the most we can expect to achieve? Then we'll go after it.

2. That isn't defeatist. Not at all. We're not looking for excuses to scale down our expectations; we just want to know *what's actually achievable.* Once we know, we'll strive toward it — and we won't be satisfied unless we reach it. Once we know we *can* get there, we *intend* to.

How to Recognize Q4 Job Goals

A Q4 job goal meets five criteria:

1. It's practical.
2. It requires optimal effort.
3. It's specific.
4. It's comprehensive.
5. It's understandable.

We'll look at each, focusing first on *business* job goals.

1. MAKE SURE THE GOAL IS PRACTICAL

A *practical* job goal can be achieved without obstructing progress toward *other* goals. It might be possible, for instance, to acquire a new account, and thereby achieve a *volume* objective, but only by spending so much time and money that it becomes impossible to achieve a profit objective. Excluding the intervention of other factors, the new-account goal, while certainly achievable, would be impractical. The first test of any job goal must be: Is it practical? Is it worth the effort? Will achieving it create more problems than it will solve? Will we be better off or worse off if it's achieved? It might be *possible* to achieve it, but not everything possible is practical. A Q4 goal should be a *desirable* goal, which means it should not get in the way of other equally important (or more important) goals.

2. MAKE SURE THE GOAL REQUIRES OPTIMAL EFFORT

A Q4 goal is neither too hard nor too easy; it requires *optimal* effort. Here's what we mean:

- An *easy* goal poses little difficulty or challenge. Contrary to popular opinion, there's plenty of behavioral-science evidence that many people *want* to be challenged. (This is one reason crossword puzzles, card games, and weekend sports are popular. Many peo-

ple enjoy being pushed to excel; in fact, they push *themselves*.)
These people may be "turned off" by easy job goals, becoming
bored and demoralized. Every organization has probably lost
good people—people *worth* keeping—because they felt their jobs
had become "dull" or "mechanical." Challenging goals might
have kept them on board.

• There's a difference, however, between challenging goals and
  goals that are *too hard*. A goal is *too hard* if the employee can't
  reach it even when he stretches. Faced with an "impossible" goal,
  most people either (a) give up very quickly (most crossword-
  puzzle fans who know only one language lay down their pencils
  when they see a puzzle with a large number of foreign words) or
  (b) stick with it (because they don't like to give up) but become
  increasingly frustrated and edgy; as they strain unsuccessfully to
  achieve the goal, their tension builds and their mistakes increase.

• Paradoxically, then, both extremes lead to the same result; goals
  that are *too easy* and goals that are *too hard* produce discomfort
  and demoralization. Many people *want* to be challenged; they
  enjoy testing their limits. But they're frustrated by challenges
  beyond their reach.

• The solution is *optimal* goals—what the ancient Greeks called
  the *golden mean*, the point between two extremes where everything comes into balance. Optimal goals require the *right* amount
  of exertion and stress—neither too little nor too much. They
  stimulate extra effort, but not hopelessness. They require stretch-
  ing, but not breaking.

This doesn't mean optimal effort always falls halfway between no
effort and extreme effort; the golden mean isn't always in the middle. Optimal effort lies *somewhere* between "too little" and "too
much." Figure 30 helps explain this.

The curve in Figure 30 must be modified to fit particular cases,
but it still helps us illustrate three principles:

a. Goals requiring little or no effort usually do little to motivate.
   The salesperson's attitude is likely to be "So what?"

b. Goals requiring excessive effort usually do little to motivate.
   The salesperson's attitude is likely to be "Why bother?"

c. Somewhere between too little effort and too much, the goal
   will be a strong motivator. The salesperson will *want* to make
   the effort.

Figure 30

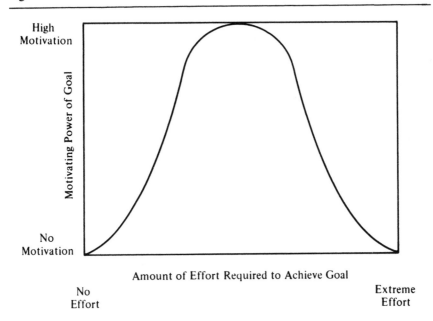

How much is optimal?

We haven't specified the point at which effort becomes optimal, because we *can't*. It varies from situation to situation and person to person. The answer to "How much is optimal?" is "It all depends." It depends on the goal and the person to whom it's assigned. A goal may be "tough but achievable" to one person, "impossible" to another. Setting optimal job goals, then, requires knowing your people.

3. MAKE THE JOB GOAL SPECIFIC

Vague goals *cannot* produce optimal results, because they don't spell out what "optimal" means. All the following goals are vague; there's no way to tell for sure if or when they've been achieved:

- Increase sales as much as possible.
- Improve your product mix.
- Trim sales expenses as far as you can.

These goals aren't even operational; they can't be intelligently *acted upon*. How can you plan to increase sales "as much as possible" unless you know how *many* sales *are* "possible"? The trouble with words like "possible" is that you can't *do* anything with them. You can't "improve" your product mix unless you know what constitutes "improvement." Is it three units more of Product A and four units less of Product B? Or three units more of Product A while holding sales of Product B constant? Or equal sales of Products A, B, and C? What does "improve" really *mean?*

Vague goals, in a word, are unusable. They may sound good, but that's all. To be *usable*, goals must be quantified or specified. For example:

Vague: Slash selling costs to the bone.

Specific: Slash selling costs by $100 a week.

Vague: Balance your calls each day.

Specific: Make four calls on Category A accounts and four calls on Category B accounts each day.

4. MAKE THE JOB GOAL COMPREHENSIVE

A Q4 goal is comprehensive; it tells the *whole* story. It *fully* describes what's to be achieved, including dates, times, quantities, and other essential details as well as the *conditions* of achievement. After all, there are certain conditions, limitations, or restrictions to which people are subject when they're pursuing goals; if these bounds are exceeded, the goal may be met, but it won't produce *optimal* results. If these conditioning factors aren't spelled out as part of the goal, you may be asking for trouble later on. A salesperson can rightly say. "I didn't achieve *that* because I didn't know I was supposed to; nobody ever told me." Here's a goal that could cause problems because it's *not* comprehensive:

"Cut selling costs in the Northeastern Territory by 1.5 percent during the next fiscal year."

This *sounds* comprehensive. After all, it spells out *what's* to be done ("cut selling costs"), *where* ("in the Northeastern Territory"), *how much* ("1.5 percent), and *when* ("during the next fiscal year"). What, then, is wrong with it?

What's wrong is that it tells much of the story but not the *whole* story. It doesn't specify the *conditions* under which the goal must be met. For example: A salesperson might cut selling costs by 1.5 percent by refusing to call on accounts on the far edge of his territory, thereby reducing his travel expenses. Would that be acceptable? Or is one of the *conditions* of the goal that all current accounts be retained while selling costs are cut? If so, the goal should say so. For instance:

> "Cut selling costs in the Northeastern Territory by 1.5 percent during the next fiscal year while retaining all current accounts and maintaining or improving this fiscal year's dollar volume of sales to those accounts."

Job goals are most commonly *incomplete* because the *conditions* under which they must be met—the boundaries within which their achievement must take place—aren't spelled out. We call these conditions or boundaries *contingencies*, because achievement of the goal is contingent upon them. When contingencies are omitted, a goal may be achieved in ways that were never intended; after all, *anyone* can cut selling costs by staying in bed all day. To avoid such "surprises," make every job goal *comprehensive*.

5. MAKE THE JOB GOAL UNDERSTANDABLE

Several guidelines will help:

- Word the goal so the salesperson can understand it. It's all right to use technical terms or jargon as long as they're clear to *him.*

- Don't worry if the goal sounds legalistic. This may be unavoidable; after all, optimal goals and legal language have something in common: they're both designed to tie up loose ends. So if the goal sounds as if it's been drafted by lawyers, that's okay, *as long as the salesperson understands it.*

- If it will make things clearer, use several sentences instead of one. No law says a goal must be covered in one sentence.

- Include *what* and *when*, but not *how*. Obviously, the salesperson should know how to achieve the goal, but this belongs in a separate plan of action, not in the goal itself.

- Use *adjectives* and *adverbs* sparingly. Most adjectives (fast, slow, high, low, good, bad, satisfactory, unsatisfactory) and most adverbs (more, less, quickly, slowly) are *too vague*. If you use an adjective or adverb, make sure it's precise. If it isn't, try to replace it with *numbers* or some more exact expression (for example: replace *more* with 2 percent).

Two Kinds of Job Goals

So far, we've discussed *business* job goals. How about *behavioral* job goals? Can they also meet our five criteria? *Yes.*

1. PRACTICALITY

Any goal that requires a salesperson to change his behavior or improve his skills is impractical if he's (a) unable or (b) unwilling to do it.

a. *Unable.* You can't get anybody to change if the change is beyond his capacity. Suppose one of your salespeople becomes very nervous before each presentation; as a result, his presentations are garbled and disorganized. You can assign him this goal: "Overcome your nervousness before presentations so that you come across more convincingly." But that may be *beyond* him; the nervousness may be something he *cannot* overcome. If so, the goal is impractical—in fact, futile. (We're *not* saying nervousness can never be surmounted; we're saying that for *some* people it may be insurmountable. If it is, then, for *them* the goal is impractical.)

b. *Unwilling.* If a salesperson isn't *motivated* to achieve a behavioral goal (or, for that matter, a business goal), the goal is impractical. This doesn't mean it can't be achieved under *any* circumstances; you may be able to *compel* achievement by Q1 tactics. But don't look for commitment unless the salesperson *wants* to achieve the goal. If he *doesn't*, all the Q1 pushing in the world may not help.

2. OPTIMAL EFFORT

What we've said about the "golden mean" applies to behavioral as well as business goals. Let's explore the three possibilities:

a. *Easy changes in behavior.* There's nothing wrong with asking a salesperson to make "easy" changes in behavior or to acquire "easy" skills if they'll improve his work. But most behavioral goals aren't "easy." Most require changes in ingrained, habitual behavior— behavior that seems like "second nature." Don't kid yourself that such changes are "easy"; they aren't.

b. *Extremely difficult changes in behavior.* These engender either apathy ("I can't do it, so why try?") or frustration ("I'm sick and tired of trying and failing"). The old adage, "You can't make a silk purse out of a sow's ear," is worth remembering; *all of us* do certain things that, for all practical purposes, cannot be changed, or can be changed only at a prohibitive cost in time and effort.

This is especially true of certain kinds of *expressive behavior. Expressive behavior* includes all the ways we express ourselves to others, either by speech, writing, or gesture. Much expressive behavior *can* be changed; in fact, we've described some ways to do it (through probing, use of presentation skills, and so on). But *certain kinds* of expressive behavior are extremely difficult to change. Someone who stammers when excited, for example, may be unable to stop doing so without intense effort (and perhaps professional coaching). Someone whose voice squeaks when he's under pressure may be unable to do much about it. And someone with traces of a foreign accent may be unable to erase them.

Similarly, certain people cannot, no matter how hard they try, *acquire* certain skills. They lack the aptitude, the intelligence, the physical dexterity, or whatever else is required. Even if *motivated* to change, they can't; the skill is beyond them.

This brings us to a key point: a behavioral goal is *legitimate* —justifiable—only if its attainment will further the attainment of a *business goal.* Thus, some of the behavioral goals we've just discussed may not be legitimate. Does it really *matter*—as far as business goals go—if a salesperson stammers occasionally? Does it make any *difference*—as far as performance goes—if his voice sometimes squeaks? Will the *bottom line* be affected if he speaks with a foreign accent? If the answer is *no*, then the behavioral goals (which are unrealistic anyway) should be dropped.

c. **Optimal changes in behavior.**   Realistic behavioral goals which require exertion usually produce the best results. Choose goals that require people to stretch without tearing themselves apart.

3. SPECIFICITY

Most behavioral job goals cannot be as specific as business job goals. But they can be reasonably precise. Here's an example:

Vague: Heal your split with Fletcher in Production.

Precise: Get Fletcher in Production to understand that you're not trying to push him out of his job and that you haven't done anything to undermine him, so that sometime during the next 30 days he agrees to give you shipping information on the telephone again.

To make behavioral goals reasonably specific, follow these three guidelines:

a. Spell out what will *happen* if the goal is met. That way, you and the salesperson can know if and when it *has* been met. Our last example clearly states what will occur if the goal is met: "so that sometime during the next 30 days he agrees to give you shipping information on the telephone again."

In other words, since a behavioral goal is legitimate only if it furthers the attainment of a business goal, *state* the *business goal* — or at least the business consequence — as part of the behavioral goal. If you cannot link the behavioral goal to a business consequence, the goal is illegitimate and should be discarded.

    b. When you can, include a *deadline.* Try not to leave the goal open-ended; specify *when* it must be achieved.

    c. If you can, *quantify* the goal. This isn't always possible with behavioral goals, but, when it is, it should be done.

4. COMPREHENSIVENESS

Like business goals, behavioral goals should include *all* necessary details; what is to be achieved, when, for what purpose, and the limiting conditions, if any. Here's an example, dealing with the acquisition of knowledge (many behavioral goals have to do with acquiring or improving knowledge or skills):

- *What is to be achieved:*   Master the details of the new state insurance code . . .
- *When:* by August 15 . . .
- *For what purpose:* so you can explain it to the district salesforce at our September sales meeting.
- *Limiting condition:* Keep any trips to the state capital for this purpose within your present travel budget.

Behavioral job goals can and should tell the *whole* story.

5. UNDERSTANDABILITY

Behavioral job goals sometimes sound clear when they're not. They're ambiguous; they can mean different things to different people. Nobody, for instance, can tell what the following goals "really" mean:

- Don't push so hard.
- Get on the team.
- Don't get excited.
- Play it by ear.
- Have a sense of humor.

These are flawed goals. They're not specific; they're not comprehensive; and they're not really understandable. They can mean many things. There's no *sure* way to know what they're supposed to mean. To overcome this problem, (1) make the goal specific by *explaining* its key terms; (2) tie it to a *business* job goal. Here's an example:

Vague	*Specific*
Assert yourself.	Make a point of speaking up at least once in each sales meeting to present your ideas on cutting costs, so the rest of the salesforce can use them to start cutting expenses.

It boils down to this: *specificity* and *understandability* go together. The more specific, the more understandable.

THE MOTIVATION PROCESS

Now that we've looked at the nature of Q4 goals, we're ready for the most important question: how can you motivate salespeople to *achieve* them? To get the answer, let's first look at what happens in motivation:

- Motivation is concerned with *performance.* When you try to motivate a salesperson, you try to get him to perform more productively—to get *more* out of the time and energy he spends on the job.

- Nobody can be expected to work hard and efficiently—which is what it takes to perform productively—unless he sees a *benefit* in it for himself. Most people are motivated to achieve a goal when they see a *reason* to do so—when they believe it will help them satisfy their own *needs.*

- Thus, motivation depends on getting the salesperson to see the *link* between his job goals and his needs. Once he sees the link, he'll understand how he can expect to benefit from achieving the goals. And once he understands that—once he realizes that hard, efficient work will lead not only to the goals but to a *personal payoff*—he should be motivated to *perform productively.*

This process can be described in a "formula"—a convenient shorthand:

$$J + N \rightarrow B \rightarrow P$$

J is the salesperson's *job goal*—business or behavioral; N is his *needs*—tangible or intangible. When J and N are *linked* (+), the linkage leads to ($\rightarrow$) B —the *benefit*: awareness of "what's in it for me if I achieve the job goal." This awareness should, in turn, lead to ($\rightarrow$) P—*productive performance.*

Let's take a closer look at *J, N, B,* and *P:*

J. Job goals, business or behavioral, are what the *company* expects the salesperson to achieve. We've stressed the word "company" for good reason. There's no assurance the *salesperson* will feel a sense of *ownership* in his job goals. Why should he? After all, the goals are designed to help the company fulfill *its* mandate; that doesn't guarantee they'll have any *personal meaning* for the salesperson. The fact that the *company* will be better off once a job goal is achieved doesn't answer the question in every salesperson's mind: Will *I* be better off?

This point cannot be overstated: *By themselves*, job goals are likely to be considered *external* to the salesperson. As long as they are, they're unlikely to generate commitment. And, when there's no commitment, productivity is usually *low*. Thus, if a salesperson asks himself, "Why should I bother to achieve this job goal?", he'll probably come up with the obvious answer: to keep my job. But if he asks himself, "Why should I *put my heart* into it—why should I give it *all I've got?*," there is no obvious answer. Why indeed? *Nothing* in the job goal *itself* answers that question.

N. If nothing in the job goal *itself* answers the question, then something *else* is needed to provide commitment. That something else is a link between the job goal—the *company's* purposes—and the salesperson's *needs—his own* purposes. Commitment—the feeling that "This goal is *mine*, and I really *want* to achieve it"—comes when the salesperson realizes that the job goal and *his* needs are intertwined, so that whatever happens to the job goal affects *him* personally.

Every salesperson—every employee—manifests two kinds of needs on the job:

* *Tangible needs:* the *substantive* rewards people seek from their work—the "things out there" that they work *for*: bigger commissions, a promotion, a bigger territory, and so on.

* *Intangible needs:* the *psychological* drives that underlie the tangible needs: the security or social or esteem or independence or self-realization needs that impel them to seek particular tangible rewards.

Figure 31. Two Kinds of Motivation.

Motivating Customers	Motivating Salespeople
1. Crystallize the customer's needs.	1. Crystallize the salesperson's needs.
2. Describe the pertinent features and advantages of the product or service you think the customer should buy.	2. Explain the job goal you want the salesperson to achieve.
3. Link the features and advantages to the customer's needs, so he sees the benefit — what's in it for him.	3. Link the job goals to the salesperson's needs, so he sees the benefit — what's in it for him.

B. You can make *any* job goal *meaningful* to a salesperson (or anyone else) if you can show that it matters to him (or help him see it for himself). Once he realizes there's a *benefit* in it for him, he'll have every reason to follow through.

P. Follow-through is essential for *productive performance.* If the salesperson's committed to the goal, and has the skills, productive performance should follow — and the goal should be met.

An Important Parallel

Obviously, there's a parallel between what we've just said about motivating salespeople and what we earlier said about motivating *customers.* To show it, Figure 31 summarizes, in one column, what's involved in motivating salespeople, and, in a parallel column, what's involved in motivating customers.

RECOGNIZING THE SALESPERSON'S NEEDS

To phrase a benefit statement for a salesperson, you must first know his needs. In the case of tangible needs, this usually presents no problem; people often talk about what they want from their jobs. Many salespeople will spontaneously tell you their tangible needs; if they don't, you can always ask. But most salespeople *don't* talk about their *in*tangible needs; either they haven't thought much about them or don't know what they are. So, if you ask about them, you may get a blank stare.

This leaves you the job of uncovering these needs for yourself. We say "uncovering" because, as we've seen, intangible needs aren't readily apparent; they're submerged beneath *behavior*. The only evidence of these needs is what the salesperson says and does. All you have to go on, literally, is *circumstantial evidence* —evidence surrounding the needs, not the needs themselves. But by analyzing this evidence, you can *infer* the needs. Let's look at the tell-tale signs.

We'll start with security needs, and work our way up the pyramid.

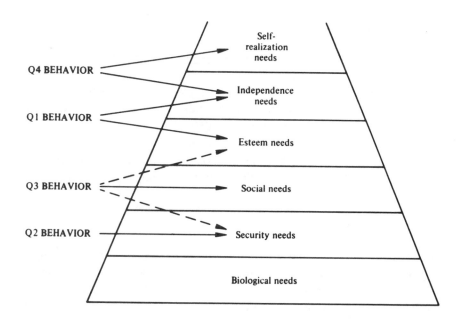

Security (Q2) Needs

The following behaviors are strong evidence of *security* needs.

1. Diffidence. The salesperson lacks self-confidence. He's timid, shrinking, apologetic, not quite sure of himself. He seems to distrust his own ability and ideas.

2. Reticence. He's tightlipped, speaking haltingly, grudgingly, or not at all. He's terse; he rarely embellishes with anecdotes or examples. His speech is sparse and colorless.

3. Caution. He's guarded and self-protective, keeping his thoughts to himself or advancing them very tentatively. He doesn't like taking chances; he uses "risk" and "gamble" as negative words. He seldom if ever proposes an original or innovative idea.

4. Neutrality. He doesn't take sides. He stays out of arguments. If asked for an opinion on a controversy, he sidesteps by saying, "I'm not sure" or "There's something to be said for both sides." It's hard to find out what he really thinks.

5. Procrastination. He handles routine matters promptly, but tries to postpone action when the stakes are high or the risk considerable. He justifies the delay by urging "further study" or requesting "more data." He likes cautionary maxims like "Look before you leap" and "Act in haste, repent at leisure."

6. Indecision. He vacillates on important matters. Or he checks to find out which decision *you* favor, and then adopts it. He rarely makes snap decisions, preferring to "mull things over."

7. Following the leader. When with you, he takes his signals from you. He seldom talks back, questions, or voices doubts. He almost never argues. He's deferential and compliant.

8. Keeping a low profile. He dislikes being "center stage" or "in the spotlight." He tries to fade into the background. He doesn't volunteer. He seldom raises his voice or tries to attract attention.

9. Preference for solitude. He prefers working alone. In a group, he hangs back and seldom jokes or socializes. He's remote, withdrawn. Some people think he's unfriendly.

10. Working "by the book." He follows policies, procedures, rules and precedents to the letter. He likes structured situations, with a detailed "game plan" and no need to improvise. He wants instructions spelled out in minute detail. Rarely, if ever, does he break rules.

11. Strong respect for tradition. He shies away from innovations; "the way we've always done it" is good enough. He prefers the tried-and-true to the new-and-unproven.

12. Pessimism. His outlook is bleak. He's more likely to see reasons why things could go wrong than right. One of his favorite expressions is "what if" ("What if the whole thing blows up in our face?"). Some call him a "wet blanket."

13. Dependency. He leans on people, and willingly lets them carry the ball. He doesn't covet important assignments. He's satisfied with back-up or support roles; he's uncomfortable in the lead.

You probably won't find anyone with all these behaviors, certainly not at one time. But a salesperson who manifests some or most of them much of the time probably has strong intangible needs for *security*.

Social (Q3) Needs

A salesperson who frequently displays some or most of the following behaviors is probably impelled largely by *social* needs.

1. Amiability. He's friendly, outgoing, easy to get along with. He seems to like everybody, and is widely liked in turn.

2. Agreeableness. He voices agreement readily, whether he means it or not. He rarely argues or pushes unpopular notions; he never belittles people or their ideas. He's exuberant and approving: "Terrific," "Great," "Fantastic." "Sensational," and so on.

3. Optimism. He has a sunny disposition and consistently looks on the bright side. Expressions like "There's nothing to worry about" or "I've got a good feeling about this" are stock phrases with him.

4. Talkiness. He talks a lot, turns short stories into long ones, uses many words where few would do, and amplifies and embroiders even ordinary topics. He carries a large inventory of anecdotes. Some people call him a "chatterbox," and occasionally avoid him because they don't have time for longwinded conversation.

5. Meandering. He has trouble sticking to the subject. He wanders from topic to topic, introduces irrelevancies, goes off on tangents, drags in trivia. He's adept at switching topics when the discussion threatens to become unpleasant.

6. Striving for acceptance. He tries hard to please and be liked. He lavishes undeserved compliments on customers, turns most sales calls into social visits, and tries to keep the conversation personal ("How are the kids?"). Not surprisingly, most customers think he's a "a nice person."

7. Intense loyalty. He often proclaims his devotion to the company, and rarely criticizes or complains about it. He's a booster ("This is the best place in the world to work," "My boss is the greatest").

8. Disorganization. He goes about his work in a loose, unstructured way. Details—especially procedural details—bore him. He's relatively unconcerned about time and territory management, paperwork, systems. He insists that what counts is not "process," but "heart" ("I don't care how you do it, as long as you put your heart into it").

9. Positive flat assertions. He makes lots of flat assertions: un-qualified statements loaded with superlatives: "He's the best cus-tomer I've ever had" ... "That's the greatest idea I've heard in a long time" ... "You always come up with something sensational" ... "This company is absolutely tops" ... and so on.

10. Sensitivity to cues. He's very alert to negative cues, and re-sponds by quickly changing his tune. If a customer frowns at some-thing he's said, the salesperson may take the remark back, or qualify it, or make a joke to imply he wasn't serious. He's good at "reading" faces and tones of voice; he's expert at detecting subtle hints of dis-pleasure.

11. Exaggeration. He usually makes things sound better than they are. He transforms good news into wonderful news, so-so news into good, and bad news into so-so (or into silence).

12. Editorializing. He has a hard time being objective. Instead of laying out the facts and letting them speak for themselves, he adds opinions that may or may not be valid. "Let me tell you something terrific ... ," "You're going to be as happy as I am when you hear this ... ," and so on.

13. Compromise. He's a mediator. If two other people in a sales meeting disagree, he's likely to become the peacemaker who advo-cates "splitting things down the middle" so that "everybody's happy." Instead of waiting until the matter's fully aired, he suggests compromise at the first sign of disagreement: "Let's not haggle ... Why doesn't everybody just give a little?"

14. Indecision. Because he's eager to please everybody, he has trouble making up his mind. He's easily swayed, deciding in favor of one viewpoint today and another tomorrow. Pressed for a decision, he'll sometimes say: "Why can't we do it both ways?"

Again, nobody is likely to do all these things consisistently. But any salesperson who displays some or all of these behaviors a good part of the time is probably motivated largely by *social* needs.

Esteem (Q1) Needs

The following behaviors—especially in clusters—are evidence of strong *esteem* needs.

1. Boastfulness. He's quick to brag. No matter what the subject, his contribution is laced with "I's" and "me's." He's always ready to take credit for worthwhile achievements, even if it means "mus-cling in" on credit someone else deserves.

2. Domination. He tries hard to be the center of attention. He monopolizes conversations, throws his weight around, and is sometimes harsh with people who threaten to push him out of the spotlight.

3. Interruptions. He frequently breaks into the middle of sentences or butts into conversations. He often interrupts customers. Some think he's rude; many consider him pushy or "nervy."

4. Obstinacy. Once his mind is made up (and it's "made up" most of the time), he's hard to budge. He digs in, sticks to his views, and seems impervious to logic. He's often called "pigheaded."

5. Self-aggrandizement. He "rewrites history" with himself as the hero. Time and again, he describes other people as bunglers or incompetents who, except for his intervention, would have "messed things up." He inflates his own reputation by deflating others'.

6. Strong views. He rarely admits he's unsure, or torn between views. He has firm opinions on everything, and he's emphatic about them ("You can bet your life . . . ," "There's absolutely no doubt . . . ," "Anybody who thinks differently ought to have his head examined"). No matter what the topic, he sounds like an expert.

7. Negative flat assertions. His speech is peppered with absolute statements—mostly negative: "That's the dumbest thing yet," "I never heard anything so impractical," "When it comes to being stupid, he takes the prize," and so on.

8. High valuation of status. He's a name-dropper, easily impressed by rank and position. He admires "winners" and "big shots"; he disdains "losers" and "pushovers." He prefers to associate with "people who count."

9. Rare credit to others. Rarely does he give credit to others, and then only grudgingly. If someone comes up with a really good idea, he's likely to urge that judgment be reserved until it's been tested ("Let's not lose our heads . . ."). If a competitor is successful, he's likely to remark that "The guy won't last . . . he's a flash in the pan" or "Anybody can make it big if he's got pull."

10. Strong need to win. He's a poor loser, and rarely acknowledges he's at fault. If something goes wrong for him, he explains it as "a bad break" or as someone else's fault ("He let me down").

11. Striving for status symbols. He's eager to surround himself with visible signs of success. A bigger company car, a reserved parking space with his name on it, an impressive title—things like this really matter to him. He's ostentatious; he not only wants to *be* important—he wants to *show off* his importance.

12. Magnifying slights. He's quick to pick up on slights and discourtesy, and treats them as serious insults. He sometimes takes remarks that most people would shrug off and converts them into "fighting words." He has no qualms about putting down others, but is extremely sensitive to being put down, and is usually ready to make an issue out of it.

A salesperson who displays a sizable number of these behaviors time and again is, in all likelihood, motivated by intangible needs for *esteem.*

Independence (Q1) Needs

Both Q1 and Q4 behavior are impelled, in part, by strong independence needs. But these needs are *expressed* differently in Q1 than in Q4. We'll talk about Q1 manifestations of independence first.

1. Argument. He carries a chip on his shoulder. He's quick to argue, sometimes going out of his way to pick a fight. It's as if he's straining to prove he does his own thinking, and that nobody is going to do it for him.

2. Rugged individualism. He's hard to supervise. He frequently listens to instructions, and then proceeds to do things his way, which he insists is *better* ("Just trust me . . . you'll see I'm right"). His confidence in his own judgment seems boundless.

3. Resistance to others' ideas. He vigorously pushes his own ideas and belittles others'. "It'll never work," "That's stupid," "It's not worth discussing" are typical responses.

4. Fixed positions. Once his mind's made up, it stays made up. His views are definite; he rarely qualifies them, or admits doubt. He speaks with great self-assurance and conviction, and refuses to be swayed.

5. Constant bids for autonomy. He tries continuously to increase his independence. He pleads with you to "let me do it my way" and to "get off my back." He seeks permission to bend the rules; if he doesn't get it, he may bend them anyway.

6. Poor teamplay. He's not much of a team player, because he has trouble subordinating his own ideas to decisions made by the team. He tries to monopolize sales meetings, makes long speeches on behalf of his own views, and scoffs at other people's.

Independence (Q4) Needs

Q4 independence is usually displayed quite differently than Q1.

1. **Self-confidence.** The sales person is self-assured but not cocky. He doesn't make a show of it. Instead of *talking* about his achievements, he lets them speak for themselves. But there's no doubt he *is* confident. He willingly undertakes high-stake assignments calling for initiative and resoluteness.

2. **Collaboration.** He's a good team player who cooperates on team projects without trying to monopolize them. He's quick to give others deserved credit. He's equally quick to admit responsibility for his mistakes; he doesn't pass the buck.

3. **Acceptance of help.** He isn't touchy about accepting help when it's needed. He's willing to be coached. No know-it-all, he's open and unembarrassed about his shortcomings, and tries hard to overcome them.

4. **Full disclosure.** He's candid and thorough; he speaks his mind without stacking the deck in his own favor. He speaks forcefully, but tries not to exaggerate.

5. **Openness to ideas.** He's receptive to other people's ideas; in fact, he's curious to know what they are. He's an attentive, courteous listener. If he thinks a suggestion's unacceptable, he says so and explains why, but doesn't "knock" it or the person who made it.

6. **Ability to work on his own.** He does large amounts of work— competently—on his own initiative. He's enterprising enough to solve many of his problems on his own; he doesn't ask for help that he can provide for himself.

Self-Realization (Q4) Needs

The need for self-realization—developing one's potential—can usually be recognized by the following:

1. **Probing.** The salesperson is curious, eager to learn. He questions, digs, tries to understand. He seldom accepts ideas just because they come from you; he wants to know if they're *good* ideas, and *why*. He has a relentless, questing mind.

2. **Candor.** He's constructively frank; he transmits information without doctoring it. He tells the whole story, not just selected parts. His compliments are sincere, his critiques worth listening to. When he

says he has good news, he's not kidding; when he says he has bad news, there may be trouble ahead.

3. Diligence. He concentrates on his job, and enjoys it for its own sake, not because it will make him look good. He's a steady, serious worker who seldom fritters away time.

4. Desire for challenge. He likes, even solicits, tough assignments. He enjoys trying things that haven't been done before. He dislikes routine, and often becomes edgy if he does monotonous work for long.

5. Risk-taking. He's willing to take chances. He's not reckless, and doesn't gamble the company's resources, but enjoys taking calculated risks. He frequently advocates untried ideas, and likes to experiment with those that promise to pay off.

6. Confronting disagreements. He acknowledges and discusses differences without rancor. He stands up for his ideas, listens, and changes his mind without embarrassment if he thinks there's good reason. In debate, he concentrates on evidence, not personalities.

7. Sharing ideas. He doesn't act as if he "owns" his ideas, doesn't "hoard" them, and doesn't use them to prove how smart he is. He *shares* them with people who can use them. A good idea, in his view, belongs to the company, which deserves full benefit from it.

8. Sensitivity. He's alert and responsive to others. He *relates* to what people say; he seldom seems wrapped up in his own concerns. He conveys interest and empathy.

Anyone who manifests many of these behaviors is probably strongly motivated by the need for self-realization—the need to *grow.*

Two Cautions

1. Bear in mind that your salespeople, being human, will display different needs at different times; deal with those needs that seem uppermost *at the time.* Yesterday's pressing needs may be less pressing today. Deal with *today's* needs. Don't expect perfect consistency in behavior.

2. In *one* brief period, any of us may display *more than one* need. A salesperson may be eager to please (evidence of Q3 social need) *and* eager to take on a tough assignment (evidence of Q4 self-realization need). If so, you'll have to deal with *both* needs. *Behavior is complex.*

A MANAGERIAL PREDICAMENT

You can infer your salespeople's intangible needs from observed behavior. But why go to all that trouble? There's a practical answer: if you *don't* know their intangible needs, you may *not* be able to motivate them. Let's see why:

- Motivating salespeople is fairly easy as long as you can satisfy their *tangible* needs. A simpleminded example will make the point:

YOU: Joe, what do you want out of your job?

SALESPERSON: To be promoted to district manager.

YOU: Okay. Close the Ajax account by the end of the month
                        and the promotion is yours.

If that's *all* there were to motivation, sales would soar.

- But that's *not* all. The fact is that *no* organization has enough tangible rewards to go around. You can't bestow a promotion, a bigger commission, or a company car on everyone who wants one. You can't assign a different territory or a different list of accounts to everyone who would like one. Tangible rewards are *always* in short supply.

This is a predicament every manager faces. The demand for the things that make motivation easiest outruns the supply. What can you do about it? Four things:

1. Satisfy the salesperson's tangible needs by using tangible rewards when you *can*. This means: use tangible rewards (a) if they're *available*, and (b) if they're *deserved*.

2. At the same time, try to satisfy his intangible needs. We'll explain how in a minute.

3. When you *cannot* fill tangible needs (either because the rewards aren't available or aren't merited), concentrate on filling *in*tangible needs.

4. In other words, if practical and suitable, satisfy *both* tangible and intangible needs. If not, at least satisfy the intangible needs.

You can now see why it's so important to observe and decipher behavior. By paying attention to what a salesperson says and does and then inferring his intangible needs, you establish a *fall-back* position for motivating him. If you don't have tangible rewards to offer (or feel you shouldn't offer them), you can fall back on *intangible* rewards—if you know his *intangible needs.*

A Caution

In motivating, remember: it's easy—all too easy—to project our *own* needs onto other people. When we project, we attribute our own ideas, feelings, or needs to somebody else, although there's no clear evidence that he thinks or feels or has the same needs as we do. We jump to the conclusion that "I feel so-and-so; he must feel the same way." In many cases, we project without even thinking about it; we *automatically* impute our ideas or feelings to others. To avoid this trap, make a *deliberate* attempt to *check* your conclusions about the salesperson's needs—especially his *in*tangible needs (it's much more common to project intangible than tangible needs). Once you've concluded, say, that he has a strong need for self-realization, ask yourself: Do I have *evidence?* Have I *observed* behavior that shows he's eager to grow? Am I assuming he has a strong need for self-realization just because *I* do? Am I trying to transform him into my psychological clone?

We all project from time to time; it's very human. But, in motivation, it must be resisted. The motivation formula *cannot* work unless you address the salesperson's *real* needs.

WHICH BENEFITS MOTIVATE?

Once you know the salesperson's needs, which benefits should you use to motivate? Obviously, we can't answer this with an exhaustive list, but we can list some of the more obvious benefits. We've done that on Figure 32. Note that *all* the tangible benefits are in limited supply—in *any* company—while the supply of intangible benefits is unlimited.

Figure 32.   Which Benefits Motivate?

NEEDS	Tangible Benefits That Are Likely to Motivate	Intangible Benefits That Are Likely to Motivate
Q1 (esteem and independence)	• Bigger salary or commission • Special responsibilities • Special or unusual assignments • Chance to handle "major" accounts • Promotion or special title • Bigger office, new furniture, company car • Freedom from paperwork required of others	• Compliments • Recognition of achievements, especially official recognition • Involvement in decision-making; opportunity to give advice • Respect
Q2 (security)	• Routinized, predictable assignments • Compensation and fringes that bolster security • Chance to work with well-established, long-time accounts	• Patience and assurance • Promises of support as needed • Absence of pressure • Working in closely-structured situations • Deserved praise
Q3 (social, esteem, security)	• Frequent opportunities to interact with others on salesforce • Chance to work with easygoing, sociable accounts • Freedom from "detail" work	• Frequent conversations with the boss • Deserved praise • Friendliness; personal touch
Q4 (independence and self-realization)	• Assignments that tap unused ability • Added responsibility • Promotion to more challenging job • Compensation tied to achievement	• Opportunity to make "extra" contribution • Candor from boss • Being kept informed • Chance to suggest new ideas • Involvement in decision-making

CONCLUSION

Our motivation formula helps clarify a subject too often shrouded in mystery. There's no reason it should be; you can understand motivation—and *do* it—by keeping a few fundamentals in mind:

1. Salespeople—like all of us—*try* to accomplish what they *want* to accomplish. They make a genuine effort to do what's *personally important and meaningful.* When they make such an effort—put their hearts and souls into it—we say they're motivated.

2. Motivation, then, is *internal*; it's a drive, an impetus, an incitement *within* the salesperson. You cannot *bestow* motivation on anyone; you can give him a raise, a promotion, or even a kick in the rear, but you *cannot* "give" him the urge, the desire, the strong wish, to achieve a goal. That must come from within.

3. What *can* you do? You can help the salesperson *become aware* that a particular goal *is* personally important and meaningful to him. You cannot create the *ends* for which he works, but you can help him find the *means* to those ends. This distinction between ends and means is critical:

- The *ends* for which the salesperson works—and we all work for certain ends, or we wouldn't get out of bed in the morning—are what we've called *tangible* and *intangible* needs. They're all the "things"—substantive and psychological—that he hopes to acquire through work.

- The *means* to these ends are what we've called *job goals.* That is, the way a salesperson can attain his ends is to attain the goals set by the company. If this *isn't* true, if the job goals cannot help him attain his ends, he's in the wrong job.

- Job goals aren't "personal." They're external to the salesperson, not a "part" of him. But tangible and intangible needs are "personal" and internal. If asked what they *really* work for, most people would answer in terms of their tangible or intangible needs—*not* in terms of their job goals. They'd say things like "I work to make enough money to put my three kids through college," *not* "I work to make sure the Ajax account is properly sold and serviced." People work for *personal*, not impersonal, reasons.

4. This poses a problem for you, the sales manager. Your job is to get people to work hard to attain their *job goals*—impersonal goals. Your job is to focus on things your salespeople consider mere *means* to ends rather than ends in themselves. How can you do this? How

can you get them to put forth effort, energy, and enthusiasm to attain *im*personal goals, when those goals aren't what they're "really" working for in the first place?

- You can do it by *linking* the impersonal goals—the job goals—to the personal goals—the fulfillment of tangible and intangible needs.

- Put another way, you can get your salespeople to see that they cannot reach their ends—fulfill their tangible and intangible needs—unless they have the *means*, unless they first attain their job goals. Once they see the *link* between means and ends—job goals and their *own* goals—they'll feel committed to the job goals.

- This is what $J + N \rightarrow B \rightarrow P$ is all about. It's what the whole subject of motivation is all about. To motivate people to attain job goals (which is what you're paid to do) you must transform the impersonal into the personal: you must take something external to the salesperson and show him why it deserves to be internalized. You can do this with $J + N \rightarrow B \rightarrow P$.

5. We're back where we started. Salespeople are *motivated*—internally impelled—to do those things that are personally important and meaningful to them. To *motivate* them—to create conditions in which they feel internally impelled—you must *personalize* their impersonal job goals by showing that these are a means to the ends *they* seek, a way to fulfill their tangible and intangible needs. If you can't do this, if you can't personalize the impersonal, you can't motivate. $J + N \rightarrow B \rightarrow P$ shows the way.

SUMMARY

1. *Motivation* is the drive to achieve a goal. The motivated person wants something enough to take action to bring it about.

2. Job goals come in two varieties: (a) *business* job goals are what the employee's paid to achieve; they focus on the external environment, (b) *behavioral* job goals are what he must do in order to achieve the business job goals; they focus on the salesperson.

3. To be Q4, any job goal—business or behavioral—should meet five criteria: (a) practicality, (b) optimal effort, (c) specificity, (d) comprehensiveness, (e) understandability.

4. The motivation process can be conveniently summarized in a "formula": $J + N \rightarrow B \rightarrow P$.

5. The motivation formula means: when a salesperson's job goal (J) is linked to his tangible or intangible needs (N), the benefit (B) of achieving the goal should become clear to him, and he should then be willing to do what's needed to achieve it productively (P).

6. There's a close parallel between motivating salespeople and motivating customers. Both depend upon crystallizing needs and then linking what's to be achieved or what's to be sold to those needs. In either case, the salesperson or the customer must see "what's in it for me."

7. A salesperson's tangible needs can usually be discerned by discussion; his intangible needs, however, must usually be uncovered by observing his behavior, looking for tell-tale clues, and then drawing correct inferences.

8. If every salesperson could be given whatever tangible rewards he seeks, motivation would be easy. But no company has enough tangible rewards to go around; they're always in short supply.

9. Therefore, if it's practical and suitable, a sales manager should strive to satisfy both the salesperson's tangible and intangible needs; if the tangible needs cannot be satisfied, however, the manager should at least satisfy the intangible needs. This is frequently the only motivational tool at his disposal.

10. Salespeople are *motivated*—internally impelled—to do what's personally important and meaningful to them. To *motivate* them—to create conditions in which they feel internally impelled—the sales manager must *personalize* their impersonal job goals by showing that these are a means to the ends *they* seek, a way to fulfill their tangible and intangible needs. If he can't do this, if he can't personalize the impersonal, he can't motivate. $J + N \rightarrow B \rightarrow P$ shows the way.

18

Coaching and Counseling

Most sales managers would probably agree that they have no more important — or difficult — job than coaching and counseling. Important because coaching and counseling — when manager and salesperson sit down to "talk things over" — is the manager's most *available* tool for helping her people *develop.* And difficult because a manger needs a great deal of *skill* to help her people develop. Coaching and counseling may look easy; it's anything but.

This chapter is about coaching and counseling: how to do it, and how to surmount the obstacles that so frequently arise while doing it. We'll offer a formal definition of *coaching and counseling* in a minute; right now — to make sure we all agree on how the term is being used — we'll offer an informal definition:

> *Coaching and counseling* is any talk between a sales manager and a salesperson that's intended to help the salesperson do a *better job.* The talk may take place in a car between sales calls, over a cup of coffee, over the telephone, in a lobby while waiting to see a customer — whenever it's timely and wherever it's convenient. The so-called "curbstone conference," where manager and salesperson stand on the sidewalk and talk over the last sales call, is a good example. What's significant about the "conference" is its *purpose*: the whole idea is to come up with an idea or ideas to help the salesperson do *even better.*

We say "even better" because coaching and counseling isn't reserved for salespeople who are doing a "bad" job. It's for all salespeople—including the best. The underlying principle is that *there's always room for improvement—and it's the sales manager's job to guide the salesperson toward that improvement.*

METHODS OF DEVELOPMENT

This chapter focuses on *coaching and counseling* as a "classic" technique for helping salespeople do a better job. But it's certainly not the only technique. Day-by-day management, formal training courses, and performance appraisal are also important. Let's situate coaching and counseling in this context:

1. **Day-by-day management.** Your day-in, day-out interactions with a salesperson—face-to-face or by telephone or my memo—are a subtle but potent technique of development. Whether intended or not, *everything* you say and do conveys a clear message: *"This* is the way *I*—the *boss*—think it should be said and done." Thus, even when not aware of it, you're a *role model.*

More than that, you can *deliberately* convert many of your face-to-face encounters into short but effective training sessions. How? With the *Five-Step Format.* It involves the salesperson and makes her think, and involvement and thought—if intelligently guided—are catalysts to development.

This is a major difference between Q4 and Q1 management. Q1 tells, instructs, dictates, imposes, and decrees, but it doesn't turn the "tumblers of the mind." It doesn't "unlock" self-discovery ("Aha!"). Because it doesn't, it's more likely to stifle development than foster it. Q4 *engages* the mind. That helps the salesperson actualize her potential. Actualizing potential—converting what *could be* into what *is*—is one of the sales manager's prime jobs.

2. **Formal training.** "Formal" training means "courses"—workshops, seminars, classes—on or off the job. Mostly, these fall into two categories: courses that impart information (product-knowledge training, for example) and courses that develop skills (a Dimensional Sales Training course, for example).

Unhappily, some sales managers equate *all* training with formal training. As soon as they spot a training need, they search for a course to fill it. They talk to the training department, study night-school catalogs, investigate outside training programs, all in the hope of finding a course which will quickly and efficiently provide what's needed. They may be disappointed.

Why? Because even if a suitable course is available, it may not provide "quick" development, especially of skills. Skills rarely develop quickly. A good course can provide the insight and know-how on which to build skills; that's why good courses are important. But the building takes time, follow-through, and practice. A course — any course — usually only begins a particular line of development, serves as a springboard to better performance. But without persevering follow-up by the salesperson and plenty of support and feedback from her manager, the better performance probably won't materialize. A course can begin the process of improvement, and cut down on the amount of time required to effect improvement, but it cannot perform miracles. (Even courses that impart information rather than skills can't be expected to pay off if the information isn't applied back on the job. There is simply no "quickie" route to growth.)

3. **Performance appraisal.** In an annual performance appraisal, manager and salesperson formally discuss: (a) how effective the salesperson's performance has been since her last appraisal; (b) why it's been effective or ineffective; (c) how she can make it more effective in the coming period. A performance appraisal can be thought of as a formal "productivity audit," in which a "balance sheet" on the salesperson's performance is drawn up, her "net worth" to the organization is calculated, and plans are made to *increase her net worth* in the next auditing period. A competent appraisal not only *leads* to development; it helps the salesperson develop *then and there.* It does this by helping her acquire insight into her performance *for herself.* The manager guides the appraisal but doesn't impose her ideas *unless* the salesperson cannot or will not figure things out on her own. The idea is to help the salesperson grow *during* the appraisal (and the periodic reviews that precede it) as well as after.

4. **Coaching and counseling.** This is the manager's most *available* tool for developing salespeople, so we'll devote most of this chapter to it. It's the most available because it's something the manager can do *whenever timely* and *wherever convenient.* There's no need to wait for a formally scheduled time or a formally designated place. Moreover, there's no need for a special budget; a manager who can't afford formal training *can* afford coaching and counseling. It's always there to be used as needed.

COACHING AND COUNSELING:
WHAT IT IS

Coaching and counseling puts the prime responsibility for training where it belongs: on the field sales manager. Most development must take place on the job. An outside seminar can help; so can the training department. But *most* development must happen while the salesperson is on the job. This means the *manager* — the person in regular contact with the salesperson — can most significantly affect her development.

Strictly speaking, *coaching* and *counseling* are different activities. Coaching develops *skills*; counseling develops *attitudes* and *motivation*. A salesperson who consistently uses closed-end questions when summary statements are called for, and vice versa, needs *coaching*. A salesperson who repeatedly refuses to submit sales reports on time needs *counseling*. (We don't mean to imply that coaching or counseling always deals with *negatives*; each also deals with *positives* — with effective performance and sound attitudes.) In the strictest sense, then, you can coach a salesperson without doing any counseling, or counsel her without doing any coaching.

Nevertheless, most coaching and counseling are tightly intertwined; it's often difficult to know where one leaves off and the other begins. For this reason, we follow common usage and talk about coaching and counseling as a *single* activity in which the sales manager deals with both skills and attitudes, although in any coaching and counseling session one or the other may predominate.

Let's start with a simple definition of coaching and counseling that isolates its major components:

A discussion (1) initiated by either salesperson or sales manager, (2) whenever either deems it advisable, (3) in which both people analyze some aspect of the salesperson's performance, behavior, or attitudes on the job, (4) in order to change, maintain, or improve the performance, behavior, or attitudes.

That's a mouthful; let's take it bite by bite:

1. Coaching and counseling can be initiated by either manager or salesperson. Usually, the manager does the initiating, but not always. Anytime a salesperson says something like, "I'm having trouble with the Ajax account — Can we talk about it?", she's initiating a coaching and counseling session, whether she knows it or not.

2. Coaching and counseling can happen whenever either party thinks it's needed. There are no set times for it; it happens because either manager or salesperson thinks it will help.

3. In coaching and counseling, both people analyze some *aspect* of the salesperson's performance, behavior, or attitudes. This differs from performance appraisal, which analyzes not *aspects* but *all* of what the salesperson is doing. Performance appraisal seeks an *overall* view of performance; coaching and counseling zeroes in on *part*.

4. The purpose of coaching and counseling is to reinforce sound behavior or attitudes so they're maintained, and to examine ineffective behavior or attitudes so they can be changed or improved. Coaching and counseling aims at *optimal productivity*.

With these four features in mind, we're ready for a fuller definition:

Coaching and counseling is the use of managerial insight and know-how to elicit self-analysis by the salesperson so as to (1) deepen her understanding of how she's doing on some aspect of the job, and why, (2) get her commitment to maintaining or improving what she's doing, and (3) get her commitment to applicable goals and action plans.

We've added three features to our definition:

1. Coaching and counseling requires *managerial* insight and know-how. You must (a) know enough about the salesperson's work to offer useful guidance and advice (you can't coach someone on how to probe a sullen, uncooperative customer unless you yourself know how); (b) know enough about human behavior to help the salesperson understand her attitude problems or interpersonal problems, if she has any; (c) know how to raise receptivity, probe, and motivate.

2. At its best, coaching and counseling elicits *self-analysis* by the salesperson. Instead of *telling* her what her problem is or how to solve it, you help her discover these things *for herself* ("Aha! Now I get it"). This doesn't always work, of course. When it doesn't, you have no choice but to tell her what she needs to know. Still and all, the aim of Q4 coaching and counseling is to elicit as much self-discovery as the salesperson can attain.

3. Q4 coaching and counseling seeks not just understanding but *commitment* to performance goals and plans. To get it, it relies heavily on the motivation formula we've described.

COACHING AND COUNSELING AND
PERFORMANCE APPRAISAL

We're ready to see how to do Q4 coaching and counseling. With minor modifications, our guidelines can also be used to do Q4 performance appraisal. Although coaching and counseling and performance appraisal are different activities, they use the same techniques. Let's make sure the differences are clear:

1. Performance appraisal is more ambitious. Coaching and counseling deals with one or a few aspects of performance; it operates in a limited area. Appraisal deals with *overall* performance and, beyond that, it provides data the company needs to (a) make optimal use of its human resources, (b) make equitable compensation decisions, (c) comply with government regulations, and (d) set yearly objectives. Thus, performance appraisal is considerably more far-reaching.*

2. Coaching and counseling, as we've seen, can happen anytime, wherever manager and salesperson find it convenient. A performance appraisal interview happens only at prescribed times (usually once a year), almost always in the manager's office.

3. Performance appraisal requires more (and more structured) preparation; coaching and counseling is sometimes spontaneous, with no preparation.

4. Performance appraisal usually takes longer. A coaching and counseling session may last ten or fifteen minutes (there's no rule about this; it could last much longer); an appraisal may well take several hours.

We repeat: in spite of these differences, both activities employ essentially the same methods and the same skills. So, although this chapter is about *coaching and counseling*, its guidelines will also prove useful in performance appraisal.

---

*For a fuller explanation of the purposes of performance appraisal, see Lefton, et al., *Effective Motivation Through Performance Appraisal*, Boston, 1980.

COACHING AND COUNSELING:
THE FOUNDATION

Effective coaching and counseling is built on five pillars: (1) trust, (2) self-analysis and self-discovery, (3) adaptive pressure, (4) the Five-Step Format, and (5) the Q4 strategies.

1. Trust. Coaching and counseling is *action*-oriented; it tries to motivate the salesperson to *do* something—improve a skill, continue doing something that's proving effective, adopt a better attitude, etc. This requires *trust*; the salesperson must believe that what you're urging her to do is in *her* self-interest. Unless she's convinced "the boss is doing this for *my* welfare," the coaching session will probably fail.

The best generator of trust is Q4 behavior. Q4—open, candid, *we*-oriented—is most likely to convince the salesperson that "the boss isn't playing games." Several Q4 guidelines are especially important for building trust.

- *Do it every day.* This is *the* basic guideline. You can't "turn on" trust like a spigot, whenever convenient. It must *be there*, all the time. If you don't build trust every day, it won't be there on special occasions.

- *Take enough time.* You won't convince a salesperson you have her best interest at heart if you hurry through coaching and counseling, impatient to get on to something else. If you don't have time to do it right, put it off until you *do*. Hurry-up coaching may be worse than none at all.

- *Start with a benefit statement.* One way to convince the salesperson the session is in her best interest is to *tell* her, at the start, "what's in it for her." A clear, believable statement of tentative benefit will help establish trust early.

- *Don't carve your ideas in stone.* Obviously, you're going to start with some ideas about what the salesperson is doing and should do. But don't treat them as immutable "laws"; treat them as "hypotheses"—educated hunches. If you become convinced a hypothesis is wrong, change it, and *admit* it. Otherwise, you may create the impression you've rigged the session—hardly a way to generate trust.

- *Keep the salesperson involved.* A Q4 coaching session is a *dialogue*, a *joint* effort to reach understanding and commitment. It is *not* a pretext for beating down the salesperson. If you Q1 her by monopolizing the session, if you expound your views and neglect hers, you'll convince her you don't care what she thinks. Trust will go out the window.

- *Don't give instant advice.* A strong temptation in coaching is to jump right in and say, "I think you should . . ." Resist it. If the salesperson's receptivity is low, your advice will drive it lower by generating resentment ("The boss doesn't care what *I* think"). So probe first, spin up receptivity, get her views, and *then* offer your advice.

- *Face up to disagreements.* Few things will lower trust faster than the suspicion that you're ducking an issue. If you won't acknowledge and discuss a difference, the salesperson's bound to wonder why ("What's the boss afraid of? Why won't she admit we don't see eye-to-eye? Is she hiding something?"). Once these suspicions take root, you'll have a hard time building trust.

- *Don't push for total agreement.* It's a rare coaching and counseling session in which both people see eye-to-eye on everything. While you want to resolve any disagreements, you don't want the salesperson's "unconditional surrender." Understanding and commitment, your ultimate goals, require fairly full agreement, but not absolute symmetry of views. If you can't get complete agreement (and, if she has strong Q1 needs, you probably won't), settle for partial. Otherwise, you'll wipe out whatever trust you may have built.

To sum up: unless the salesperson trusts you, believes that whatever you say is for her sake (as well as your own and the company's), the best you can hope for is grudging submission. *Committed* follow-up will occur only if she's convinced you're acting in her best interest.

2. **Self-analysis and self-discovery.** Q4 coaching and counseling aims at self-discovery by the salesperson ("Aha! *That's* what I ought to do"). Your role is that of a guide who brings her to realize *for herself* what's going on and what to do about it. Because the discovery *is* her own, it's more credible and persuasive than if it came from you.

Self-discovery, however, can only come *after* self-analysis. The salesperson must first *think* about what she's doing, what the consequences are, what they should be, and so on. To stimulate this analysis, *probe.* Ask pointed questions, clear the air of emotions that inhibit logic, give her time to think, keep the analysis on track, or she may never get to "Aha!" "Aha!" may sound spontaneous, but it's not; it's the result of *hard thought.*

Why bother with self-analysis and self-discovery? After all, you can much more quickly explain her situation to her. So why go to the trouble of getting her to figure it out for herself? For three reasons:

- We *retain* more of what we discover for ourselves, and we retain it longer. That's because we *work* to discover it, and the effort seems to etch the discovery into our brains.

- We *understand* more of what we discover for ourselves. By puzzling-out problems, we see things we'd otherwise miss. If we hear the solution from somebody else, we hear only the conclusion, not the steps that led to it. If *we* work out the solution, we know how it was reached. That deepens our understanding.

- Self-discovery is more likely to product a *committed* change in behavior. A conclusion *we* reach is *ours*; we own it; we have a stake in it. A conclusion imposed by someone else is hers; we don't feel any ownership; we may even resent it. It's much easier to *care* about our own conclusions, and care, after all, is what commitment *is*.

Q4 coaching and counseling *aims* at self-analysis and self-discovery, but it sometimes misses the mark. Some salespeople, as we'll see in detail later, won't or can't analyze or discover; others can do so only limitedly. Some writers liken the Aha! effect to a light bulb being turned on in the brain; using that metaphor, we can say that for some people the bulb is burned out, and for others it's very dim.

Thus, to do Q4 coaching and counseling, encourage self-discovery when feasible, and impose your conclusion when not. The imposition can usually be Q4; it need not be heavyhanded or bullying. But it must be *firm*. For *some* salespeople, coaching and counseling means compelling and constraining.

3. **Adaptive pressure.** Q4 coaching and counseling always sets a goal or goals for the salesperson; it's *action*-oriented, and action requires a goal to strive toward. As we've seen, a Q4 goal, which should emerge from Q4 coaching, demands *optimal effort* — the golden mean between "too easy" and "impossible."

This means Q4 goals must have *pressure* built in. The *amount* of pressure must be right for the salesperson being coached. A goal with the "right" amount seems neither trivial nor impossible; it seems worthy of serious, sustained effort. It asks the salesperson to stretch, but not to break. Figure 33 illustrates what the right amount of pressure means to performance. The figure helps us make four generalizations:

Figure 33. Adaptive Use of Pressure.

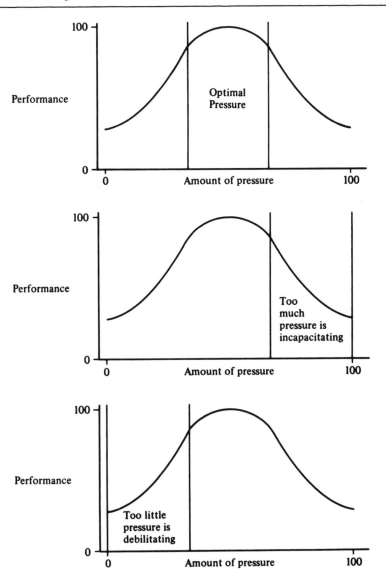

- Salespeople with strong Q1 needs can usually handle fairly heavy pressure (in fact, they usually apply strong pressure to themselves); they want to shine, to be admired ("She's a real go-getter"), so they're usually willing to tackle fairly demanding goals. They need two things: goals that require considerable exertion, and *direction*. Without direction (which they don't *want* but do *need*), they may squander their efforts.

- Salespeople with strong Q2 needs don't handle heavy pressure well; if anything, they already feel under heavy pressure (whether imaginary or real is beside the point), so they hardly require more. Thus, the pressure built into their goals must be carefully controlled, and coupled with *reassurance*.

- Salespeople with strong Q3 needs often need *more* pressure than they're getting; they tend to be easygoing, even lackadaisical. So their goals should contain both some extra pressure, and *structure* to make sure they follow through. If the pressure isn't structured, it may be wasted.

- Salespeople with strong Q4 needs usually handle pressure well; they like fairly strenuous goals, because these offer the best chance to grow. So build considerable pressure into their goals (not *too* much, of course), and give them as much *autonomy* as feasible.

It's obvious that the answer to the question "How much pressure is optimal?" is "It all depends." It depends on the *salesperson*. A goal considered "tough but achievable" by one may seem "too easy" or "impossible" to another. Thus, to set optimal goals—and do optimal coaching and counseling—you must know your people as individuals, and *individualize* your use of pressure. That's a major part of Q4 management.

4. The Five-Step Format. Q4 coaching and counseling follows its own version of the Five-Step Format. Before discussing it, we'd better clarify an earlier point.

A few pages back, we said that coaching and counseling is sometimes impromptu, with no preparation. This is true; if a salesperson walks into your office and says, "Boss, I'm stuck; there's something about this new price schedule I don't understand. . . . Will you help me figure it out?", you'll probably do some coaching and counseling then and there, without getting a chance to prepare. Quite a lot of coaching is extemporaneous.

But this doesn't mean you *shouldn't* prepare for coaching and counseling; it simply means you can't always do so. When you can, you *should*. The session is almost sure to be more productive if both you and the salesperson do some advance work. Here's what we have in mind:

a. Set objectives for the session ahead of time; be clear about them *before* starting the session.

b. Gather data you expect to prove useful. Don't risk getting bogged down during the session by a lack of information.

c. Plan the Q4 strategy you expect to use. Make sure it fits *this* salesperson.

d. Tell the salesperson why you're setting up the session, and how she can prepare. Give her as much chance to get ready as you can. Try to eliminate "surprises" at the session.

So much for preparation. Let's look at the session itself.

A FIVE-STEP PROCESS

Back in Chapter 2, we said that what happens in Q4 coaching and counseling *parallels* what happens in Q4 selling. Both are five-step processes; in both, the five steps are *basically* the same:

Q4 selling	*Q4 coaching*
1. Open the call	1. Open the talk
2. Explore customer needs	2. Get the salesperson's views
3. Present your product	3. Present your views
4. Manage objections	4. Resolve disagreements
5. Close the call	5. Work out an action plan

Because of these similarities, we won't spend a lot of time describing the five steps to Q4 coaching. A brief description should do.

Q4 Coaching

Step 1: *Start the talk*

Objectives. You want to ensure two things in this first step: (1) that the salesperson's ready to pitch in and help the discussion along; (2) that she doesn't feel threatened (remember: many people feel threatened by "discussions" with the boss; if the salesperson feels that way, her receptivity will be low).

- *Be suitably sociable.* Do what's necessary to start off on the right foot (for instance, if the salesperson has strong Q2 needs, begin on a low key; if strong Q3 needs, chat a little; and so on).

- *Explain the purpose and benefit.* Tie the benefit to her needs ("Jane, let's take a few minutes to examine that last call, so next time a customer starts yelling like that, you can calm him down and save yourself the kind of browbeating you just took").

- *Set the ground rules.* Explain how the session's going to work. A good way to do it is to run through the five steps very quickly. That way, the salesperson will understand, at the outset, the role she's expected to play.

- *Probe receptivity.* Don't be surprised if she's tense or reluctant. Many people are apprehensive about coaching; they're afraid they'll be blamed, bawled out, or belittled. So, before plunging ahead, make sure she's willing to plunge with you. If she's not, spin up her receptivity.

Step 2: *Get the salesperson's views*

Objectives. You have one prime aim in this step: to find out what the *salesperson* thinks about what's being discussed. Why should you care? First, because you may *learn* something—get hold of some useful information. Second, because you want her to feel *committed* to any decisions you reach, and she's much more likely to feel committed to a decision she's shared in shaping; it'll be "our" decision, not "yours." Why should you get her views *now—before* giving her yours? Because you're the boss, and if you disclose your views first you'll probably squelch or color hers; if you want *candor,* make sure *she* talks first.

- *Probe.* To find out what a salesperson thinks, ask her. Start with an open-end probe, and keep on until you get the whole story.

- *Promote candor.* This is often hard to do in coaching, because the salesperson may not want to talk about her shortcomings (not all coaching deals with shortcomings, but much of it does). So, instead of Q4 disclosure, you may get Q1 bravado or Q2 evasion or Q3 meandering. Stick with it; dig deep; don't settle for less than her *real* thinking.

- *Withhold your opinions.* Whatever she says, keep your reactions to yourself. Don't jump to conclusions (or, if you do, don't say what they are). If she finds out what *you* think, she may tailor her remarks to please you, and you can say goodbye to candor.

Step 3: *Present your views*

Objectives. You want to do three things in this step: (1) respond to the salesperson's ideas, (2) present your own if they differ, and (3) make sure each of you understands the other.

HOW TO DO IT

- *Tell her where you agree.*   If you go along with her ideas, say so. If any are especially good, be sure to give her credit.
- *Explain where and why you disagree.*   If some of your ideas differ, explain them, but without belittling hers. Try to prove that your ideas will work, and that they'll be good for her (this is comparable to developing benefit statements during a sales call).
- *Summarize.*   Once you're sure she understands your views, summarize the points on which the two of you agree and those on which you disagree. Don't be surprised if there's some fairly strong disagreement; after all, if you've been critical, she may take exception to your remarks. So be prepared for denial ("I did not say that"), defensiveness ("I still say I did the right thing"), depreciation ("Aw, it wasn't really *that* serious") or resentment ("You're picking on me"). Deal with all these by probing.
- *Get the salesperson's reaction.*   Probe to see if she understands and if she agrees. Watch out for automatic Q2 ("Whatever you say") or Q3 ("Terrific!") responses; try to get her *real* reactions.

Step 4: *Resolve disagreements*

Objectives.   You now want to (1) clear the air of emotions and (2) settle as many of your differences as possible.

HOW TO DO IT

- *Summarize both positions.*   Before any disagreements can be resolved, both of you must agree on what you disagree *about.* To do it, spell out each issue — each unsettled point ("Regina, as I see it, the question is whether or not you should have offered the discount so early in the presentation . . . "). Then summarize where the salesperson stands on the issue, then where you stand. Probe to make sure she agrees with—and understands—your statement of the differences.

- *Explore the positions.* Probe so the salesperson *thinks through* her position. Then explain your own. The idea is not to "knock down" her position while bolstering your own. The idea is to expose the pros and cons of both positions (it's possible that her position will prove stronger than yours). This exploration is likely to spark some heat as well as light. The salesperson may become defensive, resentful, sullen, even belligerent. So be prepared to vent these emotions. Open-end and reflective probes should help. Once both positions have been explored, see if there's a third or fourth position that's sounder than either.

- *Settle your differences.* Compare all the positions. Pick the one that promises to be most productive for everyone concerned. This may not be easy. If you can't reach agreement on one conclusion, you'll probably want to *impose your own,* unless you're not sure what the conclusion should be; in that case, you may want to let the subordinate reach her own conclusion and then try it out. This comes down to a "judgment call" on your part, and it obviously depends on factors only you can be aware of. The thing to remember, of course, is that when it comes to settling differences, you're in charge.

- *Confirm the decision.* Get the salesperson to voice her understanding of what you've agreed on, or, if you must, do it yourself. Either way, make the decision *explicit.*

Step 5: *Work out an action plan*

Objectives. Now that you've resolved your disagreements, you want to (1) come up with several solutions to the original problem, and pick the best; (2) work up a plan for carrying it out, and (3) make sure the salesperson understands—and *buys*—both the solution and the plan.

HOW TO DO IT

- *Ask the salesperson to propose some solutions; pick the best one.* She probably has some good ideas; ask for them. If the solution is one she devises, she'll almost surely be committed to it. Add any ideas you think should be considered. What counts is that the two of you come up with the best solution, regardless of who originated it. To do it, discuss the various proposals, modify them, combine them, do whatever seems best — but come up with the one *both* of you think will *work best.*

- *Make the benefit plain.* Make sure she understands that the solution will be *good for her.* (If it won't be, there's not much chance she'll follow through on the action plan.)

- *Devise an action plan.* Spell out what's necessary to *implement* the solution. Let her take as much initiative as she can in developing the plan.

- *Check understanding and commitment.* Finally, probe to insure that everything's *clear* and *acceptable* — that the salesperson knows *what* she's supposed to do and *why*, and *believes* in it. If she does, you've just finished a successful coaching session.

Two Basic Points

Whenever you coach, keep two points in mind. They're fundamental:

1. **Try for self-discovery by the salesperson.** If you can, get her to work things out for *herself.* Get her to say what it is that needs improving. Get her to say how it can be done. Guide her to the solution of her own problem. This is *self-discovery.* It's not always possible (some salespeople can't or won't do it). But where it is possible, it's the *ideal.* A salesperson is almost sure to understand and be committed to an idea she's discovered; she's not so sure to understand or be committed to an idea that's *imposed* on her (in fact, she may resent it and work to sabotage it.) In the best coaching, the salesperson, *guided by* the sales manager's probes, reaches her *own correct* conclusions.

2. **Where self-discovery is impossible, impose your own conclusions.** If diligent probing doesn't produce the "Aha! effect" ("Aha! *Now* I get it") which marks all self-discovery, if the salesperson cannot or will not figure things out for herself, do it for her. After all, you're the manager, and you're ultimately responsible for what happens in your operation. Try for self-discovery; if that doesn't work, *tell* the salesperson what's needed. One way or the other, make sure that by the end of the session she knows what's what.

THE INTERACTIONAL DILEMMA

Our last comment leads to something basic to all coaching and counseling: the predicament we call the *interactional dilemma.*

In a coaching and counseling session, you want three things to happen:

1. You want the salesperson to *contribute* something—an idea, some information, an insight, a perspective—that will help both of you accomplish more *together* than alone. You want the discussion to *synergize*—to produce results *greater* than the sum of your individual efforts (otherwise, why bother talking?).

2. You want the salesperson to *discover*—for *herself*—something she didn't know (for example, how to do her job better). Whatever the discovery, it should be one she makes (even though you guide her). You want her to experience the "Aha" effect ("Aha! *I* get it").

3. You want the salesperson to *grow*, to come out of the session knowing or believing something that will help her do a better job.

These things should always happen in coaching and counseling. But what if they don't?

• What if the salesperson cannot or will not contribute? What if she lacks intellectual ability or experience? What if she's determined—for whatever reason—to withhold her contribution? What if she tries to undermine the session?

• What if she cannot or will not discover things for herself? What if your best efforts never produce the "Aha" effect?

• What if she cannot or will not grow? What if she doesn't want to? What if she prefers to stay as she is? What if she can't grow any more?

What if Q4 management, which should produce synergism, self-discovery, and growth, doesn't? This is *the interactional dilemma.* A *dilemma* is a choice between two *un*satisfactory alternatives or sets of alternatives. It's a *bind*—in which the best you can do is pick the *least damaging* alternative. Here are the two horns of the interactional dilemma:

1. You can Q1 it—railroading your ideas and demanding that the salesperson do things your way, or you can Q2 it—shrugging

your shoulders and letting the whole matter drop, or you can Q3 it — glossing things over and insisting that there really are no significant differences between you.

2. You can Q4 it — explaining your own ideas reasonably and calmly, and then making it plain that you expect them to be followed. You can say, in effect, "I see things quite differently. . . . These are my expectations." What makes this Q4? Three things:

    a. Your action comes *after* the salesperson proves unable or unwilling to contribute and achieve self-discovery — *after* she's had a fair chance to do so.

    b. Your action is *not* arbitrary; it's accompanied by a reasonable explanation. (The Q1 railroading of ideas *is* arbitrary; it's a flat-out demand without explanation.)

    c. Your action is *not* hostile. It neither blames nor belittles. It's simply an effort to move off dead-center and get the job done. (The Q1 railroading of ideas is usually accompanied by put-downs and fault-finding.)

Which horn of the dilemma should you grab? Obviously, the *second* one. Impose your ideas without anger or acrimony. This isn't ideal — not by a long shot — but it *is* realistic. It should produce some results. The alternatives, bulldozing or going along with things as they are, are worse.

We can summarize all this graphically, in what we call the GUIDE continuum (Figure 34).

GUIDE is an acronym for *growth* potential, *understanding, insight, desire,* and *effectiveness.* In deciding where a salesperson fits on the continuum, you must answer five sets of questions:

1. **Growth** potential. How much *untapped capacity* for growth does she seem to have? Can she, eventually, take on more responsibility, or is she working at or near her limit?

2. **Understanding.** Is she *intellectually capable* of synergizing, discovering, and growing? Does she have the education, training, and intellect?

3. **Insight.** Does she have what it takes to see *herself* as she is? Can she look at herself honestly? Can she take it?

4. **Desire.** Is she *motivated* to synergize, discover, and grow? If not, can she *be* motivated? Or is she indifferent, and determined to stay that way?

Figure 34. The Guide Continuum.

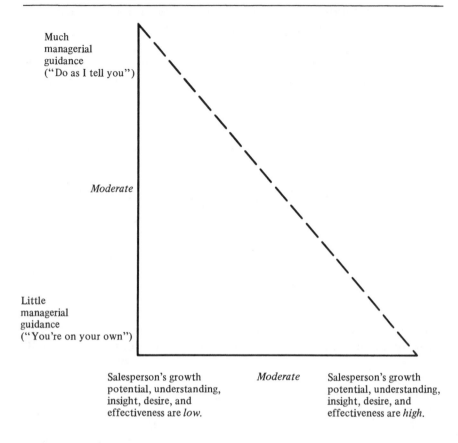

Much
managerial
guidance
("Do as I tell you")

Moderate

Little
managerial
guidance
("You're on your own")

Salesperson's growth   *Moderate*   Salesperson's growth
potential, understanding,   potential, understanding,
insight, desire, and   insight, desire, and
effectiveness are *low*.   effectiveness are *high*.

5. **Effectiveness.** What's her present level of skill and knowledge?
   How well is she currently performing?

The answers will tell you where, in general, the salesperson belongs on the GUIDE continuum. And that will tell you how much
guidance—how much *direction*—to provide.

The GUIDE continuum not only explains why different salespeople need different amounts of guidance; it illustrates the fact that
different salespeople have different capacities for development:

1. Salespeople differ in their *growth* potential. Growth transforms possibility into actuality; not all salespeople have the
   same possibilities.

2. Salespeople differ in their ability to *understand*. Their intellectual capacity varies.

3. Salespeople differ in their degree of *insight*. The ability to see yourself as you are varies considerably from person to person.

4. Salespeople differ in their *desire* to develop. The notion that everybody wants to grow simply isn't true; some people are perfectly content to stay as they are.

5. Salespeople differ in their present *effectiveness*, which means they differ enormously in the amount of development they need to reach optimal productivity.

The GUIDE continuum, then, is a guide to how much a salesperson can be expected to develop, how long it might take, and how much of your effort it will require.

A Caution

This doesn't mean you can always predict development accurately. People sometimes confound all predictions. A salesperson who seems headed for dramatic growth may disappoint us; one who seems unable to grow may surprise us. The GUIDE continuum is not infallible. Still and all, every sales manager must make some predictions about her people. All you can do is base those predictions on what you've observed; the GUIDE continuum will help *organize* your observations. Your predictions may be wrong, but, if you've been a fair, careful, objective observer, chances are they'll most often be right.

To be a fair, careful, objective observer, however, you must know if your biases are distorting your observations. If they are, you'll have to correct the distortions before predicting. Here are three distorting tendencies to look out for:

• Q1 management is usually unwarrantably pessimistic about human development. It sees subordinates as lazy or incompetent even when the facts indicate otherwise. Observation is distorted by stereotypes.

• Q2 management is usually unwarrantably pessimistic, too. A common Q2 notion is that people are what they are, so nothing much can be done to change them. Fatalism distorts observation.

• Q3 management may be unwarrantably *optimistic* about human development. Impressed by silver linings, it may ignore the surrounding clouds, and conclude that people are capable of *more* than the facts warrant.

In using the GUIDE continuum, then, always ask: Am I basing my judgment on what I *know*, or on what I *imagine?* Confront your own biases as well as the facts.

Q4 STRATEGIES

We've just said that the amount of guidance you provide in a coaching session must be tailored to the individual salesperson. But, more than that, all five steps to effective coaching (like the five steps to the sale) must be tailored, too. Basically, the strategies are the same in both coaching and selling; dealing, say, with a salesperson's Q1 behavior is a lot like dealing with a customer's Q1 behavior. Obviously, with a salesperson, you have one thing going for you that you don't have with most customers: *clout.* You can impose your ideas on a salesperson (how *successfully* is another matter) but you can't impose them on a customer. Still and all, there's a very close similarity between the two situations. For that reason, we'll describe the Q4 coaching strategies very briefly.

The Q4-Q1 Strategy

1. *Stress esteem and independence benefits.* Remember: this salesperson doesn't like coaching because it cramps her style and reminds her who's boss. So it's very important to show her how the session can enhance her self-image and enlarge her freedom.

2. *Vent hostility; probe flat assertions.* You'll probably get a fair amount of both ("Who says I didn't handle that call right? I know exactly what I'm doing"). Be prepared to do plenty of reflecting and digging.

3. *Deal with the salesperson's concerns first.* If she wants to get something off her mind, let her do it before getting into your concerns. She may become resentful and spiteful if she feels she's being neglected.

4. *Don't get annoyed.* Or, if you do, don't let it get in the way of what you're trying to do. Q1 behavior can be irritating, but if you let it get to you, and show it, it'll impair the problem-solving process. Even if you're *feeling* riled, try to stick to your Q4 game plan.

5. *Be strong, but don't Q1 it.* It's very tempting to answer Q1 with Q1, but also self-defeating. What's needed is *obvious* but *quiet* strength—Q4 strength. Speak with conviction; assert yourself; make it plain that you believe what you're saying. But steer clear of flat assertions and Q1 noise.

6. *Rely heavily on open-end probes, summary and reflective statements.* The idea is to manage the discussion without making the salesperson feel "boxed in." So leading and closed-end questions should be used sparingly.

7. *Be prepared to shift your behavior when the salesperson does.* Nobody's locked into Q1. You may be pleasantly surprised to notice a change in her behavior—especially if *you* Q4 it. Change your own accordingly.

The Q4–Q2 Strategy

1. *Stress security benefits.* This salesperson would rather not be coached. After all, coaching means *confronting* problems, which she doesn't like to do. Furthermore, most coaching ends with agreement that the salesperson do things *differently.* That's disruptive; it breaks into the comfortable Q2 *routine.* So, to coach this salesperson, you'll have to convince her it'll make her *more* secure—not less.

2. *Be patient; slow down.* If you fidget or hurry, you'll only make a nervous salesperson more nervous. Take it easy; you won't teach her much if you put her under strain.

3. *Show genuine interest.* This salesperson needs to be assured—and reassured—that you're really on her side, that you want her to succeed. That'll set some of her anxieties to rest. Be interested, and *show* it.

4. *Guide firmly but gently.* Aim for self-discovery, but realize that it'll take a good deal of probing on your part. Provide the necessary guidance, but don't try to save time by pushing her faster than she's able to go.

5. *Stress open-end probes, pauses, brief assertions.* Watch out for leading and closed-end questions; don't make her feel "cornered."

6. *Adapt your behavior to shifts in hers.* If your strategy works, she may loosen up a bit. If you pressure her, however, she may move toward Q1. Be prepared for either possibility.

The Q4–Q3 Strategy

1. *Stress mostly social (but also security and esteem) benefits.* What does it take to get this salesperson to change? Basically, the conviction that *other people will be pleased* by the changes. If you can make that point, you'll have a lot going for you.

2. *Socialize, but don't overdo it.* There's almost no way to coach this salesperson without engaging in some chitchat. There's a danger here: once you see she really *does* enjoy talking with you, you may find it hard to resist talking *too much.* Be careful.

3. *Guide firmly; be specific.* We've said it before: this salesperson *needs* structure. Vague generalities won't do; she'll provide those herself. She needs well-organized, systematic, and thorough direction.

4. *Don't be lulled.* Unless you force yourself to doubt, you may believe all the enthusiasm and goodwill this salesperson's spouting. And you may convince yourself she's ready and eager to change. That's a risky assumption. Check it out. *Probe.* You may find some strong doubts and reservations under all that exuberance.

5. *Rely heavily on closed-end questions, summary and reflective statements.* Unless you have lots of time to kill, go very easy on open-end probes and pauses.

6. *Shift your behavior if her behavior shifts.* Nobody's genial and easygoing *all* the time. Coaching does produce pressures, and these can push Q3 into another quadrant. Be ready.

The Q4–Q4 Strategy

1. *Stress self-realization and independence.* This salesperson appreciates coaching, and *expects a lot* out of it. Unless you show her how it'll help her grow and achieve, you'll dampen her enthusiasm, and water down her commitment.

2. *Be candid, but don't make flat assertions.* This sounds easier than it is. All of us, when we're candid, tend to make flat-out statements: "You're dead wrong," "I've never seen anything like it," and so on. Don't weaken your credibility by exaggeration. Be precise.

3. *Be ready to be challenged.* This salesperson will ask tough questions, request proof, and maybe tell you things you don't want to hear. Don't expect the session to be easy; it could prove very demanding.

4. *Use the full range of probes.* You might find open-end probes and summaries especially useful, but you'll probably need *every* probe before you're done.

5. *Change your strategy if her behavior shifts.* She's only human. Her behavior can and may move to another quadrant. Be ready.

THE CONTENT OF Q4 COACHING

We've covered the Q4 coaching process. But how about its content? What should Q4 coaching and counseling cover? To answer that, let's go back to our distinction between coaching and counseling.

- Coaching focuses on *skills* and *information*. A salesperson who doesn't know how to prospect or handle Q2 behavior, who lacks product knowledge or gets confused when using the price book or demonstrating the product, or who can't spin up customer receptivity or vent anger or organize her call schedule, needs *coaching*. Much Q4 coaching (but certainly not all) zeroes in on the skills discussed in this book: sizing-up skills, timing skills, communicating skills, motivating skills, strategy-planning skills.

- Counseling focuses on *attitudes* and *relationships*. A salesperson who refuses to make calls after 4:30 in the afternoon, or antagonizes customers by flippant responses to their complaints, or breaks promises to customers, or thumbs her nose at company policies, or argues incessantly with her manager, or constantly exceeds her expense allowance, or refuses to pass along leads to other salespeople in the company, needs *counseling*.

As we've said, neither coaching nor counseling need be *exclusively* about *negatives*. It frequently zeroes in on *positives*. Still and all, most coaching and counseling is triggered by problems—by things the salesperson *should* do but *cannot* or *will not do*.

One word of caution: *counseling*, as we use the term, is not counseling in the *clinical* sense. A salesperson may need clinical counseling, but, if she does, that's not a job for the sales manager; it's a job for a specialist in the appropriate mode of clinical counseling. For example, you may counsel a salesperson whose performance is being impaired by a "drinking problem," but the purpose of the counseling should be limited to getting agreement that there *is* a problem and that an *effort* should be made to solve it. Beyond that—unless you're clinically qualified to analyze and treat drinking disorders—you ought not to go. The diagnosis and treatment of the problem—the clinical counseling—should be left to an appropriate specialist. The rule is this: when counseling, counsel only in your field of competence.

DEVELOPMENT IS INCREMENTAL

Don't expect startling or dramatic results from coaching and counseling. The whole idea is to help people develop, and people develop incrementally. Incremental change happens in small steps, each built on the one before. There's seldom anything startling or dramatic about it.

Human development (except perhaps for very rare experiences outside the scope of this book) is evolutionary, not revolutionary.

Revolutionary change is sudden, abrupt, all-at-once; what existed yesterday is toppled and replaced by something else today. Evolutionary change is slow, continuing, unspectacular; what existed yesterday still exists today, but slightly modified; what exists today will exist tomorrow, but with further modifications. Each modification may be too small to be noticed; only when a number of modifications accumulate is any significant change noticeable.

One specialist who's written very convincingly about this is Thomas K. Connellan of the Management Group, Inc.* He advises managers who want to develop subordinates to (1) avoid the fad effect, (2) tolerate setbacks, and (3) be patient.

The *fad effect* is the belief in what Connellan calls "business cure-alls": training gimmicks that suddenly appear on the scene, announce themselves as panaceas, and then disappear some time later as suddenly as they emerged. The fad effect occurs because sales managers *want* to believe there's an instant remedy for every sales problem, even though nobody's yet found such a remedy or is likely to.

Everything we know about human development leads to one conclusion: it's a step-by-step, time-consuming process in which false starts and detours are almost inevitable.

This brings us to Connellan's second point: in developing salespeople, you must be willing to tolerate setbacks. There are no foolproof development techniques. No matter how carefully you plan and direct things, you're virtually sure to encounter setbacks. That's because you're a fallible human being guiding another fallible human being in situations constantly affected by still other fallible human beings. So, temporary blockages or even reversals are to be *expected*.

Finally, as Connellan says, patience is a must. Results rarely occur overnight; when they do, they're usually so small they're imperceptible. It's unrealistic to complain, as some sales managers do, that "I sent her to a seminar last week and don't see any results." It may be months or longer before results are visible.

Dimensional Sales Training seminars, which utilize the principles in this book, are a good example. These seminars are intensive; for five straight days (or sometimes three), salespeople work hard at developing timing skills, probing skills, presentation-planning skills, and so on. Yet it's safe to say that in the vast majority of cases there are no noteworthy results in the first week or two after the seminar. The salespeople return to their territories, some changes may be visible, but nothing much seems to *happen*. There are three reasons for this (all of which also apply to coaching and counseling).

*Thomas K. Connellan, *How to Improve Human Performance*: New York, 1978.

- It's difficult to replace habitual behaviors with newly-learned skills. The habitual behaviors feel "comfortable"; the new skills feel "awkward." The habitual behaviors can be performed without even thinking; the new skills can be performed only with a certain amount of strain. Not surprisingly, then, many people return to the job from DST and find themselves mixing "easy" old behaviors with "hard" new ones. They are *not* transformed into Q4 paragons overnight.

- Furthermore, the newly-learned skills have yet to be *perfected*. The seminar taught the skills in the only way they *can* be taught: in a rudimentary, basic way. Now, back on the job, they must be refined, sharpened, improved. This can be done only through steady practice and application. That takes *time*.

- The skills are designed for interpersonal situations. But interpersonal relationships are rarely transformed in a twinkling. It takes time for interactional skills to "take hold," to make a difference. Suppose, for instance, a salesperson who impresses her customers as brash and arrogant attends a DST seminar, returns to the job, and tries conscientiously to use the Q4 skills she's learned. Even if she immediately applies the skills with great assurance and polish (which is unlikely), how realistic is it to assume that her customers will immediately respond to her as if she's always Q4ed it? The question answers itself. In spite of her best efforts, it will *take time* for the new behavior to take hold and make a real difference.

The moral: no matter what you do to develop your people – coaching and counseling or anything else – don't expect miracles.

A FINAL THOUGHT

At best, coaching and counseling is hard to do – no matter what the salesperson's behavior. It's hard to do because, in most cases, it calls her performance (or part of it) into question; it criticizes (it may also praise, but, in most cases, it *does* criticize – and even *Q4* criticism is seldom fun to hear); it requires change – and change is rarely easy. That's why *self-discovery* is so important. If you can get the salesperson to call her *own* performance into question, to analyze it, and to realize for herself that change is required, you stand a *much* better chance of doing effective coaching. But you can't guide anyone to self-discovery without *excellent probing skills*. If this book has made any one point, it's this: probing is no "fringe activity." It's at the very heart of successful sales management – and successful selling. It deserves all the practice you can give it.

AN EXAMPLE

In Appendix B, you'll find the transcript of a fictitious coaching session, in which all the elements of the session are clearly marked out. It should solidify the points made in this chapter.

SUMMARY

1. Coaching and counseling is the sales manager's most available tool for helping her people develop. It's not reserved for salespeople who are doing a "bad" job; it's for all salespeople – including the best.

2. Besides coaching and counseling, day-by-day management, formal training courses, and performance appraisal are important methods of development.

3. Strictly speaking, coaching and counseling are different activities. The former develops skills and knowledge; the latter develops better attitudes and motivation. In practice, however, the two activities are usually intertwined, so they're spoken of together.

4. Coaching and counseling can be defined as the use of managerial insight and know-how to (a) elicit self-analysis by the salesperson so as to deepen her understanding of how she's doing on some aspect of the job, and why; (b) get her commitment to continuing or improving what she's doing; (c) and get her commitment to applicable goals and action plans.

5. Effective coaching and counseling is built on trust, self-analysis and self-discovery, adaptive pressure, the Five-Step Format, and the Q4 strategies.

6. To build trust, the manager must do it every day, take enough time, start with a benefit statement, refuse to carve her ideas in stone, keep the salesperson involved, refuse to give instant advice, face up to disagreements, and be willing to settle for less than total agreement.

7. Self-discovery (the "Aha!" effect) can come only after self-analysis. Self-discovery is important because we retain more of what we discover for ourselves, we understand more, and we're more likely to be committed.

8. Q4 goals demand optimal effort – the golden mean between "too easy" and "impossible." They require built-in pressure, which must vary with the individual.

9. The Five-Step Format, modified by the appropriate Q4 strategy, is as basic to Q4 coaching as to Q4 selling.

10. In Q4 coaching, try for self-discovery by the salesperson. If that's impossible, impose your own conclusion in a Q4 way. The GUIDE continuum is a useful tool for determining how much guidance you should exert in a coaching session. But it's not infallible.

11. Development is incremental; it happens in steps, over time. That's why it's rarely startling or spectacular.

19

What's In It For You?

By now, you've read nearly a whole book advocating Q4 behavior, but may still be wondering what—if anything—is in it for *you*. Do the skills really work? Can they help you get a bigger payoff from your efforts?

The answer to both questions is "yes," as we'll demonstrate in this chapter. More than that, we'll explain how you can make Q4 skills part of your everyday routine. After all, reading a book is one thing, putting it to use is something else. We'll explain how you can put *this* book to use.

WHAT'S THE EVIDENCE?

A large number of major corporations use Dimensional Sales Training–II, which teaches Q4 skills to salespeople by employing the concepts in this book. Many of these companies, eager to make sure that they get what they're paying for, maintain close follow-ups on the results of DST–II. Figure 35 (page 287) is a composite of the findings of a number of these companies.

The figure makes two things clear:

1. The vast majority · who go through a DST seminar find the skills useful—provided they're *used*. *If applied on the job*, the skills taught in this book can improve sales performance.

280

2. While *all* the skills are useful, *probing* skills are the most useful. That's probably because they're a component of every other skill. If you don't know how to probe, you cannot (except by accident) do Q4 exploring of needs, Q4 demonstrating of benefits, Q4 closing, or Q4 anything else. Probing skills are fundamental.

Figure 36 (page 288) provides additional evidence for the usefulness of Q4 sales behavior. To help you understand it, we'd better explain the "Model Sales Strategy":

In a DST-II seminar, each salesperson selects an *actual* prospect or customer—a real "target" account—who meets two criteria: (a) the prospect or customer must represent good sales potential, and (b) the potential must so far have proven "impossible" to convert into a sale. In other words, the salesperson selects a customer he's supposed to but *cannot* sell. Working with his seminar team, the salesperson plans a detailed "Q4 strategy" for making this "impossible" sale. During the seminar, he practices the strategy and fine-tunes it. After the seminar, he uses the strategy in the field with the *real* prospect or customer. Figure 36 shows how many of these strategies have produced *closed sales* in four major (and very different) companies. The figure is a good illustration of two points:

1. A remarkable number of "unsellable" prospects—whom the salesperson "knows," from experience, cannot be closed—*can* be closed when Q4 skills are used. Very frequently, a salesperson who says, "I've tried to make that sale, and it cannot be done," really means, "I've called on that prospect, used a Q1 or Q2 or Q3 approach, and found that it doesn't work." When the same salesperson tries again, using a Q4 approach, the results are very often reversed.

2. The format used for planning the Model Sales Strategy can be used repeatedly. It's not a one-shot device; it can be applied again and again.

Figure 37 (page 289) offers still further evidence for the value of Q4 skills. It details the experience of a major oil company which has used DST-II for many years. As the first four items show, *all* the salespeople who have gone through the program have used DST skills to *change* the way they prepare for calls, conduct calls, present benefits, and handle objections. Have these changes improved *results?* In 92 percent of the cases (item #5), the answer is "yes"; Q4 skills have helped *close sales.*

From all of this (and much similar evidence is available) it's pretty clear that Q4 skills *do* work and *will* help you get a bigger payoff from your selling efforts—*if* you put them to use. The big question is: "How can you do it?" The answer is: "By systematic self-development." We'll use the rest of this chapter to explain.

FOUR WAYS OF SELF-DEVELOPMENT

To develop yourself means to change yourself. The change may be dramatic or subtle, but *change* there must be. By definition, *development* means *improvement*, and that requires *changing* the way things are now. Most self-development—change in behavior—involves the following:

1. The self-perception gap. We can best explain the self-perception gap by urging you to do something we mentioned earlier: re-take the questionnaire on your own sales or management behavior in Chapter 2. If you do, and if you discover that your *present* behavior isn't what you want it to be—that you usually display more Q1 or Q2 or Q3 and less Q4 than you'd like—*that's* a self-perception gap— a realization that there's a *distance* between where you are *now* and where you'd *like* to be. A simple diagram should help you visualize what we're talking about:

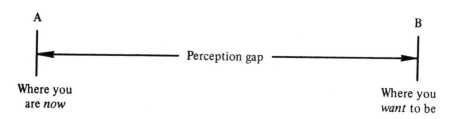

Line A is your *present* "behavioral position"—the way you typically interact now with customers or salespeople. It may be largely Q1 or Q2 or Q3 or some combination of them. Line B is your *ideal* "behavioral position"—the way you'd *like* to interact. Naturally, since you've now read virtually all this book, we'll assume that B consists entirely, or at least largely, of *Q4* behavior.

The diagram helps us make the crucial point: if your present interactional behavior isn't all you'd like it to be—if you perceive yourself at Line A but would like to be at Line B—there's only one way to close the gap: *by mastering Q4 skills.* The skills we've presented in this book are the bridge that will take you from A to B—from where you are to where you want to be.

We're saying, in effect, that experiencing a self-perception gap is a good thing—because that's how most self-development begins:with the awareness of a gulf between our *actual* behavior and our *ideal* behavior—between the things we *do* and the things we feel we *ought* to do.

This isn't surprising. After all, as we've seen repeatedly, all of us are *motivated* to do things when we feel that doing them will fill a need and thereby make us better off. The self-perception gap is the awareness of a *need*—a need to change behavior and thereby become more effective. If you take a reasonably candid and objective look at your present behavior and conclude that it *is* very largely Q4, then of course you'll see no need to change—and feel no motivation to do so. But if you take a reasonably candid and objective look at your present behavior and conclude that it's largely Q1 or Q2 or Q3 or a combination—and if you're convinced that more Q4 behavior will help you do a better job—then you will see a need to change—and be motivated to do so.

One good way to start the process of self-development, then, is to cast a cold eye on your present behavior and ask: "Is it all I'd *like* it to be? Would I get a bigger payoff for my efforts if I exerted more Q4 skills more often?" If the answer to the second question is *yes*, then you have all the reason you need to *master* Q4 skills.

2. Practice. This is essential. Any bridge between your present behavior and Q4 will be mightly rickety unless you consistently *practice* Q4. We'll say more about this later. For the moment, suffice it to say that *all* behavior—playing the piano, selling, managing salespeople—must be practiced over and over to become genuinely effective. There are *no* short-cuts.

3. Modeling. The power of example is important in changing behavior. If you want to make your behavior more Q4, single out people in your company who display Q4—and then, when you can, watch them in action. Note the way they interact with others or with yourself, in meetings, in discussions, under stress, and so on. You don't want to *copy* their behavior, but *emulate* it—use it as a *basic pattern* for your own.

4. Feedback. Seek out feedback about your behavior from people in your own company (as well as friends and relatives) who display Q4 behavior and whose opinion you respect. Don't be shy: *ask them* what they think about your behavior. Explain that you've embarked on a program of self-development, and that they can help you. If what they tell you doesn't seem fully candid, try out your probing skills in an effort to spin up their candor. Remember, the truth may sting a little, but there's no better way to find out what you're doing that you should do differently.

THE NEED FOR Q4 GOALS

We've said there's only one way to close the self-perception gap: by mastering Q4 skills. This takes more than good intentions; it takes *Q4 goals.* "I want to be a better salesperson" is *not* a Q4 goal. Neither is "I want to get ahead in my company." These are wishes or hopes or aspirations, but not Q4 goals, because they don't require optimal effort (in fact, as worded, they don't require any definite effort at all), they're not specific, and they're not comprehensive. We won't repeat what we said on this topic earlier; we'll simply say that *yearnings* are not to be confused with *goals.* Yearnings cannot, by themselves, lead to *action*, because they're not *operational*; they cannot be put to *use.* Goals, on the other hand—genuine Q4 goals— *are* operational; they *can* be put to use. Q4 goals are signposts; they mark the point you want to reach. Without them, you can only stumble around, looking for an unmarked destination called "Self-Development."

Here's a technique that should prove useful in closing the self-perception gap:

1. List a couple of *specific business events* facing you in the coming week. If you're a salesperson, pick sales calls; if you're a sales manager, pick coaching and counseling sessions.

2. Spell out, on paper, your *goals* in the events you've selected. Write out the goals in *Q4* terms.

3. Develop a plan-of-action for achieving each goal. Make sure the plan incorporates the use of Q4 skills.

4. Repeat the process the following week. This time, pick three or four events. Keep *expanding* your use of Q4 skills each week until they become "second nature."

Here are a couple of examples:

Event	Goal	Plan-of-Action
(For salesperson) August 4. Sales call on Hal Casper of Federal Plastics.	Persuade Casper to replace his current extrusion equipment with our Model 270G; get signed agreement to have new equipment delivered and in operation by December 15.	A. Plan and practice presentation evening of August 3. B. Review plan shortly before call. C. Follow Five-Step Format during call. Be especially sure to probe carefully during Step 2; Casper is usually pretty tight-lipped about his needs. D. Rely heavily on Q4 strategy for Q2 behavior (unless Casper's behavior changes during course of call).
(For sales manager) August 6. Performance review with Delores Holt.	Find out why Delores' sales have slumped 20% in last 3 months. Work out plan-of-action to bring sales up to former level.	A. Review chapter on probing in Dimensional Selling book. B. Write out examples of probes that would be especially helpful in finding out what's happened to Delores' sales. Remember her receptivity will probably be low. C. Practice these probes on tape recorder the evening before the meeting. D. Follow the Five-Step Format during meeting. Use Q4 strategy for Q1 behavior.

The important thing, of course, is not *our* examples but *yours*. Set your own goals, work out your own action plans, and follow through. There's no other way to get from *here* — where you are today — to *there* — where you want to be. Even with the best intentions in the world, you can't close the self-perception gap without Q4 goals and action plans.

THE IMPORTANCE OF DOING

This brings us to our final point: it takes more than *reading* to develop Q4 skills. Reading is important; it provides the knowledge so vital to development. But knowledge isn't *know-how*. Know-how is the ability to put knowledge to work — to make it produce results. And know-how comes from *doing* what you've read about, *applying* knowledge again and again until "people insights" become *people skills.* The strongest claim we can make for this book, then, is that it's a start. If you set it aside and forget it, it will make no difference at all in the results you get. If you keep it near at hand and *apply* it, we confidently predict you'll develop into a more productive salesperson or sales manager. If you read it and follow it up by participating in a Dimensional Sales or Sales Management Training seminar, where you'll systematically practice Q4 skills and receive feedback, we confidently predict you'll become even more productive. How *much* more productive we can't say; a lot depends upon your present skills, upon how diligently you apply the ideas in the book, upon the support from your company, upon a myriad of circumstances. Nevertheless, we stick with what we've just said: if you *do* what you've read about, you'll become more productive.

It's up to you.

Figure 35. How Dimensional Sales Training Improves the Selling Process.

(Composite findings of a number of companies using DST–II)

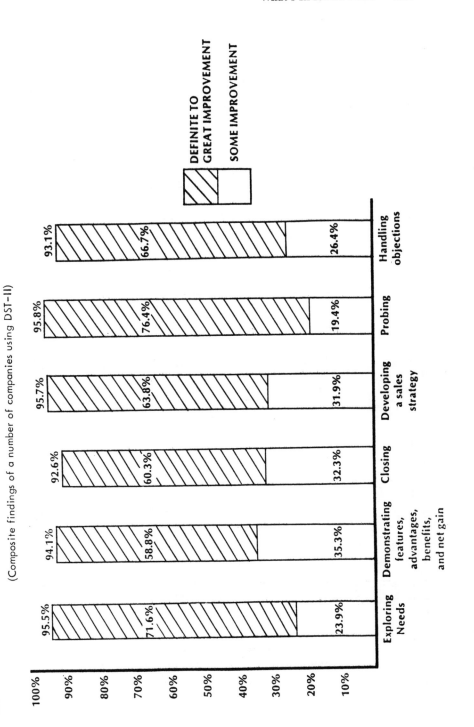

Figure 36. "Unsellable" Customers Sold After Dimensional Sales Training.

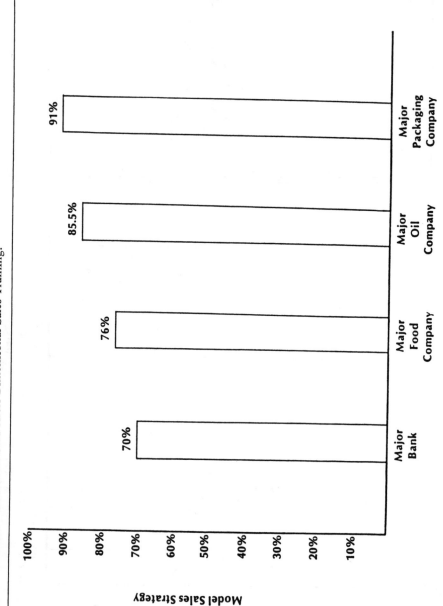

Figure 37. Changes Produced by Dimensional Sales Training.

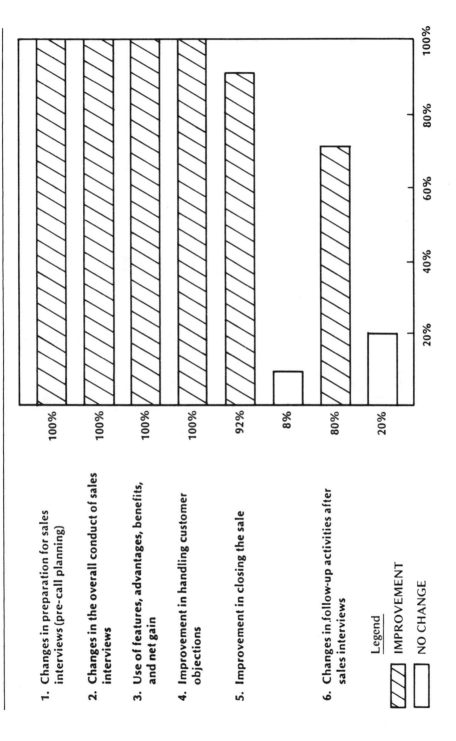

A Q4 Sales Presentation

You've read a lot *about* Q4 selling, so you'd probably like to see an example. The following "transcript" illustrates the use of Q4 sales behavior in a situation where the customer's behavior is mostly Q1. While the presentation follows the Five-Step Format, we've tried to make it sound natural, not mechanical. For example, we've had the customer raise objections earlier than Step Four, just to show that, in the real world, customers rarely conform to a preconceived scheme. Nevertheless, we've tried to show that it's *still* possible to follow the Five-Step Format; there's no reason for a salesperson to be thrown off-track by a wayward customer.

Step 1: Open the Call

	Salesperson	*Customer*
Greeting: Open-end probe	Mr. Wood, good to see you. How's it going?	
		Could be better.
Suiting sociability to the needs of the customer	Yeah. I figured that out on the phone. You sure sounded hassled.	
		You would, too, if you were in the middle of overhauling a whole operation. We're revamping our production procedures—

Salesperson	*Customer*
	all of them. The geniuses in our engineering department dumped the project on me—without any warning. Everything would be fine if those clowns stopped sticking their noses in my business and let me run things the way they ought to be run.
No wonder you're hassled. Surprises like that can really make things tough.	
	You're telling me. Outside interference always causes problems. In fact, there's so much turmoil around here that you're lucky I agreed to see you. We've got to get our copier situation squared away . . . real fast. Otherwise, I wouldn't give you the time of day.

Statement of purpose and benefit

Checks willingness to proceed
Open-end probe

That's why I'm here: to help you square away your copier situation. While I'm at it, I can also show you how our Model F copier will help you run things the way you want. How's that sound?

I'll reserve judgment. Let's get on with it. I don't have all day.

Step 2: Explore Customer Needs

Open-end probe (opens up broad topic)

Okay, then. Let's zero in on the essentials. I know you're one of those managers who thinks things through for himself . . . so you must have given this copier business a lot of thought. Tell me . . . overall, what do you want out of a copier?

I'll tell you in four short words. Speed. Reliability. Service. Quality. We make a lot of copies that go straight to customers, so they've got to be good.

	Salesperson	*Customer*
Summary statement	Let me jot this down. Speed. Reliability. Service. Quality. Right?	
		Right. And I'm not going to buy unless I get all of them. I'm not about to get stuck with another piece of junk.
Neutral probe (narrows topic; seeks amplification)	You're right. You shouldn't. Tell me what you're looking for when it comes to speed.	
		When it comes to speed, you're in trouble. I've already talked to a couple of your competitors and they've both got faster machines than yours. And I'm not about to buy a slow machine. The people around here are slow enough on their own. They don't need help from the equipment.
Acknowledges objection Neutral probe (seeks further amplification)	You're wise to compare. That's the only way to buy. And speed's important—you're right on that, too. Tell me more, though, about why you're stressing speed.	
		Because nobody . . . nobody . . . is going to accuse my department of dragging its feet. Sometimes we duplicate technical manuals— hundreds of copies of hundreds of pages. For our engineering department. And I'm not going to let those guys over there take a shot at me for being slow.
Neutral probe (seeks amplification)	I can appreciate that. I'd feel the same way. Tell me . . . how frequent is *sometimes?*	
		Hard to say. Two, maybe three, times a year.
Open-end probe (opens up new aspect of subject)	Two or three long runs each year. Fill me in on the rest of your copying jobs.	
		Boy! You *are* inquisitive. Okay . . . most of the stuff we do requires 1 to 4 copies—letters, memos,

Salesperson	*Customer*
	proposals, stuff like that. Remember . . . everybody in the building uses the same machine— the one in my department. That's another reason we need speed. I don't want all those outsiders standing around the machine any longer than necessary, talking to *my* people. It's just one more form of interference.

Summary statement followed by closed-end probe

So mostly the copier's for short runs. Right?

Yeah. Mostly. But don't forget... when we do long runs, we do *real* long runs.

Open-end probes

Okay. How about reliability? What are you looking for there?

No mystery. I've got to have a copier that works and works right . . . all the time. We've got a terrific volume of copies, and we can't handle it if the machine breaks down. Remember what I said: this is the *only* machine in the building. When it goes hay- wire, we're in trouble.

Closed-end (fact- finding question)

You've had breakdowns before?

You better believe it. And I'm sick of it. Sure . . . any ma- chine's going to break down once in a while. But that's where service comes in. When we got the copier we're using now, we were promised service within 3 hours of a call. Not *told*, mind you. *Promised.* And that prom- ise has been broken—lots of times. That's one big reason I'm talking to other manufacturers.

	Salesperson	*Customer*
Open-end probe	What happened?	
		A complete foul-up, that's what. Sometimes we wait two days for service, and then half the time the service reps don't know what they're doing. They really don't. Either they don't have the parts '... or they fix it and five minutes later the machine breaks down again.
Summary statement	So you can't rely on the machine or the service. When I describe our Model F, let's make sure I cover the service feature.	
		Don't worry. I'll make *plenty* sure. There's no way you're going to avoid *that.*
Summary statement	You can depend on it. Let me recap what I hear you saying. You say at least four things are important. Speed. Reliability.	
Closed-end question	Service. And quality of copies. Anything else?	
		No . . . that's it.
Checks receptivity	Okay. What do you say if we look at the Model F and see how it fills the bill?	
		Go on. But don't waste my time on blue-sky claims. I don't want to hear that stuff. Just give it to me straight. I'll make up my own mind.
	Fair enough.	

Step 3: Present the Product

	Let's start with speed.	
		Start wherever you want. But... like I said . . . you're in trouble on speed. I've already found two machines faster than yours.
Proof cycle #1	Well . . . you can look at speed two ways: copies per minute . . . and short-run time.	
		That doesn't make sense.

Salesperson	Customer

Salesperson

It will—as soon as I explain. Copies per minute is important on long runs . . . like those technical manuals. It measures the copies you get once the machiine actually starts copying.

Customer

What's that got to do with short-run time . . . or whatever you call it?

Short-run time is *all* the time it takes to make copies . . . starting with walking up to the machine, warming it up, loading it, getting your copy, and leaving.

So?

Establishes benefit by linking feature and advantage to customer need.

So short-run time is the real measure of efficiency. Our Model F has the lowest short-run time in the industry. Thirty seconds or less, from walking up to the machine to walking away. With all the short runs you do, that could be real important. No long lines at the machines. How does that sound?

Seeks confirmation
Open-end probe

It sounds like you're side-stepping a big issue. Long-run time. How long do long runs take?

Leading question

Long-run speed is 50 copies a minute . . . just a little slower than some machines. But, since you only do 2 or 3 manuals a year, isn't short-run time what really counts?

I'm not so sure. We do have to copy technical manuals. And I don't like losing time on them. Time's money, you know.

Checks receptivity

You're right. So let's look at some numbers. Exact numbers. Okay with you if we compute some actual times?

Now you're talking. Show me some numbers.

	Salesperson	*Customer*
Closed-end (fact-finding question)	Okay. What's the average number of pages in a manual, and the average number of copies?	
		About 150 pages. And a couple of hundred copies.
Closed-end probe	Okay. I'll work this out on the calculator. That's . . . uh . . . 30,000 pages. And the Model F turns out 50 pages a minute, so actual copier time is 600 minutes. Ten hours. Right?	
		No argument. But one of your competitors does 60 copies a minute.
Acknowledges objection and gets customer to provide own answer	Alright. 30,000 pages at 60 a minute is . . . uh . . . around 8½ hours. An hour-and-a-half saving every time you copy a manual.	
		I see what you're up to. At 3 manuals a year, that's a saving of 4½ hours. no big deal . . . is that what you're thinking?
	Not exactly. Four-and-a-half hours is nothing to sneer at. It's just that 4½ hours over a full year has to be stacked up against what you do *every day*.	
		So you're back where you started: short-run time is most important.
Seeks confirmation Open-end probe	That's how I see it. How about you?	
		I'll think about it. But speed's not the whole story. I need reliability . . . and service . . . and quality. Speed doesn't mean a thing if we get lousy copies . . . or the machine goes dead.
Checks receptivity Closed-end probe	I'll buy that. So let's look at quality. Okay?	
		Shoot.

	Salesperson	*Customer*
Proof cycle #2	Here's a bunch of originals . . . not copies, originals. Some photos and some technical drawings . . . the same kind of thing you turn out. And here's a stack of the same stuff . . . only these were copied on the Model F. How do	
Open-end probe	they look?	
		I've seen worse.
Open-end probe	How would you feel about copies like these going to your customers?	
		I'd settle for that. Can I keep these? I want to compare them to the others I'm evaluating.
	Sure. We'd welcome the comparison.	
		Y'know, these samples bother me. After all, you made them on your own machine. You guys probably tune up that machine twice a day. No wonder it turns out good copies. How do I know the one that's delivered to me will do as well? After all . . . I won't have a bunch of service reps taking my machine's pulse every day.
Checks receptivity Closed-end probe	You're right. So that brings us to reliability. Can we talk about that?	
		Go ahead.
Proof cycle #3	Mr. Wood, copiers are our business. Our only business. My company sinks or swims with its copiers. There's nothing else to keep us afloat. So we can't afford to market a mistake. That's why three years of testing went into the Model F. No machine in the industry has ever been as thor-	
Open-end probe	oughly debugged. How does that sound?	
		Very unconvincing. Look . . . tests don't prove anything. I want *proof*. *Prove* your machine won't break down.

Salesperson	Customer

	Salesperson	Customer
	I can't prove it'll *never* break down, but . . .	
		Okay. Stop right there. You guys are all the same. Lots of blue sky. Lots of poetry. But no hard proof. I can't live on words. I need *dependability* . . . *guaranteed* dependability. If you can't give it to me, there's no point in going on.
Reflective state-ment to vent customer's feelings.	You really feel pretty strong about that.	
		Sure I do. The guy who sold me my present machine talked about testing, too. And debugging. And his machine's sitting down the hall right now . . . *completely unusable.* I was played for a chump once . . . but not again. I don't like to look bad. And that machine sitting there makes me look bad. So I'll ask you one last time: can you *prove* your machine's reliable . . . or can't you?
Acknowledges and answers objection	Yes, I can. Here's a brochure . . . prepared by an independent research agency—an outfit that's completely unaffiliated with my company. It spells out the per-formance record of every major copier on the market.	
		Performance record?
	It's all here. Details on the Model F compared to our competitors. See for yourself how we stack up.	
		I see. Number one, huh? Hmmm. Here's another copier I looked at. Number seven. Okay if I keep this?
Closed-end question (seeks confirmation)	Sure. Convinced?	
		Yes and no.

	Salesperson	*Customer*
Open-end question	What do you mean?	
		Look, the book says your copier's number one. But that doesn't mean it *never* breaks down. And when it *does*, everything depends on *service*. To me, that's what really counts. *Service*. What I want to know is: how good is your service? You promised you'd come back to that.
Closed-end question	I did . . . and I will. Right now. But first, are you convinced about our reliability?	
		Yeah. I guess so. But I don't want to talk about reliability. I want to talk about service.
Proof cycle #4	Y'know, service is largely a matter of organization, and we're *organized* to provide fast, effective service. We've got a service center . . . a big one . . . right downtown here, with a full line of parts. And we've got a staff of five service technicians. They've all been with us at least two years. So if you've got a problem with the Model F . . . any kind of problem . . . we'll have a technician over here fast . . . and he'll have access to whatever parts he needs. You won't have to wait overnight while a part's brought in from out of town.	
		How fast is fast? With the machine we've got now, we usually wait two whole days before the technician even sticks his head in the door. This "fast" stuff doesn't impress me.

Salesperson	*Customer*

Acknowledges objection and answers it

I understand that. But we don't operate like that. We've got a long history of fast responses to service calls. One to three hours. So your downtime will be minimal.

> Sounds good. But I'm not in the market for sounds. I'm in the market for service. I got the same song-and-dance from our present supplier. I want a *guarantee* that I'll never have to wait more than three hours for your service rep. How about it?

We don't have a formal, written guarantee. But we've got the next best thing: a list of customers who can verify our service. I'll give you the list . . . and you can call as many as you want. How's that?

Open-end probe

> Okay. I was going to ask for references anyway.

I'll get the list over to you today. But I should warn you about one thing. Not *everybody* on the list can tell you about our service.

> Why not?

Because many of them have never *called* for service. They haven't had any problems.

> That's okay. I want to talk to some of them, too. Believe me, I intend to check out your machine—all the way. I got burned once. It won't happen again.

I know it won't. Not with the Model F. I'll get that list to you . . . so you can start checking us out today if you want. Now . . . have we covered everything?

Closed-end question

> Yeah, I guess so. I got these sample copies. And this brochure. As soon as I get that customer list, I guess I'll have everything.

	Salesperson	*Customer*
Closed-end question to uncover remaining objections	Good. Now, about those doubts you expressed . . . have we settled them?	
		No. Not really.

Step 4: Resolve Objections

	Salesperson	*Customer*
Reflective statement. Open-end probe	Okay . . . something's still bothering you. What is it?	
		I just don't think your machine's right for me.
Acknowledges objection (neutral probe) and probes for details (open-end probe)	It's not right for you. How come?	
		Too slow. Just too darned slow. Every time engineering wants a technical manual copied, there's going to be a delay.
Summary statement followed by closed-end question to confirm	You're still concerned about long runs. Right?	
		Absolutely.
Summary	You don't feel the short-run advantage outweighs the few hours you'll lose on long runs.	
		No, I don't. My problem's with engineering, and engineering needs long runs.
Neutral probe (seeks amplification)	Expand on that.	
		It's simple. Two or three times a year, those wise guys develop a new technical manual. Then they dump it on *my* department for duplicating. And they breathe down my neck 'til it's done. I don't like that. This is *my* operation . . . and I run it *my* way. I don't like anybody coming in here telling me what to do. See?

	Salesperson	Customer
Brief assertion (to show interest and continue flow of information)	I'm not sure. Keep going.	
		Look, I want a machine that'll do the job *fast* . . . so I can get engineering's nose out of my business. As long as *my* people are running copies of *their* manuals, they can come in here and lean on us. *And I don't like being leaned on.* I don't want to be criticized for buying a slow machine, either. Not by *those* guys. I'm not giving engineering an excuse to take a swipe at me. Get it?
Summary statement followed by closed-end probe to confirm	I get it. The extra 4½ hours a year it'll take to do those manuals on the Model F will put you at a disadvantage with engineering . . . because it'll open you up to interference and criticism. Is that about it?	
		Yeah. That's it. And that's why the Model F's wrong for me.
Begins to answer objection	Mr. Wood, you said you'd talked to a couple of competitors whose machines are faster on long runs.	
Closed-end probe	Did they leave samples?	
		Yeah. Just like you.
Closed-end probe	Have you got them handy?	
		Right here in the drawer.
Closed-end probe	Mr. Wood, if you were convinced . . . really convinced . . . that the Model F would make *better* copies than any other copier . . . and if you could show engineering you'd bought a machine that produced better copies than they'd ever had before . . . would that make a difference?	
		Yeah . . . I guess so.

Salesperson	*Customer*

Alright, then. Why not compare
our samples with the competitors'
. . . right now? I'll sit here and keep
quiet . . . and let you convince
yourself. You're a toughminded guy
with a lot of savvy. I'll abide by any
decision you come to.

> Fair enough. Let me get the
> samples out of the drawer . . .
> Hmmm . . . maybe you're right.

**Probes for
confirmation**   See any difference?

> Yeah, yours are a little clearer.
> More black-white contrast. No
> gray smudges.

Fine. Doesn't that prove you can
impress engineering . . . get their
applause instead of their criticism
Leading question   . . . with *our* machine?

> I don't know. I'm impressed,
> okay. But, remember: these are
> *samples.* Naturally, you checked
> them out before giving them to
> me. I still don't know that a
> *regular* run of copies will look
> this good.

Good point. Let me make you an
offer. Come on over to our service
center any time today or tomorrow
that's handy. Bring 150 sheets of
anything you'd like copied. We'll
run 20 or 30 copies of everything,
just as if we were running technical
manuals. You can watch the whole
operation, and when we're done
you can see for yourself if the
copies aren't as good as those
Closed-end probe   samples. Fair enough?

> Fair enough. I'll do it.

	Salesperson	*Customer*

Step 5: Close

Summary of benefit	Fine. Mr. Wood, let's take stock. You said you wanted four things in a copier: speed . . . quality . . . reliability . . . service. You've seen that the Model F gives you speed . . . especially on short runs . . .	
Probes for confirmation	and comes fairly close to its competitors on long runs. Right?	
		Yeah, I'd say so.
Probes for confirmation	As far as quality goes, you've seen the samples. And you'll see the demonstration at our service center. How's that sound?	
		Fair enough.
Probes for confirmation	Alright. Now . . . on reliability . . . you've got a copy of the performance record showing we're number one. And . . . on service . . . you're going to call our customer list. Agreed?	
		Agreed.
Asks for commitment (trial close)	Okay. Why don't I call you Thursday . . . day after tomorrow? By then, you'll have had a chance to talk to some of our customers and watch the demonstration. If everything checks out, we can get the order signed and set up	
Open-end probe	delivery. How's that sound?	
		Hold on a minute. If you're trying to stampede me, you've picked the wrong guy. I'm not about to be rushed into anything. There are two or three machines I still want to look at.
Acknowledges objection and begins to answer it	Mr. Wood, I'll repeat what I said before: you're right to compare. That's the way to buy. And that's exactly what the performance record will help you do.	
		What do you mean?
	Well . . . the performance record compares us with *every* major	

Salesperson	*Customer*
copier on the market. And that's an independent comparison, remember.	
	Yeah . . . I guess that's true.
Mr. Wood, do you recall your exact words when I first got here?	
	My exact words? No. Why would I?
Well, I do. You said . . . and I think this is exact . . . "We've got to get our copier situation squared away . . . real fast. Otherwise, I wouldn't give you the time of day."	
	You've got a good memory. I did say that.
You also said: "Nobody is going to accuse this department of dragging its feet."	
	I've got to hand it to you. I said that, too.
Okay. You've given me the time of day. As a result, you've seen how you can get your copier situation squared away . . . real fast . . . so nobody can accuse your department of dragging its feet. Now . . . from *your* point of view . . . if the customer check and the demonstration both pan out . . . wouldn't it be to *your* benefit to order the Model F?	
	Alright. I'll go along with that. You know, this department's got a reputation . . . a *deserved* reputation . . . for getting things done. I don't want that reputation tarnished. And I don't want to give engineering a chance to swipe at us. Set up the demonstration. How early does your service center open tomorrow?
Eight o'clock.	
	Good. Make it eight, then.

Side annotations:

Closed-end probe

Repeats customer's own words to show he was listening (appeals to Q1 need)

Leading question for final commitment.

Salesperson	*Customer*
Fine. I'll alert our service manager.	
	And call me Thursday. How long will delivery take?
We can have the machine installed one week after the order's signed.	
	Okay. The sooner the better.

Works out action plan

Salesperson	*Customer*
Mr. Wood, we'll see you tomorrow ... 8 a.m. ... at the service center. Third at Spruce. Plenty of parking behind the building. And I'll drop off the customer list this afternoon. Leave it with your secretary.	
	Good.
One last thing. Thanks very much for giving me the time of day. I think it's been beneficial to both of us. I even think it'll pay off for your engineering department.	
	Those idiots! Who cares about them?
I thought *you* did.	
	Ha! I take back everything I just said. You've got a *lousy* memory.
See you tomorrow ... 8 o'clock.	
	Okay. Take it easy, wise guy.

A Q4 Coaching Session

Here's a "transcript" of a fictitious coaching session. The salesperson's behavior is mostly Q3.

Step 1: Open

Sociability

So tell me, Rose! How's it going?

Great Frank! You know, I think we got a green light from Stan McDonald over at Pacific Air Transit. I went by again yesterday . . . and it sounds like they might upgrade their alarm system and go with our A3900. So we'll not only have the Monitor in place, but we might get all their electronic alarm business. In *all* their centers!

Brief
Assertion

Sounds good.

"Good"? Fantastic! They have distribution centers up and down the coast. Dozens of them. That'd be a great piece of business. And the way they're expanding, we'd expand right along with them. Their business has already changed over the last few years. Now they're into Industrial.

Reflective	You're pretty excited about the add-on.	
		I'll say. It's great to know a customer likes what he's got so much he wants more.
Closed-end	If it goes through, it'll be just about your biggest sale so far, won't it?	
		Uh huh. It's a good thing I took the time to go back to see Stan. You know, he's a good guy. Good businessman, too. He was telling me about some of the things going on at Pacific . . . some of the stuff he has to keep track of, I'll tell ya . . .
Interrupts, refocuses Reflective	Excuse me, Rose, I'm glad you and Stan hit it off so well. And it's great to know we have a shot at the A3900. I'm sure you're proud.	
		Well, Frank, I've had a lot of support from you.
Closed-end *Back on track*	And you'll keep on getting it. Now . . . whaddya say we get on with the meeting?	
		Sure, Frank. Whenever you say.
Closed-end	Good. Keep me posted on Pacific Air, will you?	
		Sure. Glad to.
General purpose *General benefit* Closed-end	Now . . . what we wanna do is take stock of how you're doing . . . a progress report . . . come up with some ways to help you land more customers and keep 'em on our side—like Stan at Pacific Air. Okay?	
		Go to it. I've been trying *real* hard, you know that. Anything that'll help me get more accounts like Pacific sounds good.

Specific purpose *Specific benefit* Closed-end	Good. Let's narrow in on a couple of things: call reports and price quotes. There may be some things we can improve upon, okay?	
		To tell you the truth, I thought I was doing all right there. But ... you know ... I'm always ready to listen.
Ground rules *Probe* *receptivity* Closed-end	Good. Let's take'em one at a time. I'll ask you for your thinking first ... then tell you how I see things. Then we can iron out any wrinkles, come up with some improvement goals, and figure out how to reach them. Sound all right?	
		Sure. Whatever you say.

Step 2: Get Salesperson's Views

Open-end	First, call reports. What specifically do you recall about your most recent call reports?	
		Well, let's see. I think I'm getting them all in.
Neutral Closed-end	You "think." Not sure?	
		Not absolutely, but I think I've given you all of them. Haven't I?
Closed-end	Not as far as I can tell. I don't have anything on Piazzolla Foods. Remember doing that one?	
		Piazzolla. Hmmm. That's interesting. I don't recall. I seem to remember writing something down; maybe I just didn't put it down on a call report. I'll check it out. Either way, I'll get you a copy. Rest assured.
Closed-end	Okay. Piazzolla's one I didn't see. Any others?	
		Could be. I'm not really sure, Frank. Sometimes I don't have the call report forms with me. And sometimes I go right from one call to another ... you

know, I hate being late. You can't very well tell a customer you showed up late because you were filling out a call report. So . . .

Interrupts   Rose?

Yes?

Closed-end   Can we say it just boils down to not always having your call reports made out?

It sure looks that way. I guess I've been a little careless about them sometimes.

Open-end   Okay. Let's move on to the reports you do turn in. How timely would you say they've been?

Timely? Well, I guess I have been a *little* late sometimes, but, in the scheme of things, getting sales is more important than the form. Isn't it?

Closed-end   Sure, getting the sale's important. But that's another matter. The question is, are you getting your reports in on time?

Not very often, I guess. I have a tendency to put off certain things. Like paperwork.

Open-end   Why?

Well, the sales part of the job . . . you know, talking to the customer . . . takes up most of my time. Every sale's important to me. And so's every customer. I'm putting a lot of time and effort into keeping up with them. To tell the truth, Frank, when I started, I never realized selling was gonna be so consuming. But that's what I really like about it. Meeting people . . . talking to people . . . who really *need* our products and . . .

Interrupts   Rose?

| | | Uh . . . sorry, Frank. I guess I'm getting off the track. But, you see, my point is, I'm so busy selling, I don't have time for paperwork. In fact, when I *do* do paperwork, I get the feeling I should be out there, selling. |

Summary

And that's why your reports don't get in on time.

I suppose it is. I just hate giving up selling time.

Shows listening
Summary

You're saying call reports, overall, aren't really a very high priority.

Yeah . . . I guess so. You know, I really have had a lot to learn. I've only been in the field six months, and some of our products are pretty technical. It takes a while to get a handle on them.

Open-end

I don't see the connection. What's product knowledge got to do with call reports?

Well, it takes time to learn our line. You know . . . all that electronic data. All those product manuals.

Closed-end

You're saying that's also a higher priority than call reports?

I guess that's what it comes down to, Frank. But don't forget . . . I do *do* them. I may be a little lax here and there, but I'm sure not saying call reports don't matter. I know they do.

Summarize
understanding
Closed-end

Okay. What you *are* saying is, some call reports don't get turned in, and some get turned in late, because selling counts more than paperwork. Anything else, Rose?

I don't think so. Y'see, Frank, to me, what's important is being with customers. That's the real payoff. And the real satisfaction. Take Pacific Air. I spent hours talking to Stan. You can't believe . . .

Interrupts Closed-end Closed-end	Rose . . . can we stick to the call reports? You want to add any- thing about them?	
		No, that's about it.
Closed-end	Fine. Can I add a few thoughts?	
		Sure. Say anything you want, Frank. You know more about these things than I do.

Step 3: Present Own Views

Present agreement	First, Rose, you deserve credit for trying as hard as you have. You've thrown yourself into the job . . . and that's been a big plus.	
		Thanks, Frank. That's good to hear. I appreciate it.
Present disagreement	Still and all, I think we have to beef up your paperwork . . . the call reports.	
		Anything you say, Frank. Just tell me what you want and I'll follow through. I admit . . . I have been kinda late at times. Like I said, I've been going after sales. And that takes time. But it's worth it.
	We'll get to that. First, let me explain something.	
		Sure. Go ahead.
Present views *Proof* *Check understanding* Closed-end	You've conceded you've given a low priority to call reports. I understand your thinking, Rose, but it's mistaken. The fact is, call reports are *crucial.* I can't run this district without them, be- cause I can't know what's *going on* without them. If I don't get call reports, I end up stumbling around in the dark. Can you see that?	
		Absolutely. Believe me, Frank. I never intended to make trou- ble. I'll start getting them in on time.

Step 4: Resolve Disagreements

Check acceptance	You're in complete agreement?	
Closed-end	No other reactions?	
Closed-end		

None at all. If you say you need call reports, you need call reports. I'll cooperate 100 percent. Believe me, Frank, I'm a team player. I'll do what's best for the team.

Premature agreement

Rose, I appreciate that. But I wanna be sure you buy what I'm saying because you're *convinced*, not just because I said it.

I *am* convinced. I know you're right. That's why you're manager. Believe me, from now on, you'll get call reports . . . all of them . . . on time.

Check commitment
Open-end

Rose, why do call reports make sense to you now when they didn't before?

Because of what you just said. You shouldn't have to stumble around in the dark . . . and I'm sorry I made that happen. I wouldn't say I'm crazy about paperwork, but I do know it's important. And I wanna do what's best for you.

Closed-end

I know that. See any problems in filling out the reports?

No.

Summary

None at all.

I don't think so.

Probe objection
Closed-end

The reason I'm asking is, you said before selling was what counted— not paperwork. Now you're taking a different tack. You don't see any problems?

Well, maybe just a small one.

Brief assertion

Go on.

Well, it's just that I don't have much time, and . . . you know . . .

Brief assertion	Keep going.	
		Well . . . you know, Frank . . . it could cut down on my ability to get out and sell. I mean . . . like I said . . . time in front of customers is the big thing.
Acknowledge objection Open-end	Good point. Let's talk about it. Rose, what do you mean by "selling"?	
Probe objection		"Selling"? You know . . . getting out . . . meeting people . . . getting to know them . . . finding out how you can help them. Persuading them they'll benefit from your product. Getting them to trust you. Having a good long-term working relationship.
	Okay. I'll buy everything on your list. But there's one thing you left out.	
		What's that?
Answer objection with benefit	What happens after the order's signed. Making sure the company's got all the information it needs to follow through and provide full satisfaction to the customer. After all, the transaction's not completed in front of the customer. It's completed afterward.	
		You're saying I left out the paperwork.
Expands on benefit *Proof*	Uh huh. Paperwork's not busy-work. Paperwork's essential. We can't complete the sale without it. We need it for delivery . . . service . . . all those things. Without it, this business would grind to a halt.	
Closed-end	That make sense?	
		I see that, Frank. I just never thought about it before.
Discuss consequences	Rose, to show you how important paperwork is, it's one of the things you're expected to learn during probation.	

You mean it'll be part of my evaluation?

Open-end	Right. How would you evaluate yourself on it right now?

Falling short. I have to admit it. I never confused paperwork with busywork . . . but I guess I never appreciated its full importance, either.

Probe for understanding Closed-end	And you do now?

I really think so.

Closed-end	Good. Let's pin down what we're gonna do about it. Okay?

Fine with me.

Step 5: Work Out Action Plan

Ask for proposal Closed-end	Any ideas on how to make your reports solid . . . and on time?

Let's see. Well, I outline most of my calls now. Sort of. I could do a better job of that. You know, make *sure* I take time to get it down on paper.

Open-end	Okay. How you gonna insure you'll fill them out and on time?

Just have to *make* myself, I guess.

Closed-end	Can I suggest something?

I wish you would. I could stand some pointers.

Offer alternative *Work out* *specific action* *plan*	How about outlining each call on audiotape? You can even do it while you're driving to your next call. That way, you'll get everything down while it's fresh. Then you can transcribe it onto a call report form.

That would make it easier to remember what happened. I could fill out the report faster that way.

Open-end	Okay. Now, how about getting them in on time?

What if I list every call, right afterward? Then, later in the day, check it to be sure I've filled out a report on every call on the list.

Follow-up
Closed-end

Good. Can I see your first couple of lists?

Sure.

Pin down details
Closed-end

Fine. When will the first one be ready?

I'll start tomorrow . . . first call in the morning.

So I'll see it the day after. (Writes down)

Yeah. I'll show it to you before starting out.

Closed-end

Anything else on call reports?

Not that I can think of. Frank, this talk's been real worthwhile. I appreciate your taking the time.

Check under-standing
Open-end

Glad you feel that way. To wrap things up, give me a quick summary of what you're gonna do.

First, record information . . . right after each call . . . on a cassette. Then make a daily checklist . . . to make sure I get my reports in on time. Show you the first one day after tomorrow.

Check motivation
Open-end

Sounds good. One other thing, Rose. How's all this gonna help you?

That's pretty obvious. I'll have a better chance of getting through probation and making the team. Believe me, I'm really learning. I guess this business is more complex than I expected. I thought selling would be mostly a matter of just talking to people. It turns out it's a lot more. I never worked this hard when I was a service rep. In fact, I used to . . .

Meanders

Interrupts Closed-end	Rose, let's move on. Okay?	
		Sure. What next?
Refocus Closed-end	Price quotes. Can we talk about them?	
		Absolutely.
	To start with, tell me what . . .	

Do the Dimensional Models Fit the Facts?

In reading this book, you may have wondered if the Dimensional models actually fit the facts of human interaction as verified by behavioral science. The answer is yes. This appendix explains how the model and the research fit together.

Every training-and-development specialist has been exposed to various models of human behavior; happily for the training profession, all of the most widely used and respected models resemble one another to a striking degree. But no model has been subjected to such intensive empirical research as the one on which Dimensional Training is based. This is the pioneering "interpersonal classification system" developed in the late 1940s by psychologists Coffey, Freedman, Leary, and Ossorio. To check the validity of this system, and develop it further, the Kaiser Foundation and the U.S. Public Health Service began, in 1950, to sponsor research, the final results of which were published in 1957. Since then, a number of studies have amplified and tested the validity of this research. The most recent of these studies* is only one in a series which demonstrates that the Dimensional models are valid classifications of interpersonal behavior, and are therefore *dependable* tools for understanding that behavior.

Journal of Consulting and Clinical Psychology, 1979, Vol. 47, No. 6, 1030–1045.

To explain how this validation came about, we'll go back to the beginning.

THE EARLY MODELS

In its simplest form, the interpersonal classification system developed by Coffey and his associates looked like this:

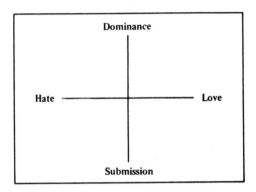

The 1957 Kaiser version of this model, based upon years of additional research, was more complex. It looked like this:

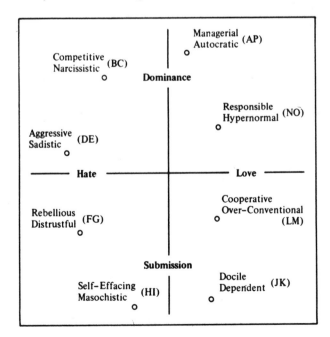

Anyone familiar with Dimensional Training will quickly recognize the strong resemblence between these two models and the various Dimensional models. Small wonder. The Kaiser research was published while Psychological Associates was developing the first Dimensional Training Program—Dimensional Sales Training. We already knew of the Coffey model, and were impressed by it; when the Kaiser research appeared, it confirmed our belief that, with suitable modifications, the model could be used to describe *business* interactions. The modifications were necessary because:

1. The language of neither model—Coffey or Kaiser—was entirely appropriate for business interactions. "Hate" and "love" were obviously too strong, and didn't really describe what's involved in most business transactions.

2. The Kaiser model was too unwieldly for business use. Eight behaviors presented no problems for clinicians and other specialists in human behavior (for whom the Kaiser research was intended), but businesspeople needed a model that could be more readily mastered and used.

THE DIMENSIONAL MODELS

The original Dimensional model, then, like all later ones, was an adaptation of the Coffey model to the world of work. Moreover, it was based on the extensive research funded by the Kaiser Foundation. So we knew at the time that the model had "worthy ancestors." Our model, in its most general form, looked like this:

DOMINANCE

Q1 behavior:	*Q4 behavior:*
• Cocky, brash, pushy • Overcontrols • Tries to dominate others and monopolize conversations • Motivates by threat or coercion	• Strong, self-assured, dynamic • Gets other person involved • Reaches decisions through candid give-and-take • Motivates by understanding and commitment

HOSTILITY ———————————————————— **WARMTH**

Q2 behavior:	*Q3 behavior:*
• Withdrawn, indecisive, diffident • Gives in easily • Tries to avoid close interpersonal situations • Makes no effort to motivate	• Friendly, easygoing, highly optimistic • Doesn't argue • Seeks out close, relaxed interpersonal situations • Motivates by affection and loyalty

SUBMISSION

Since 1958, we've adapted this model, with its quadrants or Qs, to a variety of business behaviors (sales, management, appraisal, etc.). But many users of the model have probably been bothered by a couple of doubts: (1) Can interactional behavior really be explained in terms of only *two* dimensions? (2) If so, are the two dimensions used in the Dimensional models the *right* ones?

A series of independent studies has answered *yes* to both questions. We'll describe the most recent of these studies.

The Truckenmiller–Schaie Study

A report published in 1979 in the *Journal of Consulting and Clinical Psychology*, on research done by Truckenmiller of Wilkes College and Schaie of the University of Southern California, concludes:

> Our results principally confirm the general validity (of the 1958 model) with respect to the number and nature of dimensions found to subsume interpersonal behavior ratings.

The purpose of the T–S Study was to test the validity of the Kaiser model. In very general terms (the original report is very technical and statistical), here's a summary of the work done by Truckenmiller and Schaie and the conclusions they reached:

- The study involved 150 subjects from West Virginia University, separated into 14 groups; each person did a self-rating and a rating of five others in terms of how closely they measured up to one or another of the behaviors on the model.

- To do the ratings, the subjects responded to selected items on a testing instrument called the Interpersonal Check List (ICL) and to the pictures on a group of cards known as the Thematic Apperception Test (TAT).

- In responding to the ICL items, each subject was asked to endorse or not endorse each item depending on whether or not it described the person being rated.

- In responding to the TAT cards, each subject was asked, among other things:

  What is going on in the picture? . . . How do the people feel about each other? . . . How does the story end?

- The subjects thus produced three different kinds of information: (a) ratings of *other* people's *observed* behavior, (b) ratings of their *own* behavior, and (c) *imaginary* analyses of interpersonal situations.

These three kinds of information were then analyzed (by methods too intricate to describe here) and correlated with the model. Here are the results:

1. The ratings of other people's observed behavior and the ratings of the subject's own behavior lend support to the model.

2. The imaginary analyses of interpersonal situations lend somewhat more modest support to the model. (This is hardly sur-

prising. Ever since the first Dimensional Training seminar, Dimensional trainers have been advising participants that, when analyzing behavior, they should focus *only* on *observed* behavior — what they've actually seen and heard — and ignore "fantasy production" — what they *imagine*. Fantasy production is often wishful thinking; in the imagination, meek Walter Mittys easily become heroic earthshakers. If a model purports to describe real behavior in the real world — as the Kaiser model does — then it's reasonable to assume that the model will receive its strongest corroboration from ratings of *overt* behavior.)

3. Behavior can be explained in terms of two major dimensions.

4. The two dimensions identified by the model (dominance-submission and love-hate) thoroughly correspond to the findings of the study.

Significantly, Truckenmiller and Schaie don't claim that their findings stand alone. As they put it: "Our results seem consistent with a body of literature analyzing the structure of interpersonal behavior ratings." They then list a number of studies whose results generally coincide with theirs.

CONCLUSIONS

The Truckenmiller–Schaie study lends strong support to the claim that the Kaiser and Coffey models and, by extension, the Dimensional models, stand up in the real world. Readers who use the models can be confident of their validity.

Dimensional Sales and Sales Management Training

Dimensional Sales and Sales Management Training (DST and DSM) are skill-building programs that teach salespeople and managers how to get better results in interaction with others. The seminars show salespeople and managers how to *use* the skills and concepts described in this book.

DST and DSM exemplify what Psychological Associates calls "the pragmatic approach to training." This approach contends that a training program can *only* be justified if it produces *results on the job*. To make sure this happens, a training program should follow a 12-step format. We'll list the 12 steps, then explain how each of them is carried out in DST and DSM.

1. Spell out the training goals.
2. Develop or select a learning-engineered system for teaching them.
3. Provide "cognitive maps" of pertinent behaviors.
4. Develop sizing-up skills so trainees can "position" themselves and others on the cognitive maps.

5. Teach people skills appropriate to the positions observed on the maps.
6. Model the skills.
7. Provide plenty of skill practice.
8. Give trainees feedback on how they did in practice.
9. Set individual goals based on the feedback.
10. Develop plans of action to achieve these goals.
11. Review the results of the plans of action.
12. Research the results.

This system is pragmatic in the root sense: it's concerned with *results* (Steps 11 and 12) and with how to get them (Steps 1–10). Here's how the 12 steps fit together:

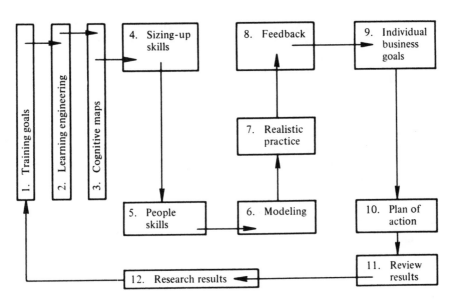

The Dimensional System

Let's look at each step:

Step 1: Spell Out the Training Goals

Starting a training seminar with vague goals is like starting out on a trip to "somewhere in North America"; you'll burn up a lot of fuel and energy going nowhere in particular. The goals of DST and DSM are clear and precise: to help salespeople and sales managers become more productive by developing Q4 skills.

Step 2: Develop or Select a Learning-Engineered System

Clear, precise training goals aren't worth much unless there's an *assured way* to reach them. In DST and DSM, this assured way is called *learning engineering.* Learning engineering is the use of scientifically-established learning techniques to make it easier to acquire, retain, and apply Dimensional skills; it's step-by-step training in which each step follows logically from the preceding step, and all steps utilize *validated* learning principles.

Research has shown that skills training is most likely to "take" when four conditions are met:

   a. **Motivation.** The training must promote a *desire* to learn; without it, the training will be an exercise in futility.

   b. **Practice and involvement.** The training must provide ample opportunity to *learn by doing*; trainees must be active, not merely passive, in the learning process.

   c. **Modeling.** The training must *demonstrate* skills as well as talk about them; trainees must have a model they can emulate when trying out the skills on their own.

   d. **Reinforcement.** The training must provide *feedback* on the quality of the practice; the trainee must know, *immediately* after trying a skill, how effective or ineffective he was, so that he can quickly correct any ineffective behavior before it hardens into habit.

DST and DSM have been carefully designed—engineered—to fulfill these essential conditions of learning.

Step 3: Provide Cognitive Maps

Imagine taking a course on "Discovering Buried Treasure" and learning, first, how to use a compass, second, how to use a divining rod, and third, how to use a shovel. Then the instructor shakes your hand and says: "Get out there and put your skills to use." After stumbling around for a while, you realize that what you need before anything else isn't a compass or a divining rod or a shovel; it's a map! Before you can start, you must know what's "out there." Where is the treasure believed buried? What's the terrain like? Where are the danger spots—the swamps and ravines and so on? Without an *organized* idea—a map—you cannot know what it's like "out there" or what direction to go in—and you'll probably give up in frustration.

Some training is like that. It teaches skills, but never provides a map—a *cognitive map*—an organized description of the behavioral terrain through which trainees must move. Without such a map, the *motivation* to move ahead will probably dissipate pretty quickly. Rather than "wander around in circles," many trainees decide it makes more sense to stay where they are.

This situation is easily corrected. In recent years, behavioral scientists have drawn a number of excellent maps of the "psychological topography" in which people have to work. And, like all good map-makers, the behavioral cartographers have charted the "danger spots" that lie in wait, like quicksand, to trap the unsuspecting.

DST and DSM use several cognitive maps, all of which we've discussed in this book: The Dimensional models, the Pyramid of Intangible Needs, and the GUIDE Continuum.

To sum up: salespeople and sales managers, like searchers for buried treasure, can most readily get from here to there, from where they are to where they should be, if they know what's *between* here and there. Once they know that, they're more likely to be motivated to make the trip; they know that once they start moving, they've got a good chance to reach their destination, and that it's therefore worth the effort.

Step 4: Develop Sizing-up Skills

Cognitive maps have no value unless they're used. To produce results, the information on the maps must be applied—put to work. Salespeople and sales managers must use the concepts to size up their own behavior and that of the people with whom they work. A pragmatic training program should teach them to answer questions like: (a) What is my behavior usually like with each of the people with whom I work? (b) What kind of behavior does each of them usually display with me? What patterns can I detect in their behavior? (c) What can I learn from all this that will help me boost productivity? Without the sizing-up skills that make it possible to answer these questions, the payoff from training will be lower than it should be.

Step 5: Teach Other "People Skills"

To become more productive, you need more than sizing-up skills. You need skills that incorporate your diagnosis and enable you to do *something* with it. Imagine, for example, that you become proficient in diagnosis and, putting your proficiency to use, you develop two behavioral portraits, one of your own sales behavior and one of a customer's.

> SELF-PORTRAIT: I Q3 it a lot. I put being liked ahead of everything else . . . I waste a lot of time on chit-chat . . . I emphasize the positive and down-play the negative . . . I back away from tough subjects . . . I'm too quick to agree . . . I feel uncomfortable asking for the order.
>
> PORTRAIT OF CUSTOMER: He shows a lot of Q1 behavior. He considers me a pushover . . . grabs control of the presentation and tries to keep me off balance. He's quick to applaud himself . . . and refuses to budge from his position. He's not interested in listening.

These are examples of sizing-up. But so what? What difference will these portraits make? How will they affect results? The answer is: they won't make *any* difference unless they're coupled with action — the use of skills. It isn't enough to know why you have trouble dealing with people. You must also know what to *do* about it. Sizing-up skills therefore *motivate* trainees to master *Q4* skills.

Many of the activities used in DST and DSM to develop sizing-up skills are also used to develop other people skills — in raising receptivity, demonstrating benefits, generating involvement, gathering information, presenting ideas, breaking through resistances, handling negative emotions, and so on. We'll see how this is done in the next two steps.

Step 6: Model the Skills

A basic principle of learning engineering is that people can best "try out" new skills if they've seen them correctly modeled. So, modeling is a fundamental part of DST and DSM. Trainees watch scenarios in which "salespeople" and "managers" *use* people skills; they see Q4 behavior in action. They *observe* sizing-up being done, they *observe* receptivity being raised, they *observe* probing, and so on. This is much more vivid than merely hearing about Q4 skills; the scenario becomes a kind of "mental template," a pattern to follow when practicing the skills.

The idea, of course, is not to provide models that trainees imitate; the idea is to provide models that can be shaped and adapted to fit any situation in which the trainee finds herself. The models bring Q4 to life as descriptions alone can never do.

Step 7: Practice the Skills

People best learn how to do things by doing them. So DST and DSM do much more than model Q4 skills; they provide plenty of opportunity for *using* them—for *practicing*. The ultimate teacher is *experience*.

Much of this experience is acquired in role plays, most of which deal with real-life situations. The role plays have two major purposes.

a. In each role play, the trainee who plays the primary role must size up, on the spot, both her own and the other person's behavior and then adapt her own to fit the situation. This lets her try out new ways of behaving—experiment with the skills she's seen modeled. She finds out, for example, maybe for the first time, what it's like to probe, patiently and tenaciously, until a tight-lipped subordinate opens up. Because most of the role plays are based on on-the-job situations, they have the ring of authenticity.

b. Other trainees observe the role play and then *analyze* it. Ordinarily, role playing occurs in five-person teams. Two people play the roles while the other three observe. The observers, using a structured Analysis and Feedback format, dissect the role play—take it apart and examine each part to see what made it tick. Then they feed back their findings to the trainee who played the key role. As they do, they not only help her, they sharpen their own sizing-up skills and their understanding of interactional dynamics.

Step 8: Give Feedback

We've just described how team members give feedback. We'll add one important point: developing feedback in small groups is *synergistic*. It would be possible, of course, to set trainees in front of a TV set, by themselves, show them a series of interactions in which they played roles, and have them analyze their own behavior. But it's doubtful they'd acquire much insight that way. They'd probably "judge themselves by their intentions" rather than by their actions— and actions count far more than intentions in explaining the *results* of interactions.

In small groups, however, each team member gets the benefits of the others' thinking. Insights rub against one another, viewpoints are weighed against other viewpoints, one interpretation triggers others. The team as a whole is more productive than the sum of its parts, and each trainee emerges with broadened perspective and understanding.

More than this, in small-team feedback, a trainee learns that his way of looking at things isn't the only, or even the best, way. A long-winded salesperson who usually starts each call with three or four anecdotes and then observes another salesperson doing the same thing in a role play may evaluate it as "a great way to begin a call." He'll then be startled to hear teammates evaluate it as a "real waste of time." For the first time, he may realize there are other and better ways to open a call, a realization that might never have dawned without small-group feedback.

Step 9:   Set Individual Goals

Ultimately, each trainee must ask: What do I do with all the insight I've acquired? How do I bridge the gap between the snug world of the seminar and the not-so-snug world outside? The answer: set business goals to be attained in the real world—goals that require using Q4 people skills. Here's how DST and DSM help trainees build this bridge:

a. Each trainee works on an actual interactional problem that's currently hampering him back on the job, and then uses Q4 skills to work his way through the problem in a role play. This is a dry run for the real thing. When the trainee gets back on the job, he can implement what he's learned to resolve the real problem.

b. Toward the end of the program, each team gives each member *summary feedback*, a candid profile of the trainee's interactional strengths and weaknesses as observed during the seminar. This gives him a rounded view of his behavior as seen by a group of fellow trainees who have had plenty of chance to observe him at close range.

c. In addition, the team gives each member recommendations for improving her interactional effectiveness. Each member gets to "see herself as others see her." The question now becomes: What is she going to do about it?

d. The answer: Set some hard-headed improvement goals—goals she can achieve only by changing or modifying her behavior. Thus, each trainee leaves the seminar with clear-cut improvement objectives, and clear-cut plans of action for achieving them.

Step 10: Develop Action Plans

The point cannot be overstressed: goals, *by themselves*, aren't worth much. All of us set goals we never achieve (New Year's resolutions are a good example)—not because there's anything wrong with the goals, but because we don't have a plan for achieving them. A good training program should culminate not merely in goal-setting, but in action-planning. Without explicit procedures for attaining the goals, goal-setting is really wheel-spinning.

Step 11: Review

Plans of action should not be carved in stone. They should be tentative, subject to revision in the light of subsequent experience. A good plan of action is like a good hypothesis in science; it represents your best current thinking, which must then be tested. In business, as in science, the empirical approach, the willingness to be guided by experience, pays off.

So, in Dimensional Training, the plan of action may be changed or improved as experience dictates. It's the final payoff that counts.

Step 12: Do Research

Since the final payoff *is* what counts, it's critically important to know what the final payoff *is*. If pragmatism is both a concern for results and a concern for the process by which they're achieved, then pragmatism demands that the results of training be studied so that, if necessary, the training process can be modified to get the intended results. Psychological Associates helps those companies that want to verify the results of DST and DSM set up post-seminar monitoring systems by which the impact of the programs can be measured.

Bibliography

Readers who want to know more about the behavioral science concepts on which Dimensional Sales and Sales Management are based will find the following books and articles well worth their while.

Allen, Louis A., *The Management Profession*, New York: McGraw-Hill, 1964.

Argyris, C., *Personality and Organization*, New York: Harper & Row, 1957.

Asch, S., *Social Psychology*, Englewood Cliffs, N.J.: Prentice-Hall, 1952.

Bales, R.F., *Personality and Interpersonal Behavior*, New York: Holt, Rinehart and Winston, 1970.

Bamard, C., *Functions of the Executive*, Cambridge, Mass.: Harvard University Press, 1968.

Bavelas, Alex, "Communication Patterns in Task-Oriented Groups," *Journal of the Acoustical Society of America*, 1950.

Bennis, W., *Changing Organizations*, New York: McGraw-Hill, 1966.

Blake, R. and J. Mouton, *The Managerial Grid*, Houston, Texas: Gulf Publishing, 1964.

Buzzotta, V., D. Karraker, R. Lefton, and M. Sherberg, *Effective Motivation Through Performance Appraisal*, Cambridge: Ballinger Publishing, 1977.

Cartwright, D., *Studies in Social Power*, Ann Arbor, Mich.: Institute for Social Research, 1959.

Connellan, T., *How to Improve Human Performance*, New York: Harper & Row, 1978.

Dollard, John and Neal Miller, *Personality and Psychotherapy: An Analysis in Terms of Learning, Thinking and Culture*, New York: McGraw-Hill, 1950.

Drucker, P., *Managing for Results*, New York: Harper & Row, 1964.

Drucker, P., *Age of Discontinuity*, New York: Harper & Row, 1969.

Etzioni, Amitai, *Modern Organizations*, Englewood Cliffs, N.J.: Prentice-Hall, 1964.

Festinger, L., *A Theory of Cognitive Dissonance*, Palo Alto, California: Stanford University Press, 1957.

Fromm, E., *Man for Himself*, New York: Rinehard, 1947.

Gardner, J.W., *Excellence*, New York: Harper & Row, 1961.

Gordon, T., *Leadership Effectiveness Training*, New York: Wyden Books, 1977.

Haire, M., *Psychology in Management*, New York: McGraw-Hill, 1964.

Herzberg, F., B. Mausner, and B. Snydeman, *The Motivation to Work*, New York: John Wiley, 1959.

Horney, K., *The Neurotic Personality of Our Time*, New York: Norton, 1937.

Hovland, C. and I. Janis, (Eds.), *Personality and Persuasibility: Vol. 2 Yale Studies in Attitude and Communication*, New Haven, Conn.: Yale University Press, 1959.

Hull, C.L., *Principles of Behavior: An Introduction to Behavior Theory*, New York: Appleton-Century-Crofts, 1943.

Leary, T., *Interpersonal Diagnosis of Personality*, New York: Ronald Press, 1957.

Leavitt, H.J., *Managerial Psychology*, Chicago: University of Chicago Press, 1958.

Likert, R., *New Patterns of Management*, New York: McGraw-Hill, 1961.

Likert, R., *The Human Organization*, New York: McGraw-Hill, 1970.

Maier, N., *Principles of Human Relations*, New York: John Wiley, 1956.

Marrow, A.J., *Behind the Executive Mask*, New York: American Management Association, 1964.

Maslow, A.H., *Motivation and Personality*, New York: Harper & Row, 1954.

Maslow, A.H., *Eupsychian Management*, Homewood, Illinois: Dorsey Press, 1965.

McClelland, D.C., J.W. Atkinson, R.A. Clark, E.L. Lowell, *The Achievement Motive*, New York: Appleton-Century-Crofts, 1953.

McClelland, D.C., J.W. Atkinson, R.A. Clark, and E.L. Lowell, *The Achieving Society*, Princeton, N.J.: Van Nostrand, 1961.

McGeoch, J.A. and A.L. Irion, *The Psychology of Human Learning*, 2nd ed. New York: Longmans Green, 1952, 1953, 1954.

McGregor, D., *The Human Side of Enterprise*, New York: McGraw-Hill, 1960.

McGregor, D., *The Professional Manager*, New York: McGraw-Hill, 1967.

Moreno, Jacob, *Sociometry, Experimental Method and the Science of Society*, Boston: Beacon House, 1951.

Murphy, Gardner, *Personality: A Biosocial Approach to Origins and Structures*, New York: Basic Books, 1966.

Murray, Henry, *Exploration in Personality*, New York: Oxford Press, 1938.

Schien, E.H., *Organizational Psychology*, Englewood Cliffs, N.J.: Prentice-Hall, 1965.

Schutz, William C., *The Interpersonal Underworld (FIRO)*, Palo Alto, California: Science and Behavior Books, 1966.

Sherif, Muzafer, *Intergroup Relations and Leadership*, New York: John Wiley, 1962.

Sullivan, H.S., *The Interpersonal Theory of Psychiatry*, New York: Norton, 1954.

Tannenbaum, R., I.R. Weschler, and F. Massorik, *Leadership and Organization: A Behavioral Science Approach*, New York: McGraw-Hill, 1961.

Whyte, W.H., *The Organization Man*, New York: Simon and Schuster, 1956.
Whyte, W., *Money and Motivation*, New York: Harper, Hayser and Row, 1955.
Zaleznik, A. and D. Moment, *The Dynamics of Interpersonal Behavior*, New York: John Wiley, 1964.

Index